# QUASI-MARKETS IN
# THE WELFARE STATE

**Studies in Decentralisation and Quasi-Markets**

This series of working papers examines the introduction of 'internal' or 'quasi-markets' throughout the welfare state. There are seventeen titles published to date. Please contact SAUS Publications for further details.

# QUASI-MARKETS IN THE WELFARE STATE

## The emerging findings

**Edited by Will Bartlett, Carol Propper
Deborah Wilson and Julian Le Grand**

First published in Great Britain in 1994 by

SAUS Publications
School for Advanced Urban Studies
University of Bristol
Rodney Lodge
Grange Road
Bristol BS8 4EA

Telephone (0272) 741117
Fax (0272) 737308

British Library Cataloguing in Publication Data
A catalogue record for this book is available from the British Library

SAUS Study 14

ISBN    1 873575 70 X
ISSN    0268-3725

The School for Advanced Urban Studies is a centre for research, post-graduate and continuing education, and consultancy at the University of Bristol.    The School's focus is the analysis, development and implementation of policy in the fields of employment, health and social care, housing, social management, and urban change and government.  Its aim is to bridge the gaps between theory and practice, between different policy areas, and between academic disciplines.  SAUS is committed to the wide dissemination of its findings and in addition to courses and seminars the School has established several publications series: **SAUS Studies, Occasional Papers, Working Papers, Studies in Decentralisation and Quasi-Markets, DRIC Reports and SAUS Guides and Reports**.

SAUS is working to counter discrimination on grounds of gender, race, disability, age and sexuality in all its activities.

Printed in Great Britain by The Alden Press, Oxford, OX2 0EF.

# CONTENTS

vi *Contents*

# ACKNOWLEDGEMENTS

We are grateful to the ESRC, the Nuffield Foundation and the Joseph Rowntree Foundation for their financial support of the conference on 'Quasi-markets: the emerging findings' held at SAUS in March 1993. The contributions to that conference form the basis of this book.

We would like to acknowledge the helpful comments of participants at that conference on the draft versions of several chapters in this book.

We would also like to thank Jane Raistrick for her editorial input and to Linda Price for her invaluable contribution in the organisation of this book.

# LIST OF CONTRIBUTORS

*Carol Propper, Will Bartlett and Deborah Wilson,* School for Advanced Urban Studies, University of Bristol.

*Linda Challis, Patricia Day, Rudolf Klein and Ellie Scrivens,* Centre for the Analysis of Social Policy, University of Bath.

*Rosalind Levacic,* Centre for Educational Policy and Management, Open University.

*Ron Glatter and Philip Woods,* Centre for Educational Policy and Management, Open University.

*Stephen Ball, Richard Bowe and Sharon Gewirtz,* Centre for Educational Studies, King's College London.

*Geraint Johnes,* Department of Economics, Lancaster University.

*Martin Cave,* Faculty of Social Sciences, Brunel University.

*Martin Knapp and Julien Forder,* Personal Social Services Research Unit, University of Kent.

*Gerald Wistow and Brian Hardy,* Nuffield Institute for Health, University of Leeds.

*Robin Means, Lesley Hoyes, Rachel Lart and Marilyn Taylor,* School for Advanced Urban Studies, University of Bristol.

*Paul Hoggett,* Centre for Social and Economic Research, University of the West of England.

*Ewan Ferlie,* Centre for Corporate Strategy and Change, University of Warwick.

*Calum Paton,* Centre for Health Planning and Management, University of Keele.

*Manos Matsaganis and Howard Glennerster,* London School of Economics.

*Julian Le Grand,* London School of Economics.

# INTRODUCTION

## Carol Propper, Will Bartlett and Deborah Wilson

Throughout the 1980s the Conservative government pursued a radical programme of market oriented reforms. State owned industries and public utilities were privatised and the financial services sector was deregulated in the 'big bang' of 1986. The powers and influences of local authorities were reduced by the contracting out of services and the sale of council houses. However, the welfare state escaped unscathed throughout most of the decade and continued to be organised through a number of large state bureaucracies.

Between 1988 and 1990, however, the focus of change was turned to ways in which the process of 'marketisation' could be extended to the provision of public services in areas such as health, education and community care. The legislative programme which underpinned these changes included the Education Reform Act of 1988 and the NHS and Community Care Act of 1990. Despite the breadth and diversity of the sectors affected, the reforms had a number of common features. These included the separation of purchaser and provider functions within each service, the devolution of managerial autonomy to individual provider units, changes to funding mechanisms involving the introduction of formula funding of providers in some cases and the creation of a system of contracting between purchasers and providers in others. In general, bureaucratic mechanisms of service delivery were replaced by competitive systems based on quasi-markets (Le Grand, 1991). In contrast to standard markets, these systems are set up in such a way that the provision of services remains free at the point of delivery: no money changes hands between the final user (eg pupils, patients) and the provider of services (eg schools, hospitals). Thus the state has retained its role as a funder of services within the welfare state, but the task of providing services has been transferred from an integrated set of state owned and managed enterprises to a variety of independent provider organisations including not-for-profit organisations, private companies and state owned units under devolved management.

The quasi-market reforms were intended to overcome the perceived defects of the bureaucratic organisation of the welfare state, particularly in the areas of efficiency, choice and responsiveness. Some attention was also devoted to the issue of equity of service delivery, a fundamental principle of the founders of the post-war welfare state.

Early research on the operation of quasi-markets was necessarily largely confined to establishing the conditions under which the objectives of the reforms could be met and to analysing the very early phases of the reforms (Le Grand and Bartlett, 1993; Robinson and Le Grand, 1993). But the research literature is now increasing rapidly. Inevitably the study of new social innovations has proved to be a hugely attractive area for researchers in the social sciences and a large number of new research studies are being carried out on the problems raised by the quasi-market reforms. Some of these are beginning to bear fruit and in this book we present some of the emerging findings on their effects in health care, social care and education in the UK.

The chapters in this book are a selection from a conference held at the School for Advanced Urban Studies at the University of Bristol in March 1993 to examine the impact of these changes. They range across several quasi-markets. The researchers have different concerns and foci and reflect a variety of intellectual perspectives. Some of the findings relate to quasi-markets which are at more advanced stages than others. Other chapters are necessarily rather more speculative, reflecting the early stage of the changes and the case study nature of much of the data. Nevertheless, a set of common themes and concerns emerges.

First, there is a concern that market failure will be a major problem in these welfare quasi-markets. The issues of information asymmetry, barriers to entry, poor information on outcomes and monopolistic relationships are raised in most of the chapters. Second, there is a concern that the current contracts between funder and supplier of care or between funder and the agent responsible for purchase of care cannot on their own solve these problems of market failure. Several chapters point to the potential for cream-skimming or cost reduction rather than service improvement. Third, there is widespread concern over the lack of skills in the organisations acting as the users' agent. Purchasers, care managers and even parents may not have sufficient skills and information to make efficient or equitable choices. Finally, through several of the chapters, runs a rather broader concern over the extent to which large purchaser bodies can be accountable to both user and the state. These chapters suggest that the tension between user empowerment and the meeting of central government aims is not solved by the present organisational forms. The reforms may not be able to achieve their goals simply through separation of funding and provision.

Challis, Day, Klein and Scrivens (Chapter 1) examine regulation of quality in the markets for health, social care, education and social housing. They advance two hypotheses. The first is that the form and level of regulation will differ in the different markets because each is characterised by different structures. The differences are in the levels of information asymmetry, in the extent to which quality can only be judged ex-post, in the costs of changing suppliers and the extent to which the end-user is also the purchaser. The second hypothesis is that, not withstanding these differences, the level of regulation will be a systematic function of the extent of concentration on either the purchaser or the provider side of the market. This relationship will be a negative one: the more diffuse either the provider or the purchaser side, the greater the extent of regulation.

They conclude that initial evidence confirms these hypotheses. The different quasi-markets are regulated in very different ways. Yet across the markets, it appears that where the market is more diffuse (on either the purchaser or the provider side) there is more regulation. This interesting result contrasts with the nature of regulation in other markets and perhaps also with what economic theory might recommend. Utilities regulation, for example, tends to be greater where there are fewer, rather than more, sellers. Challis et al suggest that transactions costs between buyer and seller of service may offer some explanation for their result.

In Part 1 four studies report the emerging research findings on the effects of quasi-markets in education. Levacic (Chapter 2) focuses on the impact of formula funding of schools' budgets, and local resource management within schools. She notes that under formula funding, the prices set in the formula are determined politically and not by the forces of supply and demand.

Nevertheless, the formula funding system is leading to greater efficiency, since it penalises schools with above average unit costs. Evidence on equity is less clear-cut, but there is some indication that schools with more disadvantaged pupils may be penalised by the system. Increased autonomy and local management of schools may, in principle, give rise to problems of inequity linked to the issue of selection. However, Levacic finds little evidence of cream-skimming in her study. Nor is there any evidence that falling rolls were associated with the proportion of socially disadvantaged pupils at a school. There is evidence that schools are beginning to group together into consumer cooperatives (clusters, consortia) recreating some of the missing services previously provided by the LEAs.

The unanswered issue Levacic raises is whether local management of schools (LMS) can improve school efficiency by stimulating those processes which are associated with educational effectiveness. This may be doubted, since rarely did head teachers in the study have the time to be both chief executive of the school and the professional leader of the school as an educational institution. In addition, in all but the largest schools, LMS did little to empower classroom teachers.

Chapter 3 by Glatter and Woods looks at competition from the consumer viewpoint. They emphasise the importance of social class in determining the effects of the reforms. They argue that there was a long tradition of competition between schools in the UK even before the reforms, and that there has been a great deal of autonomy for schools to develop their unique characters. Falling school rolls have been instrumental in giving rise to competitive pressures. In this context, Glatter and Woods analyse the factors which affect consumers' experience of choice and competition.

The chapter shows that, surprisingly, middle class parents are less likely to feel they have a choice than working-class parents. The study found no evidence of schools selectively discriminating against children from working-class homes, but the middle class children were over-represented in the 'better' schools. The authors link this to the narrower range of choice exercised by working class parents, who tend to value proximity more highly than middle class parents, both because of transport cost and because of views about the importance of children being with their friends. They point out that the availability of different types of schools also limits choice, as does the topography of the local area. As a result a large degree of discretion remains with the schools and consumer choice is constrained.

Ball, Bowe and Gewirtz (Chapter 4) also argue that the implementation of the education reforms is affected by local factors, particularly the class and social composition of the local population. To support their argument they present two local case studies. In one, a Social Democrat council supports comprehensive education and discourages competitive behaviour. The local education authority (LEA) produces schools' prospectuses in a common low-key format, and schools' admissions are also managed centrally. The LEA adopts a corporatist approach and tries to encourage cooperative non-poaching agreements between schools. Even so, this policy is coming under strain as competition begins to be felt.

The other LEA is Conservative controlled and is committed to competition and choice. It has pursued an active policy of developing a quasi-market. The LEA has also encouraged the entry of a new Church of England school and has begun to publish surveys of attendance and test results for primary and secondary schools. In reaction to this policy, some schools have opted out to preserve their comprehensive status and identity and to avoid becoming part of the selective LEA school system.

Ball et al highlight the importance of local and historical factors in shaping the market and argue that social class is an important factor in parental selection of schools and hence in driving LEA policy implementation. They argue that the evolution of the quasi-market is not a spontaneous process. Rather it is being created in different ways by different authorities.

Johnes and Cave (Chapter 5) describe and evaluate recent attempts to enhance competition between the providers of higher education in the UK and the implications that these attempts have had for quality of the product. They argue that the changes in institutional management arrangements and in the funding system have had a remarkable effect. To the extent that the aim of policy has been to expand provision and reduce costs it has clearly worked. However, they hold serious reservations about the adequacy of mechanisms for quality control. They argue that the present system distorts the market towards the production of a uniform product, and so fails to offer customers (students and employers) a range of quality.

The three studies in Part 2 explain the early effects of introducing quasi-markets in the area of community care which took effect rather later than the changes in the education system. Knapp, Wistow, Forder and Hardy (Chapter 6) examine the opportunities for, and the barriers to, the development of markets in social care. They argue that while the mixed economy of care is not a new phenomenon in social care, the form of market organisation set by the reforms may be prone to market failure. They identify the main sources of potential failure as coming from structural imperfections, the specialised nature and heterogeneity of the product delivered and asymmetry of information. In terms of structure, many of the authorities surveyed by Knapp et al felt that entry barriers were such that market entry would be insufficient to ensure competition. Product heterogeneity would exacerbate this lack of entry, allowing suppliers to differentiate themselves, so avoiding direct competition. Product heterogeneity may also promote quality rather than price competition. Many of these problems are familiar from the long experience of 'contracting out' in the USA, but the effect that these factors will have upon cost savings, quality and choice is still very unclear in the UK. What is clear is that to achieve the goals sought by the community care reforms, considerable changes in local authorities' organisational and incentive structures are required.

Whether these changes in social care markets are likely to empower users is also unclear. The study by Means, Hoyes, Lart and Taylor (Chapter 7) found rather different levels of enthusiasm in four authorities for implementation of a quasi-market in social care. They also found that users and carers groups expressed rather different concerns to funders. Some felt that their local authority had a commitment to increasing user involvement. But few saw such processes as being likely to lead to user empowerment. Further, the lack of resources, as distinct from the form in which these resources were packaged, was seen as a crucial issue. Means et al conclude that any potential of the reforms to empower will depend on the level of funding. Inadequate funding will limit the development of user empowerment, regardless of the forms through which this funding is channelled. However, even a well funded quasi-market system will not go far enough. At best, the market allows for exit and voice: it has little to offer in the way of rights. Further, the quasi-market mechanism has built into it a conflict between the role of the local authority as rationer and broker/advocate. This conflict may undermine the extent to which professionals attempt to empower users.

In another study of social care, Taylor and Hoggett (Chapter 8) examine the extent to which policies intended to develop a mixed economy of care are providing the conditions under which such an economy can develop. They pose two questions. Will the current policies produce a genuine mixed economy in which there is genuine diversity for the user? And should the government have any role in this market? Their evidence suggests that despite current community care guidelines which demand that over 60% of funds ring-fenced for expenditure by the lead local authority be spent on care provided in the private and voluntary sectors, the answer to the first question may well be 'no'. They argue that contracting is likely to reduce the extent of diversity, reduce the number of relationships based on trust and discretion, increase the amount of regulation and decrease the scope for user responsiveness and worker altruism. There will be no guarantee that the service user will have greater choice.

Given this, they argue that the answer to their second question must be 'yes'. However, government action must change from its present form of 'testing quality out'. Government should seek to act as a social entrepreneur whose task is to stimulate, through funding and other powers, a market of alternative providers. This requires a focus on democracy and pluralism in the public sphere.

Part 3 turns to the effects of the introduction of quasi-markets on the provision of health services. In Chapter 9 Ferlie argues that to predict the effect of the NHS reforms it is necessary to shift the focus of the analysis towards the micropolitics of a public sector organisation. He advances the proposition that the NHS quasi-market is best seen in terms of sets of relationships between different participants, and that these relationships are - and will continue to be - socially and institutionally embedded. Using material from a longitudinal case study of purchasers and providers, he argues that the reforms have brought about significant managerial and organisational changes which may significantly change the social relationships within the NHS.

Changes in the NHS are analysed by Paton (Chapter 10) using an explicit policy analysis perspective. He argues that such a perspective is necessary as the NHS quasi-market operates in an area in which both centralist and political forces remain strong. He identifies the four salient features of the NHS quasi-market as: first, the need for regulation of the providers; second, the extent of distinction between providers and purchasers; third, the global cash limits on the service; and fourth, the need to incorporate publicly defined rights into agreements between purchasers and providers. These features will determine the outcome of the operation of the market. Regulation of providers may limit the extent of competition. Purchasers' priorities may dominate those of local people. Cash limits may encourage cost cutting at the expense of allocative efficiency. And the (political) imperative to prevent the emergence of differences across the NHS may limit the extent to which local wishes can be reflected in purchasing plans. Paton argues that the combined operation of these forces requires that some form of planning should be undertaken. The specific challenges that this planning function (wherever located) will need to address include mechanisms for deciding priorities, the extent of purchaser regulation, coordination of the purchasing function and regulation of provider provision to ensure cost-shifting is minimised.

General Practitioner (GP) fundholders have been seen as one of the key elements of the NHS reforms, increasing the responsiveness of service providers to the wishes of the end-user. But fundholders also have the opportunity to select only those patients who are low risk and hence profitable to treat. Matsaganis and Glennerster (Chapter 11) explore the extent to which cream-skimming (and patient selection more generally) by fundholders is both possible and likely.

The extent to which cream-skimming is profitable depends upon the form of payment to fundholders for patients on their lists. The capitation formula recommended by the Department of Health uses only age and sex as risk adjusters. The authors use data on a sample of GP fundholders' patient costs to examine whether these are sufficient adjusters for risk. They conclude that they are not, and that a capitation formula based only on these adjusters would make cream-skimming both technically feasible and financially attractive. The authors concede that cream-skimming does not seem to occur at present - the result perhaps of either medical ethics and/or the £5,000 limit on the cost of any treatment to a fundholder. But on the basis of evidence from other health care systems, the authors are pessimistic that such forces will halt the development of patient selection in the longer term. Their work thus points to the need to use more measures of risk in the GP fundholder reimbursement mechanism.

It is clear from the chapters in this volume that similar issues are emerging in all the markets under consideration. It is also clear that authors from different disciplines stress different dimensions of these issues. But it is also clear that the research agenda has hardly been touched. The concluding chapter of the book reviews some of the theoretical and empirical issues that need to be explored; others will doubtless also wish to add to the agenda. This book is intended as a stimulus towards further exploration of that agenda.

## References

Le Grand, J. (1991) 'Quasi-markets and social policy', *Economic Journal*, vol 101, pp 1256-67.

Le Grand, J. and Bartlett, W. (1993) *Quasi-markets and social policy*, London: Macmillan.

Robinson, R. and Le Grand, J. (1993) *Evaluating the NHS reforms*, London: King's Fund Institute.

*one*

---

# MANAGING QUASI-MARKETS: INSTITUTIONS OF REGULATION

## Linda Challis, Patricia Day, Rudolf Klein and Ellie Scrivens

One of the most striking aspects of the privatisation drive of the 1980s was that the withdrawal of the state from the ownership and production of services was accompanied by the creation of new institutions of regulation (Kay and Vickers, 1988). As industries were sold off, so a new generation of regulatory institutions was born: OFTEL, OFGAS and so on. Direct, hierarchical organisational control was replaced by regulatory instruments designed to safeguard the public interest. In this chapter, we explore the extent to which the same trend is evident in the quasi-markets in the field of social policy, and what form it has taken. The nature of the new quasi-markets created varies (Bartlett, 1991; Le Grand, 1992): rather different patterns are evident in the NHS, the social services, education and housing. Do regulatory policies and institutions also vary? And are any such variations systematically related to the characteristics of the quasi-market concerned?

First, however, it is important to disentangle the notion of 'regulation'. The new quasi-markets are all managed markets: that is, purchasers are consciously and deliberately 'creating' the market. Decisions have to be taken about whether or not to support traditional providers or how best to encourage new entrants into the field in order to create competition. Purchasers are not the only actors involved in shaping the market. There may be national policy players as well: the Tomlinson Inquiry (1992) into London's health services provides perhaps the best example of this type of intervention, reminiscent of the attempts by central government in the 1930s and subsequent decades to 'rationalise' industries with surplus capacity.

A wide definition of regulation might well encompass all such activities (see Propper, 1992). It would include all attempts to structure the market: ie to determine the quantity and distribution of resources, as well as to lay down prices and standards. In this chapter, however, we adopt a narrower definition: regulation seen as the control of standards of quality either through control of new entrants to the market (registration) or through inspection and monitoring mechanisms - and usually both. That is, the focus is not on market control but service control.

Service control in the public sector has traditionally taken the form of direct managerial supervision of the providers; the line of accountability has been hierarchical (Day and Klein, 1987). With the new split between purchasers and providers, this relationship has been broken up. There is no line of managerial or administrative accountability, for example, between an NHS trust and purchasers; the line now runs, if anywhere, directly to the Secretary of State via the Department of Health's outposts. The new instrument of control or accountability in the NHS (although not in all quasi-markets) is the contract. At the same time, however, regulatory institutions can be seen as a supplementary or alternative form of control or accountability: a way of protecting the public interest by ensuring that providers maintain adequate standards of service production.

What are the motives for the introduction of regulation and in what ways do they differ from policy area to policy area such that different regulatory regimes are apparent? The literature suggests a variety of motives. There may be information asymmetry, ie the purchasers may be at an information disadvantage or vice versa; there is the problem that quality can only be established *ex post*, the case of 'experience goods'; there may be heavy switching costs where the costs associated with changing a provider are substantial; and principal agent problems, for example where the consumer is not the purchaser.

These features may, to a limited extent, help explain the variety of regulatory regimes in different markets. In all four markets the providers are knowledgeable, but in education and the personal social services (PSS) the level of purchaser knowledge is currently rather scanty. It is also true that quality can only really be established *ex post* with three of the four areas, social housing perhaps being the exception. The switching costs associated with health and the PSS are probably greater than for education and social housing. All the case study areas - education, PSS, the NHS and social housing - are characterised by major purchasers acting as principal agents; certainly this is true in health and social housing but in the PSS as well, relatives may purchase on behalf of the consumer and in education parents decide on the school for their children. In short, there seem to be reasons for the regulation of all four areas and sufficient difference in the weight of reasons in each case to expect somewhat different regulatory regimes. However, it is the thesis of this chapter that the forms which regulation take are contingent upon the characteristics of the markets themselves. In other words, the literature may give us some understanding as to why regulation is introduced in the first place but does not really help us to explain its particular forms in particular markets.

In analysing the relationship between purchasers, providers and regulators in different social fields - and examining the way it has changed and is likely to change in future - we propose to test a simple proposition. This is that the balance between reliance on contracts and on regulatory institutions will depend on the balance between purchaser and provider power. Purchasers may be either diffuse or concentrated; similarly, providers may be either diffuse or concentrated. The nature of the quasi-markets will vary accordingly. Figure 1 illustrates the four possible combinations that emerge.

**Figure 1:   The balance of purchaser and provider power**

|  |  | Providers | |
|---|---|:---:|:---:|
|  |  | Diffuse | Concentrated |
| Purchasers | Diffuse | A | B |
|  | Concentrated | C | D |

Thus in box A diffuse purchasers are dealing with diffuse providers (the normal notion of a competitive market). In box B diffuse purchasers are dealing with concentrated providers (the situation in the case of public utilities and in some of the quasi-markets, for example if parents have to deal with a school with a local geographical monopoly or if there is only one general practice in the local area). In box C, concentrated purchasers are dealing with diffuse providers. And in box D concentrated purchasers are dealing with concentrated providers.

The starting point of this chapter is to test the proposition that reliance on regulatory mechanisms (in our restricted sense) will diminish as we move from type B situations to type D situations. There are a number of reasons for making this presumption. In type B situations, where diffuse purchasers face a concentrated provider, there has long been an assumption that regulatory instruments are required not only to prevent abuse of monopoly power but also to redress the asymmetry of information. The information costs involved for purchasers in negotiating contracts is very high. In type C situations, where concentrated purchasers are dealing with diffuse providers, we might well expect to see a mixture of contracts and regulation. Purchasers are in a strong position when negotiating contracts but the transactions costs of dealing with multiple providers, and ensuring that standards of quality are met, may be very high. Hence the case for using regulation as a means of lowering transactions costs. Finally, in a type D situation, where concentrated purchasers are dealing with concentrated providers, one might expect to see the contract predominating as an instrument of control, since transactions costs fall as the number of contracts diminishes.

The introduction of quasi-markets is incomplete in all four of our chosen policy areas; they are very much markets in transition. At present we can locate the PSS as falling within box A: care management has not yet become a fully fledged system for buying care and purchasers can be characterised as diffuse with individuals acquiring care privately and officials spot-purchasing on behalf of people who need more complex packages. The providers have not yet coalesced into corporate bodies, although there are signs that this is beginning to happen, and national policy stresses the importance of heterogeneity in supply. Health care, excluding nursing homes, can be placed in box D where district health authorities (DHAs) have evolved into purchasing consortia and where provision is made through substantial provider units. Health, however, provides a good example of the way in which the picture may change quite rapidly. As GP fundholding becomes more widespread and as more NHS trusts are created so the picture may come to fit more readily into box B or even box A. Education fits into box B with the 'purchasers', ie parents, being diffuse but the provision being concentrated, particularly in areas where there is only one local school.  Social housing has the features of box C where the purchaser, ie the Housing Corporation, represents a concentrated purchaser but the providers, a multiplicity of housing associations, are diffuse.

The next section elaborates the classification both of regulatory institutions and of our four case study areas. Subsequent sections then look at the impact of quasi-markets on regulatory institutions within each of those four areas.

## Varieties of regulation

Regulation is part of an increasingly complex machinery of control in quasi-markets.  Contracts are now a major mechanism by which quality, price, and quantity may be specified, and by which suppliers can be held to account.  This relatively new approach to public sector commissioning is still in the early stages of evolution and it is therefore difficult to judge whether the problems of contract compliance and enforcement that have arisen are part of the learning process or endemic to the system.  Similarly, we do not know whether the costs of contract specification will fall over time with more experience.  But contracts are perhaps the most obvious symbol of the import of techniques from the commercial sector into the public sector and provide clear-cut evidence of the existence of quasi-markets.  In essence, contracts are concerned with achieving value for money, making explicit the kinds of standards which must be met, and promoting an efficient and business-like approach to service provision.  They are not, necessarily, a suitable way of upholding the public interest, insofar as they leave it to individual purchasers to define desirable standards.  If the aim of policy is to ensure a check on purchasers, as well as providers, then more familiar forms of regulation may be required, specifically registration and inspection.

Registration is structural regulation, ie the sanctioning of entry into the market place, and inspection may be seen as a means of conduct regulation (Kay and Vickers, 1988), which in the past was almost entirely concerned with quality - usually defined in terms of inputs and process - rather than with charges, quantity, and so forth. The last ten years have seen the development of codes of practice and the specification of standards to support registration and inspection.  For example, in the PSS there has been *Home life*

(Centre for Policy on Ageing, 1984) and *Homes are for living in* (Department of Health, 1989), while in the NHS there has been the National Association of Health Authorities (NAHA) guidance on the registration and inspection of nursing homes (National Association of Health Authorities, 1985). In the case of education, the development of the national curriculum could also be interpreted as a move towards setting standards.

The institutional arrangements for registration and inspection have been subject to review as part of the introduction of quasi-markets. Three of the four areas discussed in this chapter are regulated by central inspectorates, the NHS being the exception; two are also regulated by local inspectorates. Not only do the institutional arrangements vary from quasi-market to quasi-market but so too does the scope of the regulation. In education, both public and private facilities are inspected; in the PSS, too, both statutory and non-statutory provision is subject to inspection, although only non-statutory provision is subject to registration; in social housing it is non-public housing which is regulated; and in the NHS it is only private care which is registered and inspected, not public care. Figure 2 sets out the relationships.

**Figure 2:  Arrangements for registration and inspection**

|  | Central only | Central and local | Local only |
|---|---|---|---|
| Public and Private | Education | PSS |  |
| Private only | Social housing |  | Health |

Note:    Private has been defined as provision outside the public
        sector, whether for-profit or not.

In education, the Office for Standards in Education (OFSTED) is the central regulatory body with local inspection teams drawn from a centrally approved list. In the PSS there is a substantial central body, the Social Services Inspectorate (SSI), which has a regionalised structure, and at the local level there are inspection units in every local authority social services authority (LASSA). In social housing, the Housing Corporation acts as a central regulator, with no local level regulation, whilst in the NHS regulation is at the district level. Moreover, as we shall see in the case studies that follow, there are also variations in the style of regulation: different types of quasi-markets appear to produce different types of regulatory regimes. The balance between inspection and consultancy varies between the different regulatory fields, as do attitudes towards the publication of inspectorial reports.

## The case of school education

The quasi-market in primary and secondary education differs crucially in one respect from the other quasi-markets analysed in this chapter (Glennerster, 1991). The purchasers in this case are the parents, not managers or professionals as in our other case studies. In effect, a quasi-voucher system has been introduced. Money follows pupils under the formula funding methodology (Lee, 1990). The new quasi-market is highly imperfect as parents are constrained by geography and other factors (Brain and Klein, 1993). The scope for choice is often very limited as is the degree of competition between schools. However, nowhere else has there been such a dramatic change. Before the 1988 Education Reform Act schools provided an example of a type C situation: LEAs were, in effect, monopoly 'purchasers' of education within any given geographical area (leaving aside independent schools), exercising direct hierarchical organisational control over the schools in their area. Now secondary and primary education provides an example of a type A situation, with diffuse purchasers dealing with diffuse providers. The role of LEAs seems certain to become increasingly marginal as more schools opt out and formula funding becomes centralised (Secretary of State for Education, 1992).

This radical change is reflected in the institutions of regulation. To see just how radical, it is important to identify the main characteristics of the regulatory system before the transformation of Her Majesty's Inspectorate of Schools (HMI) into the OFSTED.

Inspection in education has a long history. Its origins can be traced back to 1839 when the introduction of state finance for religious schools led to the creation of a system of government inspectors (Lawton and Gordon, 1987). The award of grants was made conditional upon inspection: ie the achievement of appropriate standards. In short, the purpose of inspection was twofold: the protection of public funds and the promotion of national policy goals. HMI, as it developed over the subsequent century and a half, was thus essentially an instrument of central government: very much a 'public interest' model of regulation, as distinct from a 'purchaser-directed' model.

This is evident in the work carried out - until this year - by HMI. HMI's role was, first, to assess standards and trends in schools and to advise the Secretary of State on the performance of the school system; second, to diffuse good practices; and third, to provide advice and assistance for those working in the schools (Department of Education and Science, 1983). Thus the focus was essentially on obtaining a national picture; inspecting individual schools was a means towards this end. In the case of formal visits, the reports have been published since 1983. But no such reports followed informal inspection visits designed "to contribute to the Inspectorate's collective knowledge of the educational system" (Department of Education and Science, 1986). Similarly, the heavy emphasis on the consultancy function of HMI underlines the fact that it was seen by government as an instrument for implementing national policy goals.

The national inspectorate was supplemented by the inspectorates of LEAs. However, the role of these inspectorates was ambiguous. There appeared to be considerable diversity among LEAs in the relative stress put on monitoring quality and on providing advice or promoting good practice. Less than a quarter of the inspectors and advisers interviewed in an Audit Commission survey saw the purpose of inspection as being to provide objective information for LEAs, governors and parents (Audit Commission, 1989). The emphasis was as much on professional self-improvement as on public accountability.

The regulatory system that operated until this year can therefore be characterised as being dominated by the national policy agenda and by professional concerns: precisely what might be expected in a type C situation. Only in the case of independent schools was there a requirement for registration (on the model of nursing and residential care homes), with occasional inspections to check on standards. However, it is far from clear how effective this system has been in providing information or protection against exploitation for purchasers: the fact that independent schools have developed their own accreditation system - on a voluntary basis - suggests that they did not have much faith in the capacity of the regulatory system to guarantee anything except the most basic (largely structural) standards.

The creation of OFSTED marks - in line with the move from a type C to a type A situation - a move towards a purchaser-orientated system of regulation.   It will be responsible for the regular inspection of all schools wholly or mainly dependent on public funding, whether opted out or not, over a four-year cycle. The inspections will be carried out by teams of 'registered inspectors' selected and paid by OFSTED, the government having abandoned its initial proposal for allowing schools to choose their own inspectors during the passage of the legislation setting up the new system.   The new body, apart from validating, monitoring and analysing the work of the inspectors, will continue to have a statutory duty to inform the Secretary of State about standards and performance.   The chief inspector must present an annual report to Parliament, while also being free to "report as and when he [sic] wishes on any matter related to his functions, and to publish his findings" (Department of Education, 1992).

For the purposes of this analysis, two features of the new system require noting.   First, it is a system that is explicitly designed to provide information about standards to purchasers, very much in line with the government's controversial insistence on publishing the examination league tables for schools.   Second, it is a system which requires much greater explicitness about standards than the one which it replaces.

The first point emerges clearly from the insistence, in the notes of guidance prepared by the Department of Education (1992), on making inspectorial reports widely available.   As already noted, all formal reports have been public documents since 1983, although it is not clear how wide a readership they achieved.   But under the new system there will be specific requirements on the governing bodies of inspected schools to send a summary report to every parent and to make it available to every member of the public.   Full reports must also be made available to all (at a cost of no more than 10p per sheet).   In addition, governing bodies are being urged to distribute the inspectorial reports as widely as possible to the media.

The second point is illustrated by *The framework for the inspection of schools* (Office for Standards in Education, 1992), the document prepared for the new inspectorial teams.   One of the characteristics of the old-style HMI reports was that "the focus tends to be on inspection and reporting procedures rather than clarifying and justifying the criterial basis of judgements" (Elliott and Ebbutt, 1986).   In short, the standards used tended to be implicit: a matter of following professional conventions.   Having to produce guidelines for a diverse set of inspectors - not necessarily the product of the same in-house culture - has meant much more explicit standards. Thus *The framework* sets out in great detail the indicators to be used and the questions to be asked, moving from structure to outputs. The document stops short of setting benchmarks - ie minimum standards which must be attained - and allows much scope for interpretation (eg of examination results). But it marks a major move towards explicit, publicly available, criteria.

Education thus provides a paradigm case of the regulatory system mirroring service developments. Schools were the laboratory for the Thatcher Government's first (and still boldest) experiment with quasi-markets. The result is the first, and still the only, regulatory system designed for diffuse lay purchasers - as distinct from managers or professionals - operating in a quasi-market with diffuse providers. Whether either the quasi-market or its regulatory system will work in the way intended is, of course, still very much an open question.

## The case of the personal social services

The creation of quasi-markets within the PSS is less advanced than in the NHS, education or housing, but there has been a long tradition of regulation, mainly registration and inspection, of non-statutory forms of residential and day care provision. Before Seebohm and the amalgamation of children's, health and welfare departments, there was an inspectorate in the Home Office concerned with the quality of childcare, and at the local level the new social service authorities became responsible for registering and inspecting residential provision for some adult groups, such as homes for older people and people with mental health problems; and for children, such as homes and foster homes; as well as day care for young children, such as childminders, playgroups, and nurseries. It was estimated in 1987 that there were already some 600,000 people using facilities directly regulated by LASSAs (Challis, 1987). More recently, and as an explicit part of the community care reforms and the implementation of the Children Act 1989, the role of local inspection units has increased (Challis and Hoyes, 1992), as has the role of the SSI at the central level (Day and Klein, 1990).

The PSS have always been characterised by diffuse providers ranging from the lone operator (a childminder for example) through

small private company providers (an older people's home) to the
big battalions of the large voluntary organisations (Barnardos or the
Children's Society for example). Even within the public sector, the
range and scale of the provision has always been diverse: from bath
aids to family therapy, from meals to intermediate treatment, from
Section 1 payments to residential care.   In other words, PSS
provision has been diffuse but it has also been diverse both within
and outside the public sector.   The intention is, of course, that this
diffuseness and diversity should be actively encouraged and that, in
addition, the centre of gravity of provision should shift from the
public to non-public sectors.   It is too early to say whether this
intention will be realised in practice: much depends upon the
structuring of the purchasing arrangements made since money was
transferred from the Department of Social Security to social
services departments in April 1993.

Classifying past purchasers of PSS as either diffuse or
concentrated is not easy.   Individuals with sufficient purchasing
power could buy PSS care privately, be it domestic help to
counteract physical frailty, psychotherapy to cope with emotional
trauma, or residential care to achieve total care.   But public
authorities were the principal purchasers of the services of some
large voluntary organisation provision.   Further, while the public
sector might be the principal purchaser, it was far from monolithic:
a variety of different local authorities were buying the care.   It was
also common for local authorities to buy provision from each other.
This was not just in the obvious case of highly specialised care
shared on a regional basis, but also of run-of-the-mill provision
where scarcity or the suitability of the provision to a particular
individual's needs prompted the purchase of service.

Despite the difficulties of reducing an extremely diverse set of
'purchasing' arrangements to a simple category there can be little
doubt that, in the short term at least, the government's intention is
that purchasing in the PSS should become more diffuse than has
hitherto been the case.   This is what care management is all about.
This model assumes that each care manager will purchase, on
behalf of the client/user, a package of care suitable for that
individual's needs; purchasers will be diffuse and so, too, will the
providers.   The ideal may, of course, prove elusive.   There are
signs already that purchasing will tend towards the 'block' variety
and that providers may also form consortia or coalesce into 'chains'.

This suggests that the PSS before the creation of quasi-markets
could be described as falling within box C, (relatively) concentrated

purchasers with (relatively) diffuse providers, but is now supposed to be heading towards box A, diffuse providers and diffuse purchasers. It may be, however, that its most likely destination will be box D: concentrated purchasers and concentrated providers.

How does the regulatory framework fit with this? In the past, regulation was entirely at the local level; it was not until 1985 that the Social Work Service became the SSI, and it is only in the last couple of years that the activities of the SSI have begun to catch up with its title. The main mechanism for control was registration and inspection, where the emphasis was almost entirely upon quality; it was quality control in the public interest and it was applied only to non-public provision (Challis, 1985). The reports which were produced on individual facilities were not available to the public, indeed some authorities cited fear of litigation as a reason for refusing to give enquirers any information at all, other than an address and telephone number. It was not usual for the providers to see copies of these reports, let alone to be given an opportunity to comment upon them. There was, therefore, almost no information exchange between the regulators and the private purchasers, although the public sector, in a purchasing role, was able to use the inspection reports as a guide to its own purchasing decisions.

Up to about 1986 contracts between providers and purchasers were of the most basic variety (Challis and Bartlett, 1988) and could not have provided protection for users in matters of quality. But after that time contracts came to be used more widely and formed part of the regulatory requirements. This regulatory picture seems to be broadly consistent with our proposition that type C situations will be characterised by a mixture of regulation and contracts.

The role of the inspection units has been substantially widened. First, the unit is to inspect public provision as well as private and voluntary; second, the reports of the units are to be made public; and third, the units are supported by an advisory committee (Challis, 1990). In addition, policy and practice guidance from the Department of Health has outlined further developments, namely the introduction of lay people and the possibility of global inspections, which are indicative of a belief that there must be a greater institutional regulatory presence in the new PSS. This is consistent with our proposition, since the ideal of diffuse provider and diffuse purchasers suggests a strong emphasis on regulation in order to reduce transactions costs.

If, as has been suggested, the ideal is not achieved and instead the PSS moves towards a type D situation, we may find that the regulatory institutions are somewhat out of place. It has already been suggested in some Department of Health guidance that the inspection units should have a role in inspecting contracts and cost effectiveness. It is too early to say how this would fit in with the organisation of contracting and contract compliance within social services departments. The substantial presence of the national SSI is also consistent with a move towards type A, but again if the result of the creation of quasi-markets is closer to D, then we might expect an altered role for the SSI.

## The case of the NHS

The NHS, before the introduction of the purchaser/provider split, was a clear example of control through a hierarchic managerial system. The control was by no means as effective in practice as theory would have implied: there was, in effect, a leakage of control because of the quasi-autonomous position held by the medical profession. However, there was no perceived need for any kind of regulatory or inspectorial mechanism, with one exception. This was the Hospital (later Health) Advisory Service, set up in 1969. Its function was to "advise the Secretary of State for Social Services about conditions in hospitals" for long-stay patients (Klein and Hall, 1974). It can therefore be seen as an instrument for illuminating those dark corners of the NHS where managerial control was weakest. Rather like the case of the HMI, it suggests that inspectorates will develop as tools of central government when multiple providers are intended to implement national policies and when there is either no direct control (as in the case of LEAs) or only a feeble grip because of the nature of the service being delivered (as in the case of long-stay hospitals).

However, although the NHS itself was largely unregulated, it did have one regulatory function. This was, and is, the regulation of private hospitals and private nursing homes (Day and Klein, 1985). This involves both control of entry through registration and the monitoring of standards through inspection. This can be seen as a response to a type A situation, in which diffuse purchasers have to deal with diffuse providers and where there are serious asymmetries of information (and where, as previously noted, individual purchasers may need prospective information rather than retrospective information based on what may be painful experience). However, inspection reports remain private documents - and, as such, unavailable to individual purchasers - which might suggest that the function of regulation has been perceived as ensuring minimum standards in the public interest rather than as a way of providing information to purchasers. The registration of private hospitals and nursing homes is thus a kite mark, rather than providing Michelin-style information about the facilities.

The introduction of the internal market did not lead to any strengthening of existing regulatory mechanisms or the creation of new ones. Nor is this surprising. The NHS, on the face of it, seems to be a clear-cut example of a type D situation. Concentrated purchasers face concentrated providers. The contract would thus seem to be the natural instrument for controlling standards and there would appear to be no need for any regulatory bodies. However, it is not self-evident that this situation will necessarily persist in future. There are a number of reasons for expecting the demand for the regulation of standards to increase, in order to provide information both to purchasers and to central government.

The first reason is that the NHS internal market is itself extremely diverse (Scrivens and Henneh, 1989). In some geographical areas, concentrated purchasers do indeed face concentrated providers. In effect, monopsony buyers are negotiating with monopsony producers and there is little, if any, competition. In other areas, notably London, the situation is very different, with a diversity of purchasers dealing with a diversity of providers: approaching a type A situation. Different situations clearly have very different implications for transactions costs. A purchaser dealing predominantly with one major local provider faces far fewer costs (and has less of a problem with the asymmetry of information) than a purchaser coping with a multiplicity of service suppliers.

Thus it might be argued that, to the extent that competition does become a reality, so the demand for regulatory bodies might be expected to increase. Purchasers would become increasingly reluctant to incur the costs of devising quality criteria for every contract (and, more expensive still, subsequently monitoring them) and come to see the attractions of third-party specification of standards and inspection of performance (particularly if the costs were to be carried by the providers themselves).

The other reason is GP fundholding. If this were to become the norm, then the NHS would become an example of a type B situation, with concentrated providers dealing with diffuse purchasers. Again, there would be geographical variations on this theme. In some areas, the providers themselves might be diffuse: ie there might be a genuinely competitive market. In other areas, fundholding GPs might pool their purchasing power - as they are already beginning to do by forming consortia - and thus could even end up in a type C situation.

But there is already considerable evidence that fundholding imposes considerable transactions costs on both the practices and the hospitals concerned (Duckworth, Day and Klein, 1992; Dinwoodie, 1993). As the number of contracts multiplies, so the task of managing and monitoring them becomes more complex and more expensive. In public policy terms, these costs may well be outweighed by the benefits brought about by fundholding: in particular, the way in which the new system has opened up the hospital system, challenged existing practices and changed the balance of power between consultants and GPs. But to the extent that third-party regulation could cut costs - by avoiding the necessity for fundholders to specify and monitor standards in each contract - so it might be expected to become an increasingly attractive option.

This, indeed, is what appears to be happening. There is increasing interest in the NHS in developing accreditation systems (Scrivens, 1993). The accreditation systems that have been set up so far are primarily intended to help providers to improve their own performance: they are essentially instruments for self-monitoring. The reports that they produce are designed for the consumption of the providers themselves, not for that of the public or purchasers at large. They are voluntary, not compulsory. In contrast to the regulatory systems in our other case studies, they do not regulate entry. They are also very limited in their scope: they audit organisational performance, not the quality of the medical care that is produced. In short, the emphasis is on organisational structure and process, not outcomes.

As at present constituted, the embryo accreditation systems in the NHS are therefore - at best - an adjunct to the contracting process as a means of controlling standards and quality. However, the growing interest in expanding their role may signal an awareness of their potential. If accreditation were to become compulsory, and if its scope were to be widened to inspecting and monitoring the quality of care being provided, then they could well become a means for cutting transactions costs for purchasers (whether or not they would lower the net costs of quality control is of course another, and open, question: they might simply shift the costs to the providers if, as in the USA, these were to be charged to those inspected).

However, there is a further consideration - independent of the nature of the NHS market - which is likely to shape regulatory strategy. As noted earlier, regulation has two faces: it provides information both to purchasers and to the public. It is a form of accountability and, as such, a check as much on the purchasers as on the providers. If the aim in the NHS is to ensure national standards, then there may well be a case for a national regulator: the pattern in social housing and education, though not in the social services.

## The case of social housing

Housing is rather different from our other case studies. Here the main change that has taken place is the emergence of the housing association movement as the main instrument of government policy for the development of social housing. Local authorities remain the dominant landlords in the field of social housing, despite tenant buy-outs and transfers. But the Housing Corporation, Scottish Homes and Housing for Wales have become the principal source of funding for new building. The Housing Corporation is the purchaser, the housing associations are the providers. It is a competitive market in the sense that the associations bid against each other for the funds distributed by the Corporation. In addition, following the 1988 Housing Act, the associations have to look to the private market for finance to supplement their grants from the Corporation.

This, then, seems to be an example of a type C situation: a concentrated purchaser dealing with diffuse providers. There are 2,500 housing associations, although only about 750 of these are developers and, as such, in the business of bidding for funds. The Housing Corporation alone (by far the biggest of the three) has to deal with some 540 associations when distributing its budget for development.

In what follows, this analysis will concentrate on the role of the Housing Corporation (the other two are similar in most key respects). In contrast to the NHS and the PSS, contracts do not feature as instruments of control in social housing. The Corporation controls new developments through its funding system: money goes only to those associations which put in bids that conform to local and national priorities, such as dwellings for the homeless. So the market is shaped by the purchaser's preferences and the willingness (and ability) of providers to respond to them.

Once development has taken place, the Corporation's chosen instrument is regulation, not contracting. The regulatory system of the Corporation (Day, Henderson and Klein, 1993) is designed to ensure that housing associations:

● manage their affairs not only with probity but also economically, efficiently and effectively;

● maintain adequate standards of management and service provision for their tenants;

● implement national social policy objectives such as an appropriate ethnic mix and tenant participation.

To achieve these aims, the Corporation has evolved an increasingly stringent regulatory regime. As the public funds invested in the housing association movement have increased, so have the demands of accountability. The regime is a mixture of desk-top monitoring - with increasing emphasis on the use of performance indicators and real-time financial information - and selective inspection. A set of standards have evolved, set out in the *Performance audit visit manual* (Housing Corporation, 1992). These reflect the aims of regulatory policy. One set of standards is about the managerial capacity and financial control systems of associations. Another is about the quality of the services provided to tenants, such as repair and maintenance. A third deals with the pursuit of desirable social policy goals. The onus is very much on housing associations to demonstrate that they have met these standards: that they have the managerial capacity to run their affairs in line with the policy goals set to them and that they have got the information required to assess their performance.

Finally, following inspection, associations are graded on a one to four scale: their rating, in turn, determines the follow-up action that is taken. In the case of associations with a poor rating, the Corporation disposes of a range of sanctions ranging from drafting new members onto management committees to dissolving them as autonomous organisations. In short, the Corporation has not only incentives but also the ability to intervene directly in the affairs of providers in order to mould the market: contrast its powers to the inability of NHS purchasers, for example, to exert any direct leverage on providers (apart from the threat of withdrawing custom) who, in the case of trusts, are directly accountable to the Department of Health.

So much for the strengths of the regulatory system for social housing. There are also some limitations. The Corporation's system of inspection is, as already noted, highly selective. The programme of visits is largely determined by the degree of risk to public funds. There is a high concentration on developing associations: the 1,600 plus management only associations (which, however, are responsible for less than 10% of the units in England) tend to be neglected. The emphasis on public accountability has also meant that as the regulatory system has evolved, so there has been a deliberate effort to diminish the consultancy role of inspection staff. In short, the emphasis is on using limited monitoring resources parsimoniously by concentrating on the largest associations and on the high risk ones, even at the cost of some leakage in terms of ensuring good stewardship, protecting the interests of tenants and the achievement of national social policy aims at the margins. Lastly, the regime is very much driven by accountability to the monopoly purchaser: inspection reports are private documents though associations may, if they so wish, show them to tenants or private lenders. There is no requirement (as in the case of local authorities) to make indicators of performance publicly available.

Social housing thus provides an example of a regulatory regime which appears to be successful in managing and shaping the market to its own requirements and those of public policy at a relatively low cost: the annual salary budget for the monitoring and inspection staff in England is £3,100,000, less than 0.2% of the annual funding of associations and a much smaller proportion of the total public investment. Transactions costs are largely transferred onto the providers, on whom the burden of compliance with national standards and goals falls. However, the price of making housing associations the tools of public policy is, inevitably, a diminution of autonomy which could eventually also lead to a loss of flexibility.

## Conclusions

This chapter represents a first step towards exploring a complex topic, drawing on a still continuing programme of research, and any conclusions drawn must be appropriately tentative and provisional. However, it does appear that, in line with expectations, the more diffuse a quasi-market (on both the purchaser and provider side), the more regulation there is. Conversely, the more concentrated a quasi-market, the less regulation there is. So schools and the social services are at the intense end of the regulatory spectrum, just as they are examples of diffuse purchasers dealing with diffuse providers (ie in the type A category, to return to Figure 1). In contrast, the NHS is at the opposite end of the regulatory spectrum with no regulatory machinery at all for the public sector, just as it is an example of concentrated purchasers dealing with concentrated providers (ie in the type D category). The mixed case of social housing - a monopoly purchaser dealing with diffuse providers (type C) - provides an example, rather surprisingly perhaps, of strong regulation.

Transactions costs may provide a plausible, if partial, explanation for this pattern. In the case of the NHS, the cost of writing contracts may be relatively small for those purchasers dealing with few providers (though, as noted above, this conclusion must be qualified geographically and would no longer hold if fundholding were to become the norm). In the case of education and the social services, multiple contracts with diffuse providers may impose relatively higher costs: hence the attractions of using regulation to control and monitor standards as a means of simplifying the task of writing and policing contracts. Similarly, the existence of multiple providers in social housing may explain the attractions of using regulation, rather than contracts, in order to reduce transactions costs.

However, this conclusion must be qualified. Other factors clearly have to be taken into account. First, there is the legacy of history: in some cases regulatory regimes have been inherited, as we have seen, rather than newly created, and may thus reflect as much past conditions as the demands of the new quasi-markets. Second, the four policy fields vary on one important dimension: the degree of professionalisation. Thus in the case of the NHS (in contrast to both education and the social services) the professional providers, ie doctors, have traditionally been perceived as the guardians of standards and there is a long established machinery of professional self-regulation - although the 1989 reforms of the NHS suggest that this perception is changing, while at the same time the machinery of self-regulation is coming under increasing criticism. Third, purchasers vary on more dimensions than suggested by our concentrated/diffuse dichotomy. Thus the asymmetry of information between purchasers and providers may be more pronounced in the case of parents than in that of care managers or of fundholders. So if regulation is seen as a way of minimising this asymmetry, then one might well expect a more stringent system to develop in education than in the social services or health care.

The other factor complicating the analysis is the relationship between purchasers and regulators. In the case of social housing, the purchasers are also the regulators. In the case of the social services, the regulators are semi-independent of the purchasers. In the case of schools, the regulators are totally independent of the purchasers. Thus centralised third-party regulation turns out to be the exception. Yet it is precisely this type of regulation which might be expected if the aim of policy is to monitor the standards of the purchasers, as well as those of the providers: this would be the logic, as suggested above, of introducing third-party accreditation in the NHS. Purchasers may favour regulation as a way of cutting their transactions costs, with contracts used to determine price and volume, leaving it to regulation to control standards. But, over and above that, there is the 'public interest' argument in favour of regulation as a way of controlling purchasers.

At the beginning of this chapter we stressed that, given the transitional nature of the new quasi-markets, we must expect them to develop at different rates and in different ways. One factor which may influence development is the government's political commitment to reducing the regulatory burden on small businesses. It is this which lies behind the Department of Health's recent trawl of opinion about the scope for relaxing the regulatory requirements for residential and nursing home care. A deregulatory initiative such as this would have different impacts across our four areas; it would be substantial in the PSS but, for example, less so in education where the bulk of provision is likely to remain within the public sector. In other words, the pressure for deregulation is likely to vary in strength from one policy area to another and in consequence the regulatory regimes may become yet more diverse.

In summary, then, it seems reasonable to predict that to the extent that quasi-markets develop as presently intended, and to the extent that they become competitive, and with the caveat that deregulation does not become a major policy objective in its own right, so the institutions of regulation can be expected to grow in scope and importance. Perhaps, too, there will be a move towards centralisation and a clearer divorce between purchasing and regulatory functions. However, if the quasi-markets turn out to be stunted monuments to unrealised expectations, then we may be left with institutions of regulation that have a symbolic rather than an effective role.

## References

Audit Commission (1989) *Assuring quality in education*, London: HMSO.

Bartlett, W. (1991) *Privatisation and quasi-markets*, Studies in Decentralisation and Quasi-Markets no 7, Bristol: SAUS Publications, School for Advanced Urban Studies, University of Bristol.

Brain, J. and Klein, R. (1993) *Schools: how much choice?*, Bath: Centre for the Analysis of Social Policy, University of Bath.

Centre for Policy on Ageing (1984) *Home life: a code of practice for residential care*, London: CPA.

Challis, L. (1985) 'Controlling for care: private and voluntary homes registration and inspection - a forgotten area of social work', *British Journal of Social Work*, vol 15, pp 43-56.

Challis, L. (1987) 'Regulation of private social care', in B. Lewis (ed) *Care and control: personal social services and the private sector*, Discussion Paper 15, London: Policy Studies Institute.

Challis, L. (1990) *Organising public social services*, London: Longman.

Challis, L. and Bartlett, H. (1988) *Old and ill: private nursing homes for elderly people*, London: Age Concern.

Challis, L. and Hoyes, L. (1992) *The development of social services inspection units in Wales*, Bath/Bristol: Centre for the Analysis of Social Policy, University of Bath and School of Advanced Urban Studies, University of Bristol.

Day, P. and Klein, R. (1985) 'Maintaining standards in the independent sector of health care', *British Medical Journal*, vol 290, p 1020-22.

Day, P. and Klein, R. (1987) *Accountabilities*, London: Tavistock.

Day, P. and Klein, R. (1990) *Inspecting the inspectorates*, York: Joseph Rowntree Foundation.

Day, P., Henderson, D. and Klein, R. (1993) *Regulating social housing*, York: Joseph Rowntree Foundation.

Department of Education and Science (1983) *The work of HM Inspectorate in England and Wales*, London: HMSO.

Department of Education and Science (1986) *Reporting inspections: HMI methods and procedures*, London: DES.

Department of Education (1992) *Inspecting schools: a guide to the inspection provisions of the Education (Schools) Act of 1992*, Mimeo, London: DE.

Department of Health (1989) *Homes are for living in*, London: HMSO.

Dinwoodie, M. (1993) *Report of the director of primary and community care: GP fundholding allocations*, Mimeo, London: North West Thames Regional Health Authority.

Duckworth, J., Day, P. and Klein, R. (1992) *The first wave: a study of fundholding in the West Midlands*, Birmingham: West Midlands Regional Health Authority.

Elliott, J. and Ebbutt, D. (1986) 'How do Her Majesty's Inspectors judge educational quality?', *Curriculum*, vol 7, no 3, pp 130-40.

Glennerster, H. (1991) 'Quasi-markets for education?', *Economic Journal*, vol 101, pp 1268-76.

Housing Corporation (1992) *Performance audit visit manual*, London: Housing Corporation.

Kay, J. and Vickers, J. (1988) 'Regulatory reform in Britain', *Economic Policy*, October, pp 286-351.

Klein, R. and Hall, P. (1974) *Caring for quality in the caring services*, London: Centre for Studies in Social Policy.

Lawton, D. and Gordon, P. (1987) *HMI*, London: Routledge and Kegan Paul.

Le Grand, J. (1992) *Paying for or providing welfare?*, Studies in Decentralisation and Quasi-Markets no 15, Bristol: SAUS Publications, School for Advanced Urban Studies, University of Bristol.

Lee, T. (1990) *Carving out the cash for schools*, Bath: Centre for the Analysis of Social Policy, University of Bath.

National Association of Health Authorities (1985) *Registration and inspection of nursing homes: a handbook for health authorities*, Birmingham: NAHA.

Office for Standards in Education (1992) *The handbook for the inspection of schools*, London: OFSTED.

Propper, C. (1992) *Is further regulation of quasi-markets in welfare necessary?*, Studies in Decentralisation and Quasi-Markets no 14, Bristol: SAUS Publications, School for Advanced Urban Studies, University of Bristol.

Scrivens, E. and Henneh, A. (1989) 'Working for patients: making the internal market effective', *Public Money and Management*, Winter, pp 53-57.

Scrivens, E. (1993) *Accreditation for hospitals*, Bath: Centre for the Analysis of Social Policy, University of Bath.

Secretary of State for Education (1992) *Choice and diversity: a new framework for schools*, Cm 2021, London: HMSO.

Tomlinson, Sir B. (1992) *Report of the inquiry into London's health service*, London: HMSO.

*part one*

# EDUCATION

*two*

# EVALUATING THE PERFORMANCE OF QUASI-MARKETS IN EDUCATION

## Rosalind Levacic

This chapter is an attempt at an initial assessment of the effects of the development of quasi-markets in state schooling on the efficiency and effectiveness of schools. The 1988 Education Reform Act and its subsequent implementation replaced LEA administrative allocation of pupils and resources to schools with a system of quasi-markets whereby each school manages its own budget which depends primarily on its success at attracting pupils. The empirical data which this assessment draws upon are from an ESRC funded study of the impact of formula funding on schools (the IFFS project) and further work on schools' funding formulae undertaken at the Open University between 1990 and 1992.

## Policy background

The 1988 Education Reform Act diminished LEAs' administrative control of schools in three principal ways.

- *Local management of schools (LMS).* LEAs have been required to delegate budgets to schools for governing bodies to spend as they think fit for the purposes of the school, including the power to appoint, discipline and dismiss staff.

- *More open enrolment.* LEAs can no longer manage schools' rolls since a school must admit pupils up to its standard admission number, except in the case of schools which select by ability or religious affiliation. Parents can appeal against the refusal of a place at a school with no surplus places and may be successful.

● *Opting out.* Provisions for schools to opt out of LEA control to become grant-maintained by the Department for Education.

While these quasi-market developments have been presented by the government as reducing bureaucracy and enhancing parental choice and school autonomy, they have been accompanied by considerable extension of central government control over schools. The 1988 Act introduced a national curriculum, statutory assessment and the publication of school 'league tables' of results. The Education (Schools Act) 1992 set up a new regulatory framework in the form of the Office for Standards in Education (OFSTED) which organises the inspection of all schools every four years and trains and licences registered inspectors who tender for inspection contracts.

LEAs are thus threatened with complete dismemberment, while teachers' work is more closely controlled and monitored by the Department for Education and its agencies. These forms of hierarchical control are buttressed by control of teachers and governors through contingency payments since the funding formula must allocate at least 75%[1] of school budgets according to the number and ages of the pupils at each school (Department of Education and Science, 1988). This, married with more open enrolment, increases schools' incentive to engage in activities which recruit pupils. However, the competition faced by a school is highly dependent on local factors, in particular the number of potential pupils in the area and the presence within travelling distance of other schools with spare places.

These quasi-market developments relate to two interconnected but distinct sets of transactions:

● *the output market* - or the market for pupils in which the price for educating a pupil is largely determined by the formula funding mechanism;

● *the input market* - delegated budgeting has monetised the transactions by which schools obtain the inputs which they then transform into educational outcomes.

## Criteria for assessing quasi-market performance

The following official statement encapsulates what education ministers and high level Department for Education civil servants have reiterated as the intention of their reforms:

> The Government's principal aims for schools are to improve standards of achievement for all pupils across the curriculum, to widen the choice available for parents for the education of their children and to enable schools to respond effectively to what parents and the community require of them, thus securing the best possible return from the substantial investment of resources. With this in mind the Education Reform (Act) includes provisions ... to require all LEAs to develop schemes of resource allocation to schools and to delegate budgetary control to all ... schools. (Department for Education, 1988)

The general run of the argument for greater competition and school autonomy is familiar (Hillgate Group, 1986; Chubb and Moe, 1990; Green, 1991). Competition between schools will force schools to improve standards and differentiate their product in order to attract pupils. Schools which fail to do this will be closed because of lack of funds. Published performance indicators aid parental choice by exposing 'good' and 'bad' schools. LMS gives schools the means to improve educational standards, respond to customers and use resources more efficiently than LEA bureaucracies did. Given these stated objectives, the criteria I propose to use are as follows:

● productive efficiency[2] or value for money;

● improvements in the standard of education provided;

● greater responsiveness to customer preferences which are therefore reflected in greater differentiation of the types of educational provision;

● equity, including both procedural and distributional definitions.

Much of the literature on education markets is polemical and lacks theories-in-action to explain the internal processes in schools by which autonomy and choice would lead to school improvement. One has to look to the literature on school effectiveness and school improvement for research evidence on such processes.[3] Chubb and Moe (1990) provide the best known attempt to develop and test the hypothesis that school effectiveness depends on organisational features which are created by autonomous (ie private) schools and which cannot be generated in schools subject to bureaucratic and political controls. However British educational reforms are a long way from creating schools independent of state control (Flew, 1991). Since it is only through changes in internal school processes that one can expect improved educational standards and a closer matching of schools' educational outputs to client preferences, researchers must investigate how internal school management and learning processes have been affected by recent educational reforms (Glatter and Woods, 1992; Woods, 1992).

In the rest of this chapter I shall examine in turn the output and input side quasi-market developments affecting schools and attempt to judge the impact of these in terms of the four key criteria listed above.

## The output market: formula funding as price formation

The funding formula is crucial in establishing the conditions under which schools compete in the internal market. The Department of Education and Science (1988) prescribed the formula quite closely to ensure that the bulk of a school's budget is determined by the number and ages of its pupils and that very limited discretion in funding individual schools remained with LEAs. The formula can also take account of differences in pupils' social background and educational need and differences in schools' costs because of their size and type of building (Thomas, 1990, 1991). Four year transitional adjustments enabled LEAs to phase in budget changes so that schools losing budget did not have to adjust to massive cuts over a very short period. The most controversial part of the formula was the Department for Education stipulation that the teaching cost element in the formula must, except for schools with nine or fewer teachers, be calculated on the basis of the average cost of teachers in the LEA and not on their actual cost to the school.

It is clear from the IFFS project and work done with Sheffield LEA (Sheffield City Council, 1992) that the funding formula is an instrument for transmitting LEA policies[4] regarding differential funding for special needs, support of small schools and the relative resourcing of the different age groups, as also noted by the LMS initiative study (LMS Initiative, 1992). With the transparency provided by published formulae, knowledge of differences in the funding of pupils of different ages and in different kinds of school is more widely dispersed, making the formula the focus of conflict between different interests: price in this quasi-market is therefore determined politically and not by the forces of supply and demand.

The IFFS project undertook a detailed analysis of the extent of school budget changes and factors associated with the size of budget gain or loss over the years 1989/90 to 1991/92 for all schools in 'Barsetshire' (Levacic, 1993). The conclusions reached were as follows.[5]

- The formula is by itself redistributive. Holding all school variables constant, the formula redistributes a given overall budget between schools compared to the previous allocation system.

- The formula tends to favour schools with low unit costs and has narrowed unit cost differentials. (The tendency for small schools - which have higher unit costs - to lose out under formula funding is corroborated by Bullock and Thomas, 1992 and the LMS Initiative, 1992.)

- Schools with higher proportions of socially disadvantaged pupils as measured by the index used by the authority for formula funding did not suffer budget losses.

- Having teachers with above average salaries made only a minor contribution to explaining budget changes, and was only of significance for primary schools.

Overall I think it is fairly safe to conclude that the funding formula promotes cost efficiency in that it is biased against high unit cost schools and its transparency is leading to stronger questioning of the case for retaining such schools. This tendency is intensified by financial stringency though LEAs have been reluctant to rationalise their school systems because schools threatened with closure have succeeded in becoming grant-maintained.[7]

The equity implications of formula funding are less clear cut. As far as procedural equity is concerned the formula scores in that it makes transparent the rules for distribution and minimises the scope for LEA officer and local politician discretion with respect to individual schools. In relation to distributional equity the issue is whether socially and educationally disadvantaged pupils have received proportionately less resourcing than before. My own detailed analysis of four authorities' formulae has not produced evidence to support this, though the LMS Initiative (1992) reports that schools suffering more than 10% budget loss have higher than average proportions of special needs pupils, but no statistical significance for the data is given.   The continued squeeze on education budgets and the probable imposition of a common funding formula based on standard spending assessments do not bode well for the future funding of non-statemented special needs.

## The output market: competition for pupils

One of the peculiar features of this quasi-market is the reluctance of schools to expand once they have reached full capacity: it is difficult to fund investment in plant and there is a great reluctance to create larger school communities.   This leaves competition for pupils as a possible spur to improvement only for those schools which are under-subscribed.

In Barsetshire there was some evidence of greater parental competition for places, with the number of applications for out-of-catchment area school rising, as were the number of appeals.[8]   Of the eleven schools in the IFFS study, three were close to or above capacity and unwilling to expand.   The eight schools with surplus places were not yet showing signs of competing for pupils but colluded in 'gentlemanly' agreements not to recruit from each other's catchments.   These schools responded by attempting to assert and communicate their existing perceived strengths as educational communities, for example as a family village school, as a caring community school or as a church school.

Critics of the current forms of competition for pupils have argued that these will be socially inefficient because of 'cream-skimming' of the more able pupils by schools (Glennester, 1991; Miliband, 1991).   However, there was little evidence of this in our study given the reluctance among schools to compete and the inability of non-selective schools to fine tune entry requirements, except in the case of voluntary aided schools.   Nor was there any indication in this LEA that falling rolls were associated with the proportion of socially disadvantaged pupils at the school (Levacic, 1993).   However, one school in an area of social deprivation could not attract pupils from outside its council estate, while some local parents preferred schools off the estate.[9]

## The input market: resource management within schools

Delegation to schools of management responsibilities for finance and staffing is intended to provide the means to improve by enabling schools to purchase inputs which had previously been administratively allocated.

> Effective schemes of LMS will enable governing bodies and headteachers to plan their use of resources - including their most valuable resource, their staff, to maximum effect in accordance with their own needs and priorities. (Department of Education and Science, 1988)

The IFFS project investigated the financial and resource management decision-making practices adopted by the eleven case study schools from April 1990, when the schools received fully delegated budgets, to early 1992 when the project ended. Interviews were conducted with headteachers and other senior staff, chairs of the governing body or finance committee and classroom teachers; finance committee and governing body meetings were observed and relevant school and LEA documents studied. The resulting data were analysed in various ways. A site report summarising the process of financial management was produced for each school, the data was coded in Hyperqual using codes reflecting different aspects of budget decision making and expenditure decisions at each school were classified by type. The account given attempts to generalise across the eleven schools and to summarise and so it inevitably neglects the more subtle differences between schools which a longer account would provide. Many of the IFFS findings are consistent with those of the HMI (1992) report on the implementation of LMS which studied 61 schools (all budget gainers) in 21 LEAs from 1989 to 1992.

### *Perceived benefits and costs of school based budget management*

Headteachers and other senior staff with financial responsibilities by and large welcomed LMS, as did most of the governors interviewed, though they had reservations about specific issues. Sixteen of the twenty senior teachers interviewed (and all the headteachers) welcomed LMS even in schools which had lost budget, ranking the benefits in the following order:

- greater school autonomy;
- improved financial awareness in schools;
- more efficient use of resources;
- greater flexibility in resource use;
- improved planning within schools.

(Marren and Levacic, 1994)

The reasons given by Fenmore's head were typical:

> The major benefit has been the flexibility and the ability to
> target money to where we see the need and to do the things
> that we want to do - our priorities.  It's given us a much better
> sense of planning for ourselves because the whole process of
> drawing up a budget means that we have to examine our
> priorities and sift through, trim down and reorganise and
> replan.  It's bound to concentrate the mind on the service we
> are offering, how we can improve it, how we can direct
> money to crack a certain problem; but the exasperating side
> of this is that we have had so much docked away that the
> service we are offering is going to be threatened severely.
> There is precious little money to be flexible with but it has
> helped.

Widespread support for LMS was also found by HMI (1992) and in
a national survey commissioned by the National Association of
Head Teachers (NAHT) (Arnott et al, 1992).

The major cost of LMS is the time taken both by senior staff and
governors and by administrative and clerical staff within schools,
especially in the initial years when the new financial reporting
systems were failing to provide timely and correct financial
information.  The administrative burden of LMS for the senior
teacher responsible for financial management was greater when
she/he could not depend on a capable school finance officer.  There
was also a tendency, as noted by the Audit Commission (1993) for
senior teachers managing the budget to spend disproportionate
amounts of time on routine administration.

Classroom teachers perceived the same benefits and costs of
LMS and ranked them in a very similar order but a lower
proportion of them (60% or less out of 41 interviewees) perceived
the benefits.  Their perception of benefits related more to their
degree of involvement in financial decision making and personal
interest in it than to the state of their school's finances.

*Budget decision making: operating in input markets*

This section examines the budget decisions made by the case study schools and attempts to assess the extent to which LMS promotes efficiency in resource use. This will inevitably be a qualitative judgement as the methods used did not enable any quantitative measures of efficiency to be obtained. One major problem is the difficulty of obtaining measures of educational output. There are currently in Britain very few longitudinal quantitative measures of school effectiveness in place which necessarily puts much of the onus for assessment on qualitative judgements of teaching process and pupils' work, of which the most comprehensive are those produced by HMI - now recast as OFSTED and its registered inspectors. The empirical evidence on school cost functions, most of it from North America, has not shown significant relationships between school output measures and the quantity of resources (Hanushek, 1986). The quantitative output effects of changing input use in schools are not known to practitioners, who rely on professional judgement in determining resource use. Since school effectiveness studies have shown the importance of process variables in explaining differential effectiveness, any properly specified model for testing input-output relationships would need to include these as well as physical measures of resource use.

Information on spending decisions made in 1990/91 and 1991/92 by the case study schools was obtained from interviews and from school budget print-outs and committee minutes (Marren and Levacic, 1992). Expenditure decisions were categorised by school and by type. Five of the schools lost budget due to the effect of moving to formula funding, but because Barsetshire's primary budget increased in 1990/91 and rolls rose in particular schools, only two schools actually had a lower budget in 1990/91 than in 1989/90, though two more felt tightly constrained.

A number of schools managed to balance their planned budgets for 1990/91 due to the voluntary retirement of senior staff. This reflects a national trend in the growth of early retirement of teachers from 7,500 in 1987/88 to around 12,400 in 1988/89 and 1989/90 (Hofkins, 1990). The schools did their utmost to avoid compulsory redundancies and gave teacher staffing the highest priority. The schools studied resorted to employing young and cheap teachers of necessity when tightly constrained financially. HMI (1992), though, noted a tendency among schools which were not budget losers to appoint younger staff than previously, and

Marr (1992) noted the same for small primary schools. As reported by HMI (1992, p 24), "the majority of schools manage any problems with their staffing costs by viring money from other headings".

The greater flexibility of delegated budgeting also led to more part-time staff being appointed by the case study schools, so that specific curriculum needs could be met cost-effectively. More temporary staff were appointed, largely because of uncertainty about future budgets. HMI (1992) also report an increase in the employment of temporary and part-time teachers.

The IFFS headteachers were conscious of operating in a market for teachers and needing to pay at the appropriate scale point and incentive allowance to get the specialism and expertise required. Evidence of this developing on a national scale is reported by Marr (1992). However there was no movement at all in the IFFS schools towards using the new pay flexibilities to relate pay to teacher performance (as also noted by Marr, 1992; HMI, 1992; School Teachers' Pay Review Body, 1992; Sinclair and Seifert, 1993). Incentive allowances were granted for specific responsibilities and a handful of heads and deputies were moved up the salary scale in those schools with money to spare.

It has often been noted that teachers spend too much time on tasks which do not require their professional skills and could be undertaken more cheaply by support staff (Audit Commission, 1991; Mortimore et al, 1992). Delegated budgeting has given schools greatly enlarged scope for revising job descriptions and pay, creating new posts and building up a team of people with loyalty to the school. However the scope for doing this was limited in the first four years of LMS by the requirement under competitive tendering legislation that schools take on local authority contracts for services such as cleaning, maintenance and even caretaking. All the IFFS schools spent more on financial administrative support, both in terms of more hours and giving existing staff higher pay for taking on new responsibilities. Some schools, even in the first year, made some innovative appointments: a qualified librarian, a groundsman, a parents' room organiser and classroom assistants, particularly in primary schools. The IFFS schools felt that they could obtain better value for money by employing their own contractors or employees for grounds maintenance, repair and small buildings work and especially cleaning. HMI (1992) also note the increased employment of ancillary staff and "the fact that minor works can be carried out quickly has removed a major source of frustration from staff". There was a widespread desire for further delegation of these 'operational' services, except by the smallest schools. Utilities were another area for improved efficiency. When their energy and water bills were paid by the LEA schools had no financial incentive to economise. It was notable that all the IFFS schools, except a large budget gainer, made considerable efforts to save money on utilities.

Greater value was placed by schools on LEA educational services such as educational psychologists, welfare officers, advisory teachers, curriculum initiatives, library and museums services and outdoor education centres. This is one area where a proper internal market is being developed with schools chosing between buying LEA or private sector services (often provided by ex-LEA employees) or self provision. The market allows schools to express preferences over what is supplied and so promotes both productive and allocative efficiency, though the counter-argument is the claim that LEAs make preferable distributional decisions regarding individual pupils than do schools. The countervailing efficiency factors are loss of economies of scale in the central production and allocation of such services and the contracting costs of quasi-markets. Small schools are disadvantaged by both economies of scale and contracting costs though bulk contracting and clustering (ie consumer cooperatives) are developing.

Schools now also have a financial incentive to make commercial use of their assets. For most schools income generation, apart from Parent Teacher Association activities, involves renting out premises and equipment. Among the IFFS schools it was those in straightened financial circumstances which made efforts at income generation; others felt the time involved was not worth the extra money.

*The search for efficiency*

Schools, both in Barsetshire and nationally (HMI, 1992; LMS Initiative, 1992) largely underspent their budgets in 1990/91 and 1991/92. Partly this was due to caution given the lack of data for accurate budget monitoring and also due to the desire to accumulate reserves for a future when budgets would be cut. Senior managers put in an enormous amount of time and effort, especially when funds were tight, to manage their budgets carefully and get value for money in terms of the inputs acquired. Governors by and large also took the task of budget management very seriously, though their capacity to do so was limited by their personal expertise and by the restricted amount of information supplied by the LEA and senior staff.

The evidence presented above shows that delegated budgeting and the development of quasi-markets has improved efficiency on the *input side* of the education production function. School managers are seeking and finding new ways of using and combining resource inputs. In particular they are more successful than LEA administrative allocation in concentrating the resources available to them on direct teaching and learning.

## The impact of LMS on educational standards

If LMS is to have an impact on educational standards[10] it must affect what happens in the classroom. One way for this is to occur is through a more cost-effective deployment of a given quantity of resources. However, it is unlikely that the effect of a modest increase in resources on educational outcomes could be picked up statistically when major externally imposed curriculum change is occurring as well as some reduction in the overall level of per pupil funding in real terms. Research shows that process variables rather than small differences in resourcing are important determinants of school effectiveness (Rutter et al, 1979; Purkey and Smith, 1983; Hanushek, 1986; Mortimore et al, 1988; Reynolds, 1992; Willms, 1992).

A second possible channel whereby LMS could improve educational standards is by stimulating those processes which are associated with school effectiveness and school improvement[11] (Chubb and Moe, 1990; Malen et al, 1990). It is, of course, too early to expect LMS to have led to significant organisational changes. The most a project such as IFFS can do is provide tentative evidence on the first indications of organisational change and its possible implications for school effectiveness. There are three areas of organisational change (or its absence) that are illuminated by the IFFS findings:

● the changing role of the headteacher in relation to the increased operational responsibilities placed on schools and the greater complexity of the school's external environment;

● the processes of policy formation and planning within schools;

● the lack of involvement of class teachers in resource management.

## The new role of the headteacher

Since school effectiveness research points to the importance of the leadership qualities of the headteacher, the impact of LMS on the work of headteachers is clearly important. Not surprisingly, most of the work of LMS was found to be done by headteachers and senior staff. While governing bodies' work and responsibilities had grown, active decision making about finance and resources was largely the province of the headteacher, together with senior staff in secondary schools. These conclusions are consistent with other evidence (Malen et al, 1990[12]; New, Deem and Brehony, 1993; Creese, 1992; HMI, 1992). The general pattern of budget planning was for the headteacher and, if the role existed, senior teacher in charge of finance, to put a budget plan to the governors' finance committee, which scrutinised it with perhaps minor changes, and then forwarded it to the governing body where it would be discussed and approved. In three of the schools, however, the governors' involvement in budget setting was minimal.

The crucial issue for headteachers is how to take on the role of 'chief executive' now required by LMS while also maintaining the role of 'professional leader' within the school (categories developed in Hall et al, 1986). Lack of finance to provide additional non-teaching time for other staff forces primary headteachers to take on financial management themselves. In small primary schools teaching heads have very little time for financial management. One such school in the IFFS study was struggling to cope, while the other coped well because a parent governor acted as budget manager.

A crucial question, therefore, is whether greater school autonomy in determining how to use resources contributes enough to the effectiveness with which the learning process is managed to offset the inability of the headteacher to concentrate solely on the management of teaching and learning which is a vital factor in determining differences in schools' effectiveness. The IFFS headteachers were all highly conscious of this dilemma and were resolving it in different ways. Three basic strategies were discernible:

- carry on as the professional leader and do the minimum possible with respect to LMS;

- take on responsibilities for financial management as well as the previous role;

- take on the role of chief executive but delegate finance to leave space for educational leadership.

## Planning within schools

School effectiveness has also been shown to be associated with clear and shared organisational goals. LMS has been accompanied by considerable emphasis both from the Department for Education and within the profession on school developmental planning (Hargreaves et al, 1989; Caldwell and Spinks, 1988; Hargreaves and Hopkins, 1991). In most of the IFFS schools LMS was beginning to stimulate a more comprehensive and deliberate attempt to articulate priorities and relate them to resource needs. Only Yellowstone School was observed to prepare its budget making explicit reference to a school development plan. In other schools the connections between school aims and priorities, decisions about curriculum and staffing and the consequent implications for the budget were only fully appreciated, if at all, by a small group within the senior management team. Similar observations were made by HMI (1992, p 12):

> Few school development plans link proposed action to resource allocation in order to make sure that the budget is constructed to facilitate the school's priorities.

The widely experienced difficulty of linking budget planning to the educational purposes of the school follows from the ambiguous nature of the relationships between inputs and outputs in the education production function. This ambiguity lies at the heart of the problem of trying to get a purchase on tracing causal links between school based management and improved educational outcomes.

## The empowerment of class teachers

Classroom teachers in the IFFS study remained largely remote from financial decision making. Their most active involvement was being consulted about specific decisions being made by the senior management. This occurred more in primary and middle schools, with their smaller staff numbers, than in secondary schools. Only in the three large primary schools had classroom teachers been in any way empowered by LMS in that they had been allocated budgets to spend for their class and curriculum needs. Some secondary heads of department felt less empowered because they no longer had LEA subject advisers as an alternative source of funds while the senior management were becoming more centralised in their allocation of departmental allowances. The concentration of financial management in the hands of a small group of senior staff has been noted in other studies of LMS (Broadbent et al, 1992a, 1992b; Bowe and Ball, 1992). Our data confirm that this is largely done in order to protect classroom teachers from the worry and time demands of financial management and has their tacit approval, since they are already over-stretched coping with legislative changes. Yet it is class teachers who must ultimately deliver any improvements in educational outcomes, beyond the extra resourcing secured by cost-effective resource management by senior staff. But, as HMI (1992, p 16) reports:

> LMS has not so far changed the basic structures of middle management in schools. ... LMS does not inform the long-term planning of most departments as much as it could or should.

## Conclusion

When quasi-market developments in education are examined within the context of all the other legislative changes affecting schools since 1988, they have increased the powers of headteachers (and nominally governors) over the operational aspects of managing schools. However, this has occurred within a new framework of central control whereby the educational output of schools is being tightly specified and monitored by central government. As far as the intended aims for LMS are concerned, I consider that there are good grounds for concluding that it has improved the productive efficiency of resource use, though this conclusion depends on assuming that educational output has not diminished as a result of LMS sufficiently to offset the more efficient use of inputs for a given level of output. The only caveat to this conclusion is doubt as to whether LMS is cost effective for small primary schools.

These quasi-market developments are changing internal management processes, though what the impact on educational outcomes is likely to be is still difficult to discern, especially so soon. The tentative conclusion so far must be that the evidence for any resulting improvement in educational standards is relatively sparse. As HMI (1992, p 11) concludes:

> There is little evidence yet of LMS having any substantial impact on educational standards, although specific initiatives have led to improvements in targeting of resources and staff and so to improvements in the quality of educational experience.

The NAHT national survey (Arnott et al, 1992) reported that while 41% of primary heads and 71% of secondary heads agreed that the additional workload of LMS was compensated by greater flexibility, only 30% and 56% respectively agreed that children's learning was benefiting. Malen et al (1990, p 323), in surveying the North American literature, conclude that "the link between school-based management and the evocation of effective schools is fragile at best".

In comparison with other public services, schooling is unique in the extent to which quasi-markets have been accompanied by an extension of central hierarchical control which specifies the product on behalf of the customer. This could only be justified, if at all, on efficiency grounds by the extent of market failure due to imperfect information. In these circumstances the choice facing the customer is limited and its extent will depend on whether the government continues to fund surplus places and is prepared to finance the growth of existing schools and the entry of new ones. Quasi-markets in the school sector are restricted to a set of franchised outlets, some of which compete against each other for customers, and all of which have the freedom to buy their inputs in markets rather than have them administratively allocated. Quasi-markets appear to be productively efficient on the input side but the verdict on whether in their current form and context they can promote school effectiveness remains open.

## Acknowledgement

I wish to acknowledge the receipt of grant R000 23 2234 from the Economic and Social Research Council which funded most of the research on which this chapter is based.

## Notes

1.  Circular 7/88 stipulated 75%; Circular 9/91 (Department of Education and Science, 1991) stipulated 80% of the aggregated schools budget must be allocated according to the number and ages of pupils and could include up to 5% allocated by quantitative indicators of pupils' special needs.

2.  Productive efficiency is generally defined in relation to the cost of achieving a given specification of output and does not depend on assessing the social value of the output.

3.  For example Rutter et al (1979), Mortimore et al (1988), Purkey and Smith (1983), Reynolds (1992).

4.  Or in the future Funding Agency policies for schools.

5.  These conclusions were also found in an earlier study (Levacic, 1992).

6.  Whether small schools are 'cost effective' or 'socially desirable' is a further issue.

7.  For instance a 70 pupil 5-11 school which Sheffield wished to close was given grant-maintained status.

8.  Data were obtained for three out of five areas.

9.  Willms and Echols (1992) report that increased parental choice in Scotland has lead to greater social segregation of schools but had little impact on examination results.

10. Lack of space provides a good excuse for not examining this value laden term.

11. As Reynolds (1992) points out, knowing what factors are associated with effective schools is not the same as knowing what needs to be done to improve a school.

12.  With respect to North American school councils.

## References

Arnott, M. Bullock, A. and Thomas, H. (1992) *The impact of local management on schools,* Birmingham: School of Education, University of Birmingham.

Audit Commission (1991) *Management within primary schools*, London: Audit Commission.

Audit Commission (1993) *Adding up the sums: schools' management of their finances*, London: HMSO.

Bowe, R. and Ball, S. (1992) 'Doing what should come naturally: an exploration of LMS in one secondary school', in G. Wallace (ed) *Local management of schools: research and experience,* Clevedon: Multi-lingual Matters.

Broadbent, J., Laughlin, R., Shearn, D. and Dandy, N. (1992a) "It's a long way from teaching Susan to read': some preliminary observations of a project studying the introduction of local management of schools', in G. Wallace (ed) *Local management of schools: research and experience,* Clevedon: Multi-lingual Matters.

Broadbent, J., Laughlin, R., Shearn, D. and Willig-Atherton, H. (1992b) 'Visibilities and invisibilities: a reflection on some aspects of local managment of schools', Paper presented at the British Educational Research Association Conference, Nottingham, August 1991.

Bullock, A. and Thomas, H. (1992) 'School size and local management funding formulae', *Educational Management and Administration,* vol 20, no 1, pp 30-39.

Caldwell, B. and Spinks, J. (1988) *The self managing school,* London: Falmer Press.

Chubb, J.E. and Moe, T.M. (1990) *Politics, markets and America's schools,* Washington DC: The Brookings Institution.

Creese, M. (1992) 'Can old dogs learn new tricks?', Paper presented at the British Educational Research Association Annual Conference, University of Stirling, August 1992.

Department for Education (1988) *Public Expenditure White Paper*, London: HMSO.

Department of Education and Science (1988) *The Education Reform Act: local management of schools,* Circular 7/88, London: DES.

Department of Education and Science (1991) *Local management of schools: further advice,* Circular 9/91, London: DES.

Flew, A. (1991) 'Educational services: independent competition or maintained monopoly', in D.G. Green (ed) *Empowering the parents: how to break the schools monopoly,* London: Institute of Economic Affairs.

Glatter, R. and Woods, P. (1992) 'Parental choice and school decision-making: operating in a market-like environment', Paper presented at the Quadrennial Conference of the Commonwealth Council for Educational Administration, University of Hong Kong, August, 1992.

Glennester, H. (1991) 'Quasi-markets in education', *The Economic Journal,* vol 101, pp 1268-76.

Green, D.G. (ed.) (1991) *Empowering the parents: how to break the schools monopoly,* London: Institute of Economic Affairs.

Hall, V., Mackay, H. and Morgan, C. (1986) *Head teachers at work,* Milton Keynes: Open University Press.

Hanushek, E. (1986) 'The economics of schooling: production and efficiency in public schools', *Journal of Economic Literature,* vol 24, pp 1141-77.

Hargreaves, D.H., Hopkins, D., Leask, M., Connolly, I. and Robinson, P. (1989) *Planning for school development,* London: DES.

Hargreaves, D. and Hopkins, D. (1991) *The empowered school,* London: Cassell.

Her Majesty's Inspectorate (1992) *The implementation of local management of schools,* London: DFE.

Hillgate Group (1986) *Whose schools? A radical manifesto,* London: Hillgate Group.

Hofkins, D. (1990) 'More staff retire early', *Times Educational Supplement,* 16 November.

Levacic, R. (1992) 'An analysis of differences between historic and formula school budgets: evidence from LEA submissions and from detailed study of two LEAs', *Oxford Review of Education*, vol 18, no 1, pp 75-100.

Levacic, R. (1993) 'Assessing the impact of formula funding on schools', *Oxford Review of Education*, vol 19, no 4, pp 435-57.

Levacic, R. and Marren, E. (1992) 'Responding to LMS', *Management in Education,* vol 6, no 4, pp 22-25.

LMS Initiative (1992) *Local management of schools: a study into formula funding and management issues,* London: LMS Initiative.

Malen, B., Ogawa, R. T., and Kranz, J. (1990) 'What do we know about school-based management? A case study of the literature - a call for research', in W. Clune and J. Witte (eds) *Choice and control in American education,* vol 2, London: Falmer Press.

Marr, A. (1992) 'Golden hellos and great expectations', *Times Educational Supplement,* 10 January.

Marren, E. and Levacic, R. (1992) 'Implementing local management of schools: first year spending decisions', in L. Ellison, T. Simkins and V. Garrett (eds) *Implementing educational reform: the early lessons*, London: Longman.

Marren, E. and Levacic, R. (1994) 'Senior management, classroom teacher and governor responses to local management of schools', *Education Management and Administration*, vol 22, no 1, pp 39-58.

Miliband, D. (1991) *Markets, politics and education*, London: Institute for Public Policy Research.

Mortimore, P., Sammons, P., Stoll, L., Lewis, D. and Ecob, R. (1988) *School matters: the junior years,* Wells: Open Books.

Mortimore, P., Mortimore, J., with Thomas, H., Cairns, R. and Taggart, B. (1992) *The innovative uses of non-teaching staff in primary and secondary schools project,* final report to the Department for Education, London: Institute of Education, University of London.

New, S., Deem, R. and Brehony, K. (1993) 'Reflections at the end of term', *Times Educational Supplement*, January.

Purkey, S.C. and Smith, M.S., (1983) 'Effective schools: a review', *Elementary School Journal,* vol 83, no 4, pp 427-52.

Reynolds, D. (1992) 'School effectiveness and school improvement: an updated review of the British literature', in D. Reynolds and P. Cuttance (eds) *School effectiveness: research, policy and practice,* London: Cassell.

Rutter, M., Maughan, B., Mortimore, P., and Ouston, J. (1979) *Fifteen thousand hours: secondary schools and their effects on children,* Shepton Mallet: Open Books.

School Teachers' Pay Review Body (1992) First Report, Cm 1806, London: HMSO.

Sheffield City Council (1992) *Resourcing Sheffield schools,* Sheffield: Sheffield City Council.

Sinclair, J. and Seifert, R. (1993) 'Money for value?', *Managing Schools Today,* vol 2, no 9.

Thomas, G. (1990) *Setting up LMS: a study of local education authorities' submissions to the DES,* Milton Keynes: Open University Learning Materials.

Thomas, G. (1991) *The framework for LMS: a study of local education authorities' approved local management of schools schemes,* Milton Keynes: Open University Learning Materials.

Willms, D.W. (1992) *Monitoring school performance,* London: Falmer Press.

Willms, D. and Echols, F. (1992) *The Scottish experience of parental choice,* Canadian Centre for Educational Sociology, University of British Columbia.

Woods, P. (1992) 'Empowerment through choice? Towards an understanding of parental choice and school responsiveness', *Educational Management and Administration,* vol 20, no 4.

*three*

# THE IMPACT OF COMPETITION AND CHOICE ON PARENTS AND SCHOOLS

## Ron Glatter and Philip Woods

### Introduction

The purpose of this chapter is to map some of the key elements that need to be focused upon in seeking to analyse quasi-markets in school education. The government has sought to enhance choice for parents and competition amongst schools for pupils by means of a number of policy initiatives, as mentioned in the previous chapter. To recap, these include:

- local management of schools (LMS), under which schools are funded largely on the basis of the numbers and ages of pupils attending them, and have substantial discretion over deployment of these funds;

- more open enrolment, under which constraints on pupil numbers can no longer be applied to 'popular' schools, which must take as many pupils as their physical capacity will allow;

- provision for different types of school, such as specialist schools (principally city technology colleges and a planned network of technology schools and technology colleges) and grant-maintained schools (which have chosen to opt out of local education authority control);

● more publicly available information on the performance of individual schools (national curriculum tests, public examinations, and so on).

Whether these policies are achieving greater choice for parents is a matter for empirical investigation. This chapter draws on findings emerging from the PASCI (Parental and School Choice Interaction) study which began in 1990 and which will continue until the end of 1995.[1]

## Local competitive arenas

Choice and competition are constrained by the nature of schooling. First, there are limitations on the distance parents are prepared to see or are able to allow their children to travel to and from schools, and on the distance children themselves are willing to travel. Second, the provision of schooling does not generally lend itself to being concentrated in distant production centres, though there are exceptions (for example, where it is distributed to pupils' homes through 'supported self-study' schemes in areas of scattered population, or where pupils travel some distance from their homes, as with boarding education).

In consequence, competition in schooling (where it exists) is characteristically local in nature. This feature of school choice has a number of important implications. The first is that the empirical study of school choice must largely be conducted within local areas:

> while there may be certain principles of choice and market relations, the dynamics of choice and market relations are local and specific. The principles have to be related to local conditions, possibilities and histories. (Ball, Bowe and Gewirtz, 1992, p 2)

These authors quote Giddens' description of such locales in terms of "a physical region involved as the setting of interaction, having definite boundaries which help to concentrate interaction in one way or another" (Giddens, 1984, p 375).

We refer to a *local competitive arena*, in an ideal typical sense, as an area in which schools draw from a common population of parents and pupils. This arena is the battleground upon which the schools vie with one another for parental and pupil support. In reality local competitive arenas can be more or less closed, with boundaries that are more or less apparent. The notion of a boundary in school-environment interactions is in any case problematic and is largely a matter of individual perception (Musgrave, 1988). The significance of administrative boundaries has diminished under the government's policies outlined above. The more movement there is of pupils across neighbourhoods, communities and administrative boundaries, as in large metropolitan areas such as London, the more difficult it is to identify distinct local arenas.   Indeed, such an area may be characterised as a particularly large and complex competitive arena.

A second implication of the 'localness' of most quasi-markets in school education is that they cannot be likened to industries that are able to operate nationally and internationally (such as, for example, computing, electronics and motor vehicle manufacture).

Third, issues of both social and administrative geography come strongly to the fore in examining local competitive  arenas in school education.  Bradford (1990), in reviewing research on 'the geography of choice' has pointed to the independent influence of the socio-economic character of the local area on attainment, indicating that this influence appears to be separate from, and additional to, that of the home.  He concludes that "the local residential environment of a school's pupils will affect its overall level of attainment, independently of its effectiveness" (p 15), and since published league tables are unadjusted for such effects of social geography, the marketing of schools will reflect unfair competition on this account at least.

It also seems, from the work of Raab and Adler (1988) in Scotland, that schools which attract a larger proportion of pupils from outside their catchment area obtain higher attainments than those with fewer pupils from outside their areas.

The nature of provision, or the 'administrative geography' of the school system in the local competitive arena, is also likely to be important, however.    Another study in Scotland, although conducted some time ago - just after the Scottish open enrolment legislation was passed in 1982 - is of interest in its finding that "the largest single net effect on the incidence of choice was not individual but structural, and arose from the local availability of options between which choices could be made" (Echols et al, 1990, p 215).  This finding, if generally confirmed, would clearly be highly relevant to the current debate about the future of parental choice in the context of government plans to reduce 'surplus' school places.

The geographical dimension has recently been extended by Bowe, Gewirtz and Ball (1992) who suggest that it may be fruitful to employ the metaphor of "landscapes of choice" where landscapes includes not just the physical environment but also the observer's perceptions of it. To pursue this idea in the context of a competitive arena, individuals' perceptions of who is involved in the competition, their relative 'track records', what is to be gained by joining one contestant rather than another, and indeed the rules of the game, may depend on many factors, not least where in the arena they are located, how freely they can move about in it, and whether they can transfer to a different arena entirely (this may be elsewhere in the state system or the private sector).

A final implication of 'localness' is the need to examine the historical development of competition in different arenas. It is arguable that there have long been competitive arenas in school education in the UK. As we have suggested elsewhere (Glatter and Woods, 1992), the traditional concept of the individual school as a unique, almost symbolic entity, which dates back at least to the 'great' public schools of the Victorian era, created a context in England and Wales which was relatively compatible with reforms along quasi-market lines. It is easy to forget that state schools in the post-war period had far more freedom to decide their curricula than has been the case in most other countries (Glatter, 1977), and more control over the selection of staff than has been common elsewhere. In the early to mid 1980s period of sharply falling rolls, competition intensified in many areas under the threat of closure by the LEA.

The significance of varying historical settings is shown by the following extract from a study of six rural secondary schools in Hereford and Worcester LEA. It suggests that in some areas the current trends may be running in a direction that is the opposite of much political rhetoric and popular belief:

> For a generation at least the LEA had pursued a 'hands off' policy so that curriculum, organisation and the overall purpose and ethos in each school had been almost completely determined internally. It looks as though parents were aware of this and many responded to the differences by active choices. But as the schools were being studied, the era of self-determination was coming dramatically to an end. All the schools were acutely aware of new forces that would

require their conformity, and thus greater similarity with one another and in consequence more likelihood that they would all be judged by the same criteria. (Tomlinson and Mortimore, 1992, pp 50-51)

It will be important for future research to examine the implied prediction in this statement, that in many competitive arenas the contestants will become more alike rather than more distinctive.

As well as characterising diverse parental perceptions of competitive arenas, we also need to understand perceptions from within schools. Kotler and Fox (1985) have distinguished five types of 'environment' with which educational institutions carry out exchanges: these are called the internal, market, public, competitive and macro environments. In this formulation, the competitive environment approximates to our notion of competitive arena: the others indicate a range of other exchange relationships which schools must maintain and which may constrain or enhance their performance in the competitive domain. This analysis indicates something of the complexity of our topic, and the inappropriateness of using a simple stimulus-response model of interaction. Environments are complex, and send contrasting and often conflicting signals to schools, which (as complex organisations themselves) have to make their own strategic choices between them.

We will now look more systematically at factors influencing the nature and extent of competition in such settings, drawing on aspects of the PASCI study's findings to date.

## Factors affecting competition in competitive arenas

We are looking here at competition from the viewpoint of the putative consumer.[2]  What are the factors that affect his or her experience of choice and competition?  Elsewhere one of the authors has viewed these factors as consisting of what are termed *resources* and *context* (Woods, 1993).

### Resources

These consist of those things, both tangible and intangible, on which people need to draw when operating within a quasi-market or competitive arena in schooling.  They include money, information, legal rights and cultural capital, the latter representing skills, contacts, ability to work the system, and so on (Lareau, 1989, pp 176-180). It is likely that access to them is affected by factors such as social class and ethnicity. Thus, for example, it may be hypothesised that professional and middle class parents will be able to operate more successfully in the competitive arena than other parents. They will know more about the system and have the transport (or money) to get their children to the schools of their choice.

Do more professional and middle class parents than others feel, therefore, that they have a choice between schools? Data from the PASCI pilot fieldwork in the fictitiously-named town of Marshampton (see Note 1), focusing on choice of secondary school, suggest that this is not the case. Three-quarters of working-class parents considered they had a choice, compared with just over half of professional and middle class parents (see Table 1).[3] On the face of it, then, we might conclude that working-class parents are more likely to be exercising choice. However, whilst such findings should not be dismissed, they beg several questions. For example, if working-class families are indeed disadvantaged in terms of cultural capital, the kinds of choices open to them may be more limited and their expectations lower than others. Hence, the higher proportion of professional and middle class respondents indicating they had no choice may be a reflection of different, possibly more exacting, criteria by which they judge the existence or otherwise of choice. We are continuing to investigate this and other issues raised by the quantitative data through analysis of parent interview data.

**Table 1:   Perception of choice**

|  | Professional and middle class | Working-class |
|---|---|---|
| Considered had a choice | 55.9% | 74.5% |
| Did not consider had a choice | 44.1% | 25.5% |
| (Base) | (102%) | (110%) |

Notes:   Chi-square test indicates difference significant at 1% level. This and subsequent tables exclude 'no responses' and those whose social class could not be identified.

The outcome of the quasi-market operating in Marshampton, in terms of secondary school places offered, shows evidence of significant differences according to social class. The schools in Table 2 represent a widely shared view of the 'pecking order' amongst state (non-church) schools in Marshampton: the order descends from the most sought-after school, Salix Grammar, to Endswich which has the poorest reputation. Children in professional and middle class families were more than three times as likely to be offered a grammar school place and more than five times as likely to be offered a place at Bridgerton (which is consistently over-subscribed).

**Table 2:    School place offered**

|  | Professional and middle class | Working-class |
|---|---|---|
| Salix Grammar | 12.4% | 3.6% |
| Bridgerton Comprehensive | 15.2% | 2.7% |
| Thurcleigh Hill Comprehensive | 21.0% | 13.4% |
| Daythorpe Comprehensive | 21.9% | 25.0% |
| Endswich Comprehensive | 11.4% | 32.1% |
| Other | 18.1% | 23.2% |
| (Base) | (105%) | (112%) |

Notes:    Chi-square test indicates differences significant at 1% level.

It might appear, as a result, that the chances of the professional and middle classes securing places in the 'better' schools were significantly greater than that of children in working-class homes. However only a small part of this difference can be attributed to working-class families failing to obtain their choice. The failure rate (ie the proportion not being offered their first preference) was only slightly greater for working-class families than professional and middle class families (see Table 3).

The implication is that lack of *resources* is not in some simple way acting to frustrate the wishes of working-class families. We have drawn attention to the fact that parents, according to our data, display a diversity of views and put differing emphases on factors influencing choice (Woods, 1992b). More recent analysis (Woods, forthcoming) shows that working-class families tend to put more emphasis on being near the school, which could be related to greater transport, ie resource, problems. However, this analysis also suggests that working-class parents display significant differences (compared with middle class parents) in their pattern of priorities: in particular, (besides distance from the school/travel difficulties) they attach greatest importance to their child's preference for the school and his or her friends being there. The factor most important to professional and middle class parents was the school's standard of academic education. Consequently, they were more likely to state a preference for Salix Grammar and Bridgerton (see Table 4). The question is whether the differing priorities are the result of social inequalities (manifested for working-class families as transport difficulties and a belief that certain schools are 'not for them') or whether they represent variations in values that stem from dissimilar (and equally valid) cultural perspectives.

**Table 3:   Whether offered first preference school**

|  | Professional and middle class | Working-class |
|---|---|---|
| Offered first preference school | 82.7% | 78.6% |
| Not offered first preference school | 17.3% | 21.4% |
| (Base) | (104%) | (112%) |

Note:     Chi-square test indicates no significant difference.

**Table 4:   Parents' first preference school**

|  | Professional and middle class | Working-class |
|---|---|---|
| Salix Grammar | 16.3% | 6.3% |
| Bridgerton Comprehensive | 24.0% | 15.3% |
| Thurcleigh Hill Comprehensive | 18.3% | 8.1% |
| Daythorpe Comprehensive | 13.5% | 24.3% |
| Endswich Comprehensive | 9.6% | 21.6% |
| Other | 18.3% | 24.3% |
| (Base) | (104%) | (111%) |

Note:     Chi-square test indicates differences significant at 1% level.

## Context

Context consists of two elements. The first is *availability*, ie whether the kinds of goods and services people want are produced. If what people want is not being produced or provided, it is not possible for people to obtain them, whether in a fully private or public quasi-market. Or it may be that what is wanted is not being provided in sufficient quantities to meet demand, as with over-subscribed schools, so that some form of rationing (whether by price or other means) is necessary.

The consumer is dependent upon decisions made by producers or service providers, as is indicated in the Scottish study referred to above. Thus parents are, with respect to schooling, dependent upon decisions made by local school managers and by local and central government (and increasingly by government agencies). Politicians decide levels of funding, for example, whilst significant decisions about the type of schooling and curriculum available are influenced by a range of individuals and bodies including government ministers, agencies such as the School Curriculum and Assessment Authority, headteachers and school governors. Provision of schooling in the reformed system of schooling in England and Wales is intended to remain predominantly a public matter in the sense that it continues to be funded from the public purse.

The second element is the *conditions of the consumption process*. This refers to a wide range of variable factors which affect the process of getting and using the goods or service in question, and in relation to which people use their resources.[4] With regard to schooling they include the form (as opposed to the content) of schooling provision, physical distances between schools and the home, provision or otherwise of public transport, admissions procedures, and school policies and practices concerning home-school relationships. The form of schooling provision refers to the institutional means by which schooling is offered and which affect the accessibility of schooling: for example, whether 'supported self study' schemes are provided, whether emphasis is placed on choice *between* schools (as the government does) and/or maximum flexibility and choice for pupils *within* schools. A series of questions can be asked about the form of schooling provision and the other conditions as they are experienced by parents. For example, with regard to admission procedures, are they clear to all parents, what help is available to interpret them, is the information that parents need or want available? With regard to home-school relations, do school decision makers encourage parents to contact the school, are they welcoming, do they listen and respond to parents?

## How schools are responding

It is apparent from the above that far from a quasi-market automatically placing decision-making initiatives in the hands of the consumer, there are huge areas of decision-making powers that remain in the hands of the producers (broadly defined to include political and administrative decision makers, as well as professional educators). With this in mind, the PASCI study is investigating the interaction between parental choice and school decision making: to what extent are secondary schools being responsive to parental preferences under pressure of the need to attract pupils and, by this means, funding? The argument that is articulated for market-like environments for public services is that they will lead to better, more consumer-responsive services. The PASCI study is looking at this hypothesis as it operates in competitive arenas for schooling.

The pilot fieldwork, together with a national databank of school responses to choice and competition which we have initiated, are providing indicators of how secondary schools are reacting to this new environment. We are continuing to investigate and monitor schools' responsiveness during the study's main research phase (from January 1993 to the end of 1995). Here, we highlight three of the main features of school responsiveness to date. The first of these is unsurprising and confirms what anyone familiar with schools in recent years can see for themselves, namely that schools are responding to choice and competition by increased emphasis on promotional activities (improved brochures, better links with feeder schools, etc). Enhanced choice and competition, however, will not have the benefits claimed for them (making the education system more 'consumer' responsible and improving educational achievement) if schools only respond by 'selling' themselves better.

Of key interest, therefore, is the second feature: some schools are tackling the problem of how to attract parents by making what we have called substantive changes (defined as responses concerned with how the school organises itself and with its activities as a school, such as curriculum, teaching methods, management and planning, etc). Such changes (not all carried out in any one school) include alterations to homework policy, the introduction of banding, enhanced emphasis on the caring and pastoral aspect of schooling, encouragement of staff to gain more qualifications, increased stress on extra-curricular activities and greater community access to school facilities (a more detailed discussion is given in Woods, 1992a). Whether such changes are in line with what parents want is another matter. Our data do not yet allow us to draw conclusions. However, it is apparent (from both the pilot fieldwork and databank) that in general enthusiasm for finding out what parents want is considerably less than for promoting the school to parents and the wider community. We have characterised the impact of enhanced choice and competition in the pilot case study area as consisting at this stage of a series of 'cross-currents', rather than a single discernible trend (Woods, 1992b).

There are variations amongst parents surveyed as to what most influences their choice decision. Child-focused themes such as the child's preference for a school and the child's friends being there feature strongly, though (as demonstrated above in relation to social class) priorities may differ amongst different groups of parents. The case study schools are emphasising the caring, pastoral aspect of schooling, an aspect of marked importance to most parents. This, together with early findings suggesting that pressure of competition may be encouraging schools to make it easier for all parents to become involved in their child's schooling, might be seen as an indicator that school decision makers are seeking to be responsive to the generality of parents. However, there are indications too of decision makers in the case study schools giving special emphasis to certain groups of parents, namely academically orientated and middle class parents, by making changes which will be attractive to them.

Underlying all of these developments are the restraints on what schools are able to do in order to attract parents. They cannot re-locate themselves in order to be near all parents (nearness to school and convenience of home-school travel being significant factors in parental choice, as discussed above) and they have limited budgets with which to make changes that will attract parents.

The third feature of school responsiveness that we wish to highlight here is the strength of *collaborative* responses. The emphasis on choice and competition is often associated with a consequent need for each school to stand alone, to look after its own interests, and to engage in marketing which is aimed at enhancing its own success without regard for the impact on others.

Competition, in this perspective, provides a poor environment for collaboration and cooperation between schools. This is not necessarily the case, however. Whilst there are schools which engage in aggressive advertising or concentrate on strategies of change which are intended to increase their own attractiveness to parents, many schools are actively collaborating as a means of coping with the new environment created by the government's reforms. Examples include the Federation of South Bristol Schools, in which secondary and primary schools work together to provide in-service training, mutual advice and support, curricular opportunities for pupils that no one school alone would be able to provide, enhanced influence in relation to the LEA and other common services. Other schools throughout England and Wales cooperate, often in less formal ways, in order to improve on the service they can offer individually and to diminish the level of competitive activity that might otherwise occur. There are strong arguments in favour of this, particularly in respect of smaller schools which are enabled to engage in activities or obtain services which would not otherwise be accessible to them. On the other hand, collaboration - or certain ways of collaborating - might be viewed as means by which the rights of parents to choose between differing schools are diminished: in other words, as strategems by which the producers make life easier for themselves instead of competing to please their consumers. The varying motives underlying different forms of collaboration as well as their impact therefore require careful assessment.

## The macro environment

Local competitive arenas exist within a wider *macro environment*. With regard to school education, the former are the scene of most of the actions of parents, pupils and others in the community concerned with education and of decision makers *within* schools. In the macro environment, decision making which directly affects the schooling system and provides its political and administrative context, is dominated by public authorities (increasingly by central government at the expense of local government), whilst demographic, economic, technological and social forces also have an impact in various ways upon schools and the communities in which they operate. LEAs can be seen as outside the local competitive arena for two reasons. Firstly, the competitive arena is normally an area, one of a number, within an LEA's boundaries; secondly, with LMS their role as providers of schooling is severely diminished. Of course with the growing number of non-LEA state schools in addition to private schools within many competitive arenas, LEAs have an increasingly direct interest in the outcome of struggles within these arenas.

The PASCI study is focusing its investigations on the dynamics of local competitive arenas. However, it is clear that parental and school responses are affected by the macro environment. The macro environment determines the legal framework and statutory duties that those within competitive arenas are required to follow, and it makes decisions concerning overall funding levels, funding formulae and so on. The impact of public authorities on the nature of the quasi-market and on the context in which parents make decisions is substantial. It extends to matters such as the degree to which schools are allowed to select pupils according to ability or aptitude and provision by public authorities of information and advice to assist parents when deciding their preferences (Department for Education, 1992). The local quasi-market cannot be understood without understanding its macro environment, and its relationship to it.

An important motivation for public action emanating from the macro environment is a perception that a market is failing, as a means of supply and distribution, according to certain criteria. Perceptions of what constitutes such failure are bound up with whatever values ('above' those of the market) are considered to be important: these values can be concerned, for example, with equality or a perceived need to ensure that certain curriculum areas are taught to all pupils. Public action is necessary to offset the deficiencies of a market left entirely to its own devices. Hence, Chubb and Moe (1990), in their influential case for markets in schooling, nevertheless assign significant responsibilities and powers to government. For example, in relation to the sum of public money that goes with each pupil to his or her school, they believe that public authorities should limit the amount of personal funds that families could add to it and that pupils from deprived areas or with other disadvantages should bring a higher sum to a school so as to increase their attractiveness in the market place.

The 1992 White Paper (Department for Education/Welsh Office, 1992) contained a number of references to equality. For example, the Prime Minister's foreword identified four principles underlying the government's reforms, the final one (prefixed by 'above all') being "an insistence that every pupil everywhere has the same opportunities through a good common grounding in key subjects. I am not prepared to see children in some parts of the country having to settle for a second-class education" (p iii). Later there are assertions that "we wish to treat all children the same" [including those with special educational needs] (paragraph 1.53) and that the national curriculum ensures equality of opportunity and offers a new protection against tiers of schools developing within the maintained system (paragraph 1.49). Other values, especially moral and spiritual ones are also emphasised: "schools should not be, and generally are not, value-free zones" (paragraph 1.29). All this may be indicative of what Cole (1992) has called "the contradictions between the free-market, consumerist approach to education and the authoritarian drive for social order" (p 341) but it does suggest that the influence of the macro environment, particularly as represented by central government and its agencies, in limiting and constraining market activity in local competitive arenas may well increase further in the years ahead. These interactions will need to be examined closely.

Having acknowledged that markets may have their deficiencies, we should recognise too that the macro environment (and, specifically, the public authorities within it) is vulnerable to failure. Public authorities may be deficient to the extent that they fail to meet the needs and preferences of the people they represent (West, 1970, p l).

Greater centralisation of powers brings to central government an increased risk of such failure. For example, the government is following a policy that strongly features league tables of schools based on examination and test results and a special programme of technology schools and colleges. However, it may be asked, what grounds exist for selecting these as priorities? It would be difficult to argue that such policy decisions are based upon research or public participation schemes through which it can be shown that these are indeed the priorities that most would support.

Local quasi-markets are also interconnected with the macro environment through the role of education consumers as citizens. As electors, they have (to an arguable extent) an influence on democratically elected public authorities. Thus it is possible to conceive of the reformed education system acting as a self-regulating system: awareness of market deficiencies in local competitive arenas can be communicated through the political process to the macro environment and appropriate public action taken to deal with these. This is likely to be an optimistic view, however. Much of the imperative behind the education reforms since 1979 has been grounded in the view that public provision of services is intrinsically flawed (being characterised by tendencies towards inefficiency and unresponsiveness to people's needs and preferences) and that introducing market forces into public services offers a better alternative. Those who are committed to this policy perspective are likely to be resistant to certain kinds of political action (for example, the favouring of economically deprived areas as Chubb and Moe, 1990, advocate). Somewhat gloomily, we might ask if the chief characteristic of the British education system in the 1990s is to be a surfeit of deficiencies: those of the market (in local competitive arenas) and those of political representation (in the macro environment).

The above discussion highlights the possibility of conflict and dissonance between the perspectives of people in local competitive arenas and those operating in the macro environment. To pursue the example of examination-based league tables, does their publication by the central public authority mean that these become criteria of key importance to parents? This raises the whole question of the nature and genesis of consumers or parents wishes (which was touched upon in the discussion of social class under 'Resources' above). They cannot be assumed as 'given' that arise from the individual untouched by history, culture and society. People can be seen as in a dialetical relationship with the social, both formed by it and forming it (Giddens, 1976). The formation of consumer wishes is a dynamic and continuous process within that relationship. Thus, for example, as well as (or instead of) responding to consumers' wishes, service providers may engage in attempts to alter consumer wishes or to create new ones. Equally, public authorities may alter people's perceptions by setting the agenda of public debate and focusing on issues which concern the government of the day.. The extent to which they succeed in doing this is, however, a matter for empirical enquiry. For the moment we can note that data from the PASCI study suggest that examination results are not the most important factor to parents.

## Conclusion

In Figure 1, we attempt in a very crude, selective and preliminary way to indicate possible interactive processes, of the kind we are examining in the PASCI study, between some of the factors we have been discussing in this chapter. The figure seeks to show hypothesised interactive processes between putative 'consumers' (with varying resources) and schools, in a context of choice, both within and beyond a particular local competitive arena, and also between individual schools with their varying 'characters' (comprehensive, grant-maintained, city technology college, and so forth), reputations and resource levels. It also shows the macro environment exerting a set of largely one-way influence processes on schools and on each local competitive arena as a whole (the possibility of influence from people, as citizens, in competitive arenas upon public authorities in the macro environment has been noted in discussion above, though it is not shown in the figure). This macro environment is composed both of the policy and administrative context set by central government and its agencies and by local government where relevant, as well as of the general demographic, economic, technological and social forces that affect schools and the provision of schooling.

Any such representation must inevitably leave out many important elements. For example, the specific historical, political and cultural context of particular local arenas is not represented here. The model is at a very early stage of development, and is one means by which we are attempting to clarify our thinking in this complex territory.

Kotler and Fox's (1985) notion of the *internal environment* is of particular interest in relation to our figure. The internal environment consists of all those people and groups we regard as being within the organisation (notwithstanding the problematic nature of boundaries, mentioned earlier). This draws attention to the significance of intra-organisational factors such as micropolitics, cultures and sub-cultures, and management structures and processes in influencing schools' strategic choices over the various relationships depicted in Figure 1 (and others not shown there). When looking at the 'little boxes' which stand for schools in Figure 1 it is therefore very important to bear in mind all the subtle, almost subterranean activity which they really represent as components of local competitive arenas.

**Figure 1: Local competitive arenas - processes of interaction and influence**

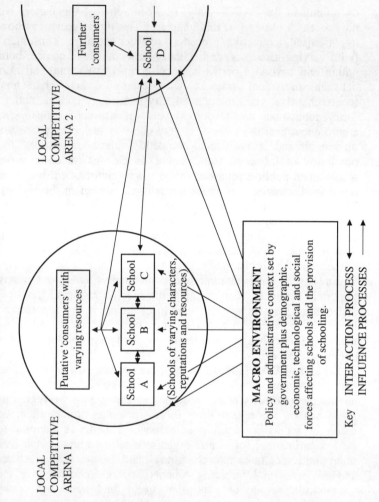

It is for this reason, as well as because of the multiple and often conflicting signals that schools receive from their various 'environments', that we regard the 'rational' stimulus-response model of the functioning of the quasi-market in schooling as untenable, although this model is often implied in political pronouncements. In somewhat similar vein, Bowe, Gewirtz and Ball (1992) have warned against the assumption of pure logic and rationality in parents choice-making processes and a tendency to neglect the non-linear and affective aspects of these processes in relevant research.

Finally, as we become more familiar with the changes discussed in this book, we are perhaps starting to take for granted both their radical nature and the style of policy making which has established them. This would be unfortunate. In particular, the frequent massive structural 'redisorganisation' (Maynard, 1993) in the public services without serious piloting or formative evaluation needs to be questioned. Alongside this style there sometimes exists a remarkable lack of humility: for example, the then Department of Education and Science's draft consultative document on LMS ended with a brief paragraph on 'follow-up' which referred to the need for evaluation but concluded with the statement: "the government's expectation is that the impact will be overwhelmingly beneficial, and that the sooner schemes are implemented the sooner the benefits will be realised" (Department of Education and Science, 1988, paragraph 129: this sentence was omitted from the subsequent Circular 7/88). We have much sympathy with Scott (1993) who recently referred with regret to the passing of the days "when evidence mattered and policy owed something to research and critical reflection". It is to be hoped that this book, and the work represented within it, will contribute to restoring the balance between certainty and enquiry.

## Notes

1. The PASCI study is funded by the Economic and Social Research Council (ESRC) (ref R000234079). The study's exploratory phase, aimed at developing methodological foundations and providing a benchmark for further study, was completed in 1992. Work undertaken in this phase included fieldwork in a pilot case study area (Marshampton), involving:

- personal interviews (31 in all) with teaching staff, governors and head-teachers of three secondary schools;

- analysis of documentary data (eg school brochures, development plans);

- postal survey of parents of children transferring to secondary education in September 1991 (262 questionnaires returned, a response rate of 66%);

- personal interviews with parents (15 in all);

- collection of data from the area's LEA on the pattern of parental choices throughout Marshampton and LEA policy on LMS and parental choice.

A national databank of school responses to parental choice and competition has also been initiated. The purpose of this is to gain insight into variations across England and Wales, and to enable case study findings to be placed in a wider context.

2.  Who the consumer is in relation to school education, and whether 'consumer' is an appropriate term, are matters of debate (see, for example, Glatter et al, 1992). We focus in this chapter on parents as the government's reforms are framed in terms of increasing parental choice and because the PASCI study is concerned with the experience of parents under the new system.

3.  Social classes are based on the Registrar General's classification of occupations (Office of Population Censuses and Surveys, 1980, *Classification of occupations*, London: HMSO): 'professional and middle class' refers to social classes 1, 2 and 3N; 'working-class' refers to social classes 3M, 4 and 5.

4.  Availability (whether the goods or service wanted is produced or not) and conditions of the consumption process (factors which affect getting and using the goods or service in question) are closely associated. It might be argued that if the service wanted (let us say the Ritz in London) by Mr X in John O'Groats is produced, it is effectively unavailable to him if he does not have the resources to overcome the distance and to pay the required service price. The argument underlying the distinction made in this chapter is that it usefully highlights

different aspects of supply-side decision making which characterise the context within which the consumer operates: on the one hand, decisions about what to produce and, on the other, decisions regarding factors that affect how people get and use goods or services.

## References

Ball, S.J., Bowe, R. and Gewirtz, S. (1992) *Circuits of schooling: a sociological exploration of parental choice of school in social class context*, Working Paper, London: King's College.

Bowe, R., Gewirtz, S. and Ball, S.J. (1992) *Captured by the discourse? Issues and concerns in researching parental choice*, Working Paper, London: King's College.

Bradford, M. (1990) 'Education, attainment and the geography of choice', *Geography*, vol 75, no 1, pp 3-16.

Chubb, J.E. and Moe, T.M. (1990) *Politics, markets and America's schools*, Washington DC: The Brookings Institute.

Cole, M. (1992) 'Education in the market-place: a case of contradiction', *Educational Review*, vol 44, no 3, pp 335-43.

Department for Education (1992) *Draft circular on admission arrangements*, London: Department for Education.

Department for Education/Welsh Office (1992) *Choice and diversity: a new framework for schools*, London: HMSO.

Department of Education and Science (1988) *Draft consultative document, Education Reform Act: financial delegation to schools*, London: DES.

Echols, F., Mcpherson, A. and Williams, J.D. (1990) 'Parental choice in Scotland', *Journal of Educational Policy*, vol 5, no 3, pp 207-22.

Giddens, A. (1976) *New rules of sociological method*, London: Hutchinson.

Giddens, A. (1984) *The constitution of society*, Oxford: Polity Press.

Glatter, R. (ed) (1977) *Control of the curriculum: issues and trends in Britain and Europe*, London: University of London, Institute of Education.

Glatter, R. and Woods, P. (1992) 'Parental choice and school decision making: operating in a market-like environment', Paper presented to the 7th Regional Conference of the Commonwealth Council for Educational Administration, University of Hong Kong.

Glatter, R., Johnson, D. and Woods, P.A. (1992) 'Marketing, choice and responses in education', in M. Smith (ed) *Reforming education: managing a changing environment*, Loughborough: Loughborough University, Department of Education.

Kotler, P. and Fox, K.F.A. (1985) *Strategic marketing for educational institutions*, Englewood Cliffs, NJ: Prentice Hall.

Lareau, A. (1989) *Home advantage: social class and parental intervention in elementary education*, London: Falmer Press.

Maynard, A. (1993) 'Bad medicine', *The Guardian*, 27 January.

Musgrave, P.W. (1988) 'What is organization theory anyway', *Curriculum Inquiry*, vol 18, no 2, pp 235-42.

Raab, G. and Adler, M. (1988) 'The tale of two cities: the impact of parental choice on admissions to primary schools in Edinburgh and Dundee', in L. Bondi and M.H. Matthews (eds) *Education and society: studies in the politics, sociology and geography of education*, London: Routledge.

Scott, P. (1993) 'Patchwork panorama', *The Times Educational Supplement - School Management Update*, 29 January.

Tomlinson, J.R.G. with Mortimore, P. (1992) *Small, rural and effective: a study of secondary schools*, Stoke-on-Trent: Trentham Books.

West, E.G. (1970) *Education and the state*, London: The Institute of Economic Affairs.

Woods, P.A. (1992a) 'Responding to the consumer: parental choice and school effectiveness', Paper presented to the International Congress for School Effectiveness and Improvement, Victoria, Canada, January 1992.

Woods, P.A. (1992b) 'Empowerment through choice? Towards an understanding of parental choice and school responsivenes', *Educational Management and Administration*, vol 20, no 4.

Woods, P.A. (1993) 'Parents as consumer-citizens', in R. Merttens, D. Mayers, A. Brown and J. Vass (eds) *Ruling the margins: problematising parental involvement*, London: IMPACT Project, University of North London.

Woods, P.A. (forthcoming) 'Choice, class and effectiveness', *School Effectiveness and School Improvement*.

*four*

# SCHOOLS IN THE MARKET PLACE: AN ANALYSIS OF LOCAL MARKET RELATIONS

## Stephen Ball, Richard Bowe and Sharon Gewirtz

The quasi-market in school level education is, arguably, the most highly developed and ideologically charged of any of the new public sector markets in the UK. That is to say, it comes closest to the ideal-type 'real' market. Individual consumers have, in theory, complete freedom of choice of school (see Ball, 1993; Ball, Bowe and Gewirtz, forthcoming). Schools receive the bulk of their budget on the basis of pupil recruitment numbers. And in areas where there is a surplus of school places schools are in competition with one another for custom. Also, schools now manage their own budgets and employ their own staff directly. Concomitantly, the planning and budgetary role of LEAs have been severely curtailed. However, state-maintained schools are constrained to deliver the national curriculum and undertake various forms of national testing.

However, this outline of the operational framework of the school market actually provides little insight into the workings and effects of specific local education markets. The diversity of local settings and the particularity of their politics, demography and history makes it difficult to generalise about market forces in education. Any conceptualisation of the market in schooling will have to incorporate aspects of these local factors.

This chapter offers some modest starting points towards such a conceptualisation. It draws upon a three year study of market forces, focused upon clusters of secondary schools in three adjacent LEAs, where place provision and geography provide for the possibilities of choice and competition. The study gives attention to three 'levels' of analysis: parents and choice (see Ball, Bowe and

Gewirtz, forthcoming); schools and competition (see Gewirtz, Ball and Bowe, 1993); and patterns of choice, access and provision across the LEAs. In this chapter we attend to the last of these and concentrate upon two of the LEAs in the study: Riverway and Northwark (Westway is the third). We will give particular attention to the effects of LEA policies (both past and present) on the nature and dynamics of the local market and discuss competition between schools and LEAs.

## Riverway

Riverway LEA is controlled by a Social Democrat council which is supportive of comprehensive education. It acts to maintain a high level of corporate identity among its schools and to dampen competitive behaviour. There is a well established but perhaps fragile consensus among the secondary schools that unconstrained competition would be damaging. Thus, the LEA produces schools' prospectuses in a common, low key format. It also manages the admissions to schools centrally (except for Corpus Christi) and a system of linked primary schools operates (see below), together with a mutually agreed 'no poaching' agreement.

Within the constraints of the government established education market the LEA works hard to ameliorate its effects. The chief education officer (CEO) of Riverway does not view his LEA as having a history of strong central direction:

> the authority is quite *laissez-faire* and gave considerable autonomy and freedom to schools ... if you talk to the Head of Parsons, who came from the ILEA, he would say that this is an authority with one policy - that we don't have any policies.

Paradoxically he sees the 1988 Act as leading to an increase in authority initiatives: "if anything we are more proactive than less".

Riverway recruits just under 40% of its secondary intake from primary schools outside of the LEA. Indeed, the out-of-LEA intake has increased between 1985 and 1992 by 13%, although the trend has reversed slightly since the 1988 peak of 39.6% out-of-LEA students in Riverway schools. In 1989/90 there were 851 Westway students and 767 Northwark students in Riverway schools. This increase is in part accounted for by the growth in secondary places in Riverway but is also a mark of the relative attractiveness of

Riverway schools compared with its adjacent LEAs, where surplus places have increased and schools have been amalgamated and closed during the same period. The location of most of the Riverway schools close to the LEA borders also encourages choices from 'outside'. Both the stability and the 'middle classness' of the Riverway schools make them attractive to out-of-LEA parents. Clearly the possibility of 'filling up' with students from out-of-LEA serves to further moderate competition between the Riverway schools. However, the schools are nonetheless keenly aware of changing patterns of recruitment and feel that they have to be image and publicity conscious to continue to attract their in and out-of-LEA choices:

> to some extent Riverway schools have always had to be fairly competitive because in secondary schools, when you had failing rolls about ten years ago, there wasn't a decision to rationalise, and we've maintained our number of schools by importing from neighbouring LEAs.    (Interview with Riverway CEO)

The issue of LEA competition is significant in Riverway for a number of reasons. The non-closure of schools means that there is a considerable local surplus of places. The LEA schools are heavily dependent upon the inflow of parents from other LEAs to keep their numbers up. This is exacerbated because the LEA loses a proportion of its own primary and secondary age students to the independent sector. In 1985/86 72.6% of year 6 children in state primary schools transferred to Riverway secondary schools, in 1991/92 the figure was 76.1% and the LEA projection for 1996/97 is 74.9%. In 1990/91 we calculate that approximately 163 (12%) moved on to independent schools and another 108 (7%) moved to out-of-LEA Roman Catholic schools. This outflow into the private sector, which occurs both at ages 5 and 11, is particularly heavy in certain parts of the LEA. For some of the Riverway secondaries competition with the private sector is as important as their rivalry with other state schools.

The schools themselves appear to recognise that the very positive perception of Riverway LEA and schools in their local area is a benefit to them all. They also fear that the development of intensified competition as a result of one or more schools 'opting out' (that is moving to grant-maintained status) would damage that positive perception. The gains and losses of opting out remain unclear and doubt seems to be the key factor in maintaining the status quo. Again though, that is not to say that there is no competition between the schools or that no tensions arise between them.

While all the schools recruit healthily the status quo is likely to remain in tact. But the LEA is attempting to retain a strange and difficult balance: it needs healthy recruitment of out-of-LEA students in order to sustain its schools, but on the other hand wants to ensure against its schools being flooded from outside. In this regard, the Greenwich judgement in the High Court creates particular problems in Riverway. In the past, pre-Greenwich, the LEA was able to defend its schools from out-of-LEA choice without much difficulty by using residence as a criterion for priority. In effect the market position of the LEA meant that the schools could be filled up from inflow choices (with the possibility of subtle forms of cream-skimming) while ensuring that all Riverway parents who wanted one got a place for their child in a Riverway school. Greenwich changed all that, LEA-of-residence can no longer be used as an entry restriction. The Riverway solution is a scheme of primary schools linked to each secondary school with priority at secondary transfer being given to link school students. Some out-of-LEA primary schools are designated as linked schools. There are two major problems with the scheme. First, the geography and designation of the schools (there is one ecumenical school and one girls' school) makes the linked scheme difficult to design. Some schools have lobbied hard with the LEA when they have felt discriminated against. Second, some parents feel they are denied choice by the workings of the scheme. If they exercise choice by nominating other than their link school for their child they may risk not getting their first choice because first priority is given to linked students, followed by siblings and distance. If their link school is their second choice they may not get a place if the school fills up on first choices.

The problem for the LEA, in selling its scheme to 'consumer-oriented' parents, is that the effects of the use of other criteria for entry (like distance) are unclear to individual consumers.

Allocations based simply on propinquity and sibling attendance would increase the proportion of non-Riverway parents in Riverway schools. The likelihood is that many fewer Riverway parents would get their first choice school than do so now. The difficulty for the LEA, in part at least, is that they are pursuing a policy based on the collective best interests of their council tax

payers when the prevailing climate is one where individual parents
are encouraged to exercise choice in terms of familial self-interest.
There is a further dimension to this. The attraction of the Riverway
schools for many (especially middle class) parents is their socio-
economic constitution. Open entry would be likely to change the
social class make up of the schools particularly in the north and east
of the LEA. Again though individually self-interested parents are
unlikely to be aware of this aspect of collective interest. Looking at
things the other way around the use of a 'closed shop' strategy by
Riverway denies free choice of school to parents outside Riverway,
even though in many cases a Riverway school would be
geographically their nearest school. Put in the most negative terms,
the protection of the local system through the linked school
arrangement protects the class privileges of Riverway parents while
ensuring that the schools remain full.

One Riverway LEA officer commented that if the link scheme
were to fail or schools to opt out then:

> the situation is now so volatile that it is impossible for anyone
> to predict what would happen. The situation is such that it is
> increasingly difficult to manage the system in the best
> interests of students or schools. (Interview with LEA
> admissions officer)

The linked school system offers secondary schools a degree of
predictability and security in the marketplace but this should not be
over estimated. Schools still find it very difficult to match offers
against admissions year on year (many parents now make multiple
place applications) and they are constantly surprised by changes in
patterns of recruitment. Table 1 demonstrates one set of year-to-
year changes. See Bartlett (1992, p 26) for a discussion of
admissions instabilities in Avon LEA.

Corpus Christi school is an anomaly: it recruits virtually all of its
students from out-of-LEA, mainly from Northwark, mostly from
Church primary schools; a high proportion of the students are
black; and the school controls its own admissions. In 1992 it had
the lowest average pass rate for five or more A to C grade GCSEs
of all the Riverway schools (30%). According to Department for
Education figures for January 1990 (Department for Education,
1993), Riverway has a net gain of 2,580 students overall when
imports are set against exports to other LEAs.

**Table 1:   Admission to Riverway schools from LEA and out-of-LEA children**

| School | 1990/91 | | | | 1991/92 | | | |
|---|---|---|---|---|---|---|---|---|
| | River-way | Out-of-LEA | Total | % Out-of-LEA | River-way | Out-of-LEA | Total | % Out-of-LEA |
| Corpus Christi | 7 | 128 | 135 | 94.8 | 13 | 118 | 131 | 90.1 |
| Blenhiem | 148 | 49 | 197 | 24.9 | 152 | 68 | 220 | 30.1 |
| Overbury | 163 | 40 | 203 | 19.7 | 153 | 33 | 186 | 17.7 |
| Parsons | 116 | 42 | 158 | 26.6 | 134 | 64 | 198 | 32.3 |
| Fletcher | 70 | 165 | 235 | 70.2 | 84 | 129 | 213 | 60.0 |
| Lockmere | 153 | 88 | 241 | 36.5 | 179 | 71 | 250 | 28.4 |
| Pankhurst | 150 | 40 | 190 | 21.0 | 125 | 52 | 177 | 29.4 |
| Goddard | 123 | 50 | 173 | 28.9 | 136 | 80 | 216 | 37.0 |

The relationships of minimal trust between the schools are maintained via a regular meeting of headteachers at which a code of conduct for promotional activity has been hammered out; for example, an agreed date for the publication of examination results. Again though, these agreements are sometimes strained by competitive pressures.   Bartlett (1992, p 23) notes a similar situation in Avon LEA.

> I was angry with Parsons last year because we felt that we had a heads' agreement, made in the tired state that one gets to at the end of term ... and I reckoned that we ought to he more worried than anybody, and yet we didn't break the agreement, and then I did see other schools as doing that ... I mean it's all very well to have morals ... (Interview with Head of Overbury)

Competitive awareness and the year on year anxieties about recruitment patterns in Riverway produce a climate of inchoate suspicion, of 'looking over one's shoulder', of the need to search for competitive edge.  The existence of the heads' agreement highlights the sorts of market behaviour that are becoming taken for granted in other settings (like Northwark).  The Riverway heads spoke of their agreement to minimise competition in two ways.  In one way with relief.  There was less to worry about, less to do in order to 'be competitive'.  But, on the other hand, they were very aware of the tenuousness and fragility of the agreement.   One school in particular is viewed as 'straining' the agreement or 'breaking ranks'.

> They are more aggressive than ... other schools.  We feel it quite keenly, because we ... because of our position and so on, are in competition perhaps with Lockmere whereas we're not with Fletcher, for example.  They are more aggressive, and it is felt that there is more of a sell rather than a reflection of the truth. (Interview with Head of Overbury)

Overall in Riverway the demand for places is buoyant, the number of year 7 pupils admitted having risen from 1,308 in 1985 to 1,591 in 1991.  The pressure on accommodation has led to investment in a school building programme.  However, despite the corporatist policies of Riverway LEA and the buoyancy of secondary school recruitment the market dynamics of competition and choice are still complex and difficult to predict.  The existence of a church school and a girls' school (Pankhurst) in the LEA, with their recruitment cutting across the other schools, is one kind of complication; geography and the spatial distribution of the schools is another; competition with the private sector another; and the attempts made by rival LEAs to retain their students is another. Furthermore, the corporate image of the LEA overlays a long-standing differentiation of schools in terms of local status and reputation.

## Northwark

Northwark is a very different authority. The Conservative controlled LEA is committed to competition, choice and diversity of provision, and has actively pursued a policy of developing a market in schooling within the LEA. The LEA was previously part of the Inner London Education Authority (ILEA) and the majority party on the council makes no secret of its antipathy to ILEA policies. In a local magazine article (October 1992), the leader of the council wrote:

> Until April 1990, education in Northwark meant ILEA: a uniform diet of all-purpose comprehensives. Every one the same and some of the worst examination results in the country. They even blew the whistle on competitive sport. And don't take my word for it. While the pupils were rattling around in half empty classrooms their pals from across the street were voting with their feet. 4,500 local secondary school places were going begging while four out of ten youngsters went to school outside the LEA or in the independent sector. (p 24)

Lying behind the concern about surplus places there is also the issue of recoupment. The LEA must pay the per capita costs of students educated in schools in other LEAs. In effect they pay twice: once for the surplus place and once for the recoupment. The leader went on to describe the council's policies and then said:

> Selection means real choice for parents and renewed motivation for pupils. Different types of school for different types of aptitude. The council publishes the results and attendance figures for every Northwark school, primary and secondary. Try getting that from Streetley! [A neighbouring Labour controlled LEA] Informed choice requires hard facts. (p 24)

The development of a market is being pursued in a number of ways. Attempts have been made to make secondary schools into 'magnet' schools with a specific curriculum specialism and to link this 'magnet' system to a system of selection by aptitude. The setting up of a city technology college (CTC) in the LEA area and a county technology college on CTC lines committed to the Japanese principle of *Kaizen* have been encouraged (LEA Parents Guide, 1992, p 23). In an interview in July 1991 the CEO of Northwark explained the thinking behind the move to establish the Carbridge Technology College:

> there was no way in which the present majority party could be persuaded to go along with the formula of the neighbourhood comprehensive school which has so patently failed. A few years ago there were four schools in Carbridge - many of them flourishing. Within a relatively short period of time there was next to none. So there would be no question of the council going along with 'well we're just going to turn the school round by giving ourselves more of the same medicine'.

These initiatives have resulted in five LEA schools using 'opting out' as a way of escaping from the LEA.

> As far as grant-maintained status is concerned, the council's view is that as long as the grant-maintained status does not damage the efficiency of the system as a whole then it will smile on grant-maintained status. (Interview with Northwark CEO)

The opted out schools are unanimous in seeing grant-maintained status as a way of maintaining their comprehensive identity and avoiding the specialisation and selection policies being pursued by Northwark.

The paradox here is that in 'driving out' some schools, which want to protect their comprehensive identity, the LEA is unable to fully pursue its objective of creating a diversified school market.

Despite the surplus places in the authority the LEA has encouraged the founding or relocation of a Church of England secondary school. Various strategies to achieve this have all thus far failed but the effort continues. This would increase diversity for parents but is also part of the LEA's corporate competition with its neighbours and its efforts to reduce its recoupment costs.

When it comes to the Church of England school, you face a situation where over a thousand Northwark children go out of the LEA for their education, for a Church of England secondary education. ... The argument is, if we had a Church of England school in Northwark it would represent no threat to the remaining schools because it would be dealing with a constituency which is already finding its education elsewhere for which the LEA has to pay a heavy recoupment. So it must be costing £2-3 million a year because we haven't got a Church of England school in Northwark. (Interview with Northwark CEO)

In particular the CEO is referring to the draw of Corpus Christi in Riverway upon Northwark students. If the authority were successful in setting up or attracting a Church of England school then the recruitment to Corpus Christi (as well as nearby grant-maintained schools) could possibly suffer markedly.

In 1991 the LEA began to publish surveys of attendance, and examination and test performance for primary and secondary schools. New tests have been introduced into primary schools as part of this process of comparison and accountability. In 1992 figures on school exclusions and ethnic minority student performance were also published. These are intended to provide effectiveness indicators and general information for parents who are choosing schools.

In 1990 the LEA announced the closure of two secondaries (one boys' school and one girls' school). The girls' school attempted to obtain grant-maintained status and was strongly supported by parents but was turned down by the Secretary of State on a technicality - that notice of closure had been announced before the moves to grant-maintained status were formally initiated.

The LEA has established a 'choice shop': a shopfront information centre to help parents in their choice of school. Overall, the Northwark CEO is committed to a model of educational provision which purports to give maximum independence to schools and a minimal role to the LEA and which involves competition between schools and school providers.

I mean the LEA does not educate anybody. There's no children educated in the town hall. There are children educated by schools and school teachers and it is better that the school should have the greatest degree of independence. ... I would like to see LEAs run their own schools in a proper degree of competition with other schools because I think well run LEAs can run very well run schools and I see no difference between the church and [CTC sponsor] and a local corporation. But I do think that the discipline of the market is a very good discipline. (Interview with Northwark CEO)

This position also intriguingly led this CEO (often seen as a key innovator in relation to radical Conservative education policies) to vociferously oppose those aspects of the 1992 education White Paper *Diversity and choice* which emphasised the need, based on cost, to remove surplus places. The CEO, like many others, recognises that the removal of surplus places would curb the market and possibilities of parental choice and shift market power back to the producers, but he also sees it as likely to stultify innovation and limit diversity. Nonetheless, the CEO also supports the use of selection: "you can't have parental choice without greater diversity, you cannot have diversity without greater specialisation, you cannot have specialisation without selection" (Northwark CEO, BBC Radio interview, November 1992).

But the policies of Northwark LEA contain their own contradictions around the issue of *planning versus choice*. As noted above, in 1990 the LEA made the decision to close Elizabeth Anderson Girls' School despite the schools' application for and parents' support for grant-maintained status. The CEO has described himself in public as an "agnostic on opting out" and told parents at a public meeting on opting out in another school that they should not believe that "opting out will allow you to escape from government policies; it won't". And as indicated in the extract above, the majority party on the Education Committee are strongly set against the idea of the neighbourhood comprehensive school. One of the effects of the LEA restructuring of its secondary schools is intended to be the destruction of the neighbourhood comprehensive principle. If this is achieved, parents who support the neighbourhood comprehensive principle will find this choice unavailable to them. The Northwark LEA has supported and advanced 'choice' and competition paradoxically by adopting a highly interventionist strategy. The independence of schools which the CEO advocates rests on terms set by the LEA.

The overall impact of these policies on choice and recruitment is difficult to gauge in the short term and the competitive position of Northwark as an LEA is becoming increasing difficult to monitor as more and more of its schools opt out, but some material from 1990 (when the ILEA was abolished) through to 1992 is available.

If these figures, presented in Table 2, are accurate then two points are worth noting. As indicated above, one of the concerns of the LEA has been the loss of primary school children to secondary schools in neighbouring LEAs. However, the retention rate in Northwark seems to have improved considerably from 1990 to 1991, and at least as regards the maintained sector, inflow from other LEAs more than compensates for the outflow. The competition with the independent sector paints a different picture. But these figures are difficult to interpret and explain. The outflow changes might indicate that Northwark's attempts to 'de-comprehensivise' its schools are encouraging more parents to stay in the system but a variety of other factors may also be at work. As regards outflow, Riverway is by far the largest single beneficiary. But these in and outflows merit closer examination. It is difficult to say much about who these students are but the London reading test scores of these students gives some indication (see Table 3). Knowing what we do about the relationships between performance on such tests and social class background, these data suggest that middle class (high ability) students are being lost (mainly to Riverway and to elite/cosmopolitan schools; see Ball, Bowe and Gewirtz, forthcoming) and working class students are being attracted into Northwark, mainly from the adjacent Streetley LEA. This is all part of a westward drift of middle class students, both black and white, from inner-city to suburban schools. Push and pull factors play a part. Streetley LEA is poorly perceived by many middle class parents and Northwark looks good by comparison. As far as outflow is concerned Northwark's history as an ILEA division also looms large.

A number of the middle class parents we interviewed in our research clearly regarded ILEA education policies as operating against the relative advantage of their children and continue to regard the Northwark schools with suspicion. According to Department for Education (1993) figures, Streetley LEA is the largest net loser of students in England, showing as at January 1992 a net loss of 5,764.

**Table 2:   Secondary transfer from Northwark primary schools**

**a. Outflow**

| To: | To September 90 | To September 91 |
|---|---|---|
| Northwark | 1,319 | 1,690 |
| Farnsea | 90 | 67 |
| Keswell | 28 | - |
| Streetley | 67 | 14 |
| City | 40 | 9 |
| Subville | 23 | 4 |
| Riverway | 198 | 182 |
| Others | 36 | 13 |
| Total transfer | 1,801 | 1,979 |
| Total out-of-LEA | 482 (27%) | * 289 (15%) |

**b. Inflow**

| From: | Boys | 1990 Girls | Total | 1991 Total |
|---|---|---|---|---|
| Northwark | 45 | 35 | 80 | 117 |
| Out-of-LEA | 257 | 155 | 412 | 486 |
| Total | | | 492 | 603 |

Note:   * Data may be incomplete.

In addition in September 1990 116 parents notified Northwark that their children were transferring to the independent sector. In September 1991 328 parents so notified the LEA. Department for Education (1993) figures on the import and export of students, as at January 1992, show Northwark with a net loss of 148.

**Table 3:** **London reading test scores and banding for Northwark students**

| Group | Mean score | Band 1 group % |
|---|---|---|
| Total year 6 1990 | 101.2 | 31.6 |
| Outflow to LEAs | 102.8 | 34.7 |
| Remaining in Northwark | 100.1 | 27.2 |
| Inflow from LEAs | 96.1 | 17.7 |
| Total year 7 1991 | 99.6 | 26.1 |

## Conclusion

It would be difficult to characterise these school markets as free markets. In general terms, through its attempts to control the information system of the education market (via national testing, local league tables and published performance indicators) the government is asserting a planning function while pursuing the rhetorics of autonomy and choice. Hayek's term for this is "ordered competition": to order competition so as to achieve *particular* social and economic goals (1980, p 111). And the school market is subject to manipulation and intervention in a variety of other ways. Riverway and Northwark both constrain and plan their local markets, although in different ways and with different effects. The former is seeking to maintain comprehensive education and the class advantage of local residents. The latter is seeking to deconstruct comprehensive education and create a new diversity among schools (related to selection). In neither case could we see the outcome as some kind of 'spontaneous order', an aggregate of individual actions. The implantation of the city technology college in Northwark is also a planned distortion of choice; an intervention which also increases surplus places while other 'popular' schools are being closed. The analysis of Northwark and Riverway as market players also raises more general questions about the role of LEAs. As competitive units, attempting to maximise the use of their school place provision and minimise recoupment costs, they act as corporations rather than small businesses (eg closing down unprofitable subsidiaries, investing in new developments, maximising market share). But their geographical boundaries are ultimately arbitrary in market terms. They cut across 'natural areas' or catchments, or spatial localities. Nationally, in 1992, a total of 186,000 students crossed LEA borders to attend school (Department for Education, 1993). Riverways' policy of importation has avoided the necessity of school closures and indeed has led to an expansion of accommodation and facilities for students attending Riverway schools. In effect these developments have been funded by other LEAs. Northwark is committed to reduce its loss of students and its recoupment costs by radical innovation and the expansion of the LEA's school portfolio. In their different ways both authorities exercise some "interpretive potential" (Duncan and Goodwin, 1988) in and around the provisions of the 1988 Education Reform Act. The contrasts between Riverway and Northwark are summarised in Figure 1.

**Figure 1:   Riverway and Northwark LEAs**

| Riverway | Northwark |
|---|---|
| Social Democrat | Conservative |
| Pro-comprehensive | Pro-selection and specialisation |
| Cartel of schools | School competition |
| LEA schools | Mixed (LEA/GMS/CTC) |
| School cooperation | School suspicion |
| Inflow problems | Outflow problems |
| Link primary scheme | Open enrolment/choice |
| Limited diversity | Planned diversity |

The market structure and dynamics in these two localities remain strongly framed and guided by LEA policies and politics. But there are many other factors (not discussed here) which need to be incorporated into analysis of local school markets. The market in education is not simply a product of the 1988 Education Reform Act and LEA decision making; markets in particular settings have long and complex histories. Those histories are part of the local folk knowledge that parents draw upon when choosing schools. Those histories construct and confer reputations upon schools. Schools are increasingly aware of and increasingly sophisticated in the management of impressions and reputation building. Markets are also informed and constrained by locality and community. Some schools have strong locational identities; the attraction of the 'local school' remains strong for many parents and is a major criteria in their choice of school. The spatial location of schools is also important in relation to enrolment. This is the one thing that schools have no control over; transport, natural barriers, traffic flows and demographic changes all impose limitations upon the possibilities of recruitment and hit certain schools hard. The history of school building, of amalgamations and of location are also important more generally in relation to competition. These are the outcomes of previous LEA decisions which were often driven by very different economic and political priorities from those now in play.

Social class (and in some cases ethnicity) is also a key factor in the dynamics of the market. There is evidence of relationships between certain class factions and preference for certain styles and ethos of schooling (see Ball, Bowe and Gewirtz, forthcoming). The class and ethnic composition of schools is also, for some parents, a criterion in their selection of schools. And social class is a key factor in understanding the movement of students between LEAs and the recruitment strategies of particular schools. The policies of both Riverway and Northwark are indirectly related to retaining or changing the social class and ethnic profiles of their schools.

What this kind of analysis begins to display is a complex interplay of planned, arbitrary, historical, spontaneous and producer and consumer factors that constitute the education market. In all this the LEA continues to have a role of some significance (at least in urban settings). None of the currently employed concepts - such as planned or regulated markets, consumer sovereignty, freedom of choice - do justice to this complexity or begin to describe or anticipate its effects either in terms of quality and efficiency or social justice and patterns of educational opportunity. We need a set of more specific and carefully grounded concepts and descriptors if the analysis of quasi-markets is to move forward.

## References

Ball, S. (1993) 'Education markets, choice and social class: the market as a class strategy in the UK and the USA', *British Journal of Sociology of Education*, vol 14, no 1, pp 3-20.

Ball, S., Bowe, R. and Gewirtz, S. (forthcoming) 'Circuits of schooling: a sociological exploration of parental choice in social class contexts', *Sociological Review*.

Bartlett, W. (1991) *Privatisation and quasi-markets,* Studies in Decentralisation and Quasi-Markets no 7, Bristol: SAUS Publications, School for Advanced Urban Studies, University of Bristol.

Bartlett, W. (1992) *Quasi-markets and educational reforms: a case study,* Studies in Decentralisation and Quasi-Markets no 12, Bristol: SAUS Publications, School for Advanced Urban Studies, University of Bristol.

Department for Education (1992) *Choice and diversity,* London: HMSO.

Department for Education (1993) *Consultative paper on new arrangements for inter-authority recoupment,* London: DfE.

Duncan, S. and Goodwin, M. (1988) *The local state and uneven development,* Cambridge: Polity Press.

Gewirtz, S., Ball, S. and Bowe, R. (1993) 'Values and ethics in the education market place: the case of Northwark Park', *International Studies in the Sociology of Education*, vol 3, no 2, pp 233-54.

Hayek, F. (1979) *The constitution of liberty,* London: Routledge and Kegan Paul.

Hayek, K. (1980) *Individualism and economic order*, Chicago: University of Chicago Press.

*five*

# THE DEVELOPMENT OF COMPETITION AMONG HIGHER EDUCATION INSTITUTIONS

## Geraint Johnes and Martin Cave

### Introduction: the political context

Universities typically aim to enhance or maintain their academic reputations. Such prestige is gained by achieving high positions in rank order tournaments where the goal is to recruit the ablest students, to publish in the top journals, or to secure the most lucrative research contracts. This being so, higher education institutions in the UK have considerable experience of competition, and that competition has fostered what many regard as a high quality system. Discussions about quasi-markets in the field of higher education, therefore, usually focus on new methods designed to introduce competition specifically for financial resources, taking competition for prestige for granted (Glennerster, 1991).

The new policies which we are describing are set against the background of major changes in the structure and decision taking processes of higher education institutions. It has been argued (Cave et al, 1992) that before the 1980s the objective function of higher education institutions was determined largely by their employees. They could thus be regarded as a form of not-for-profit labour cooperative in which academics were able to realise their preference for research over teaching, buttressed by substantial excess demand for student places. The Conservative government, following the recommendations of the Jarratt Report (Committee of

Vice-Chancellors and Principals, 1985) resolved to shift the balance of power in universities from their academic staffs to their councils and to strengthen the role of the vice-chancellor as chief executive. It is likely that the effect of these changes was to shift the objective function of the institutions in the direction of profit or output maximisation, and to focus attention upon efficiency.

There are at least two possible ways of specifying the new objectives sought by the government. The first is to regard them as being aimed at ensuring the continued provision of the quality service, but to do so with increased efficiency; thus universities pursue, as before, the goal of excellence while the new tools encourage them to reduce both $x$-inefficiencies and (in a partial sense) allocative inefficiencies. This goal is pursued subject to some arbitrary expenditure constraint. The second possible goal of the new policies is to encourage universities to maximise some more complex function, such as surplus or profit. If profit were maximised the institution's only concerns with quality would be indirect: either quality is a determinant of profits or it imposes an arbitrary constraint. This would be consistent with the aim of achieving overall economic efficiency (albeit narrowly defined). If the aim of government (which still provides most higher education finance in the UK) is to secure economic efficiency, while that of the universities is academic excellence, the development of new funding systems may usefully be regarded as an attempt to find solutions to a classic principal-agent problem. Since the funding councils buy student places on behalf of the consumers of education (that is, students and - possibly - employers), a further principal-agent problem is apparent; it is in this respect that education is traded in a quasi-market.

The funding mechanisms which we shall discuss below have been developed in response to a stiffening of the government's resolve to ensure that incentives faced by agents in the university system are compatible with the goals of the principal. This increased determination has its roots in both political philosophy and pragmatism. The laissez-faire approach of the Conservative administration first elected in 1979 has been consistent with the desire to bring the social and private returns to higher education more into line with each other. Hence the 1985 Green Paper on the development of higher education into the 1990s stated:

> There is continuing concern that higher education does not always respond sufficiently to changing economic needs.

> This may be due in part to disincentives to change within higher education, including overdependence on public funding. ... The government believes that ... more income for higher education can be obtained from business and private sources. (HMSO, 1985)

More recently, the former Parliamentary Under-Secretary of State for Education and Science has stated that

> Market forces are effective tools for improving the match between the services provided by the higher education system and the needs of its users and funders. (Howarth, 1991)

Nevertheless, the funding cuts of 1981 resulted, not from education policy considerations, but from the government's decision to pursue an overall deflationary macroeconomic stance. Necessity is the mother of invention, and institutions of higher education responded by seeking alternative sources of finance. The gradual move away from dependence on funding council monies is illustrated in Table 1. Simultaneously the advantages of diminished reliance on public funds were beginning to be understood in the universities (Marris, 1986). The decision to expand higher education, signalled at Kenneth Baker's famous Lancaster speech (Baker, 1989), likewise was the result of adjustments which the universities were already making; the absence of cash limits on tuition fees, together with the gradual increase in the value of fees, meant that universities could receive at least partial funding for all the extra students they were willing to enrol (The Higher, 1992). In order to expand higher education at a time when the electorate favoured reductions in rates of direct taxation, innovative and market-oriented methods of bringing private funds into the university system have been sought.

Given the role played by exigency in formulating higher education policy over the period under consideration, moves towards the quasi-market have often occurred by accident rather than by design. They have enjoyed correspondingly mixed success.

The concern of this chapter is the allocation by the various funding councils of monies for teaching in higher education institutions. First, a brief history is given of funding mechanisms used since the 1970s by the University Grants Committee (UGC), the Universities Funding Council (UFC), the Polytechnic and Colleges Funding Council (PCFC), and the Higher Education Funding Council for England (HEFCE). We then provide

theoretical and empirical analyses which throw light on aspects of
the operation of these systems.  Quality regulation is then discussed
and finally we draw conclusions and look ahead to further possible
reforms.

**Table 1:    General recurrent income by source**

|  | 1979-80 | 1989-90 |
|---|---|---|
| Total recurrent income: | | |
| current prices | £1,604 m | £4,040 m |
| June 1992 prices | £3,380 m | £4,499 m |
| | | |
| Exchequer grants | | |
| (block, equipment and furniture) | 62.9% | 47.4% |
| Full-time fees: | | |
| home rates | 13.2% | 5.7% |
| other rates | 3.4% | 5.0% |
| Part-time fees | 0.4% | 0.7% |
| Research training and other support grants | 0.2% | 0.4% |
| Endowments, subventions and donations | 0.9% | 3.3% |
| Computer board grants | 0.7% | 1.0% |
| Other general recurrent[1] | 2.7% | 6.8% |
| Research grants and contracts | 12.7% | 18.9% |
| Other services rendered[2] | 2.8% | 10.8% |

Source:    *University Statistics*, Volume 3, Finance, various issues

Notes:      1.  The 1989/90 figure includes depreciation allowance and
                 fees for short courses, and fees for liberal adult education
                 courses.
            2.  The 1989/90 figure includes revenues from residences and
                 catering.

## Systems of higher education finance in the UK

The system of finance of higher education systems in use up to the
1970s has been expertly surveyed by Williams (1988) and will not
be discussed here.  In choosing to describe systems in operation
during the last two decades, we highlight the nature of recent
developments as a response to inefficiencies which were built into
the funding allocation mechanisms of earlier years.

During the 1970s neither market forces nor the performance of the universities played much of a role in allocating funds between higher education institutions. The UGC determined planned student numbers for each university, these being based in part on the availability of space within each institution's buildings. Small and financially vulnerable universities received more than their share of the total resources available in each year; that is, the allocation between universities was made by deficiency grant. This was a recipe for the generation of $x$-inefficiency.

The first moves in the direction of the quasi-market as a means of allocating resources in higher education concerned research rather than teaching. The UGC introduced the first of a series of research selectivity exercises in 1986. These were intended to inform, and so render more efficient, the allocation of resources for the purposes of research. Since the focus of this chapter is on the development of the quasi-market in the provision of teaching services by higher education institutions, we do not discuss research selectivity further here.

More competitive systems for the allocation of teaching funds across institutions were introduced separately by the PCFC and UFC in 1989 and 1990 respectively. In both cases the new mechanisms were intended to allocate the councils' contribution to teaching costs more efficiently than under the block grant system. The fee element of provision was essentially unaffected, though it is worth noting that at around this time the level of fees increased substantially. The systems introduced by the two funding councils had a number of similarities (for instance they both involved a process of bidding for students) but they also differed in some crucial respects. While one of the schemes achieved moderate success in securing efficiency gains, the other collapsed in ignominy.

The UFC's method of allocating teaching funds took the form of a bidding process or auction (Cave, 1990; Johnes, 1992a). Bids were solicited from the universities in 1990 and the outcome of the exercise was intended to determine resource allocation for the planning period from 1991/92 through 1994/95 and beyond. As an aid in the bidding process, the UFC published 'guide prices' for some 20 subject areas; these were based upon historic unit costs faced by the council, and the hope was therefore that institutions would bid to take students at a cost to the UFC at or below these guide prices. Within each subject area, each university would bid to take $x$ students at a price of £$y$ each. Alternatively, universities could choose to bid in a slightly more complicated fashion; that is, they could bid to take $x_1$ students at a price of $£y_1$, plus a further $x_2$ students at a lower price of $£y_2$. The UFC would then decide, on the basis of these bids, how many students should be allocated to each university on a subject by subject basis. The lowest price bids would win the auction subject to a quality constraint. The UFC provided detailed guidance about what expenditures should be included in calculating unit costs for the purposes of bidding. A prescribed allowance for overheads was included, but research costs, local taxation and London salary allowances were not. Moreover, while bids were submitted in 1989/90 prices, the UFC could not guarantee full indexation of funds allocated during the lifetime of the scheme. For these reasons, bids did not reflect anything resembling true unit costs, but rather were measured in an esoteric metric which became known as 'Chilver pounds' in honour of the chair of the council. The system thus imposed exceptionally heavy demands upon the institution's capacities to make rational decisions, and its complexity may have contributed to the outcome.

Following the submission of bids in 1990, the UFC declared that 93% of all student places tendered were offered at the guide prices - a remarkable degree of concord. Since it was "disappointed by the scale of economy" which these bids represented, the UFC abandoned its auction system without ever putting it to use as a means of allocating resources.

The PCFC bidding process was first used to allocate recurrent funding for the 1990/91 year (Turner and Pratt, 1990; Pratt and Hillier, 1991). Some 5% of total recurrent funds were withheld by the council for allocation by competitive means, the remainder being allocated across institutions as a block grant. (In the second year of operation of the scheme, the proportion withheld for competitive allocation doubled to 10%; following that, the system met with increased resistance from the institutions.) As in the UFC auction, polytechnics and colleges were invited to submit bids for both quantity (number of student places) and price (funding per student). Bids were tendered subject by subject. Lower price bids were favoured by the PCFC, other things being equal, but a number of other criteria also entered the council's optimand. In particular, quality, student demand, and the widening of student access to higher education were all characteristics sought by the PCFC in determining which bids should be successful. These were factors which contributed directly to the optimand of the PCFC; they did not merely serve as constraints. Thus the bids submitted to the

PCFC within any given subject area could vary widely because the student places offered referred explicitly to courses which, though similar in content, differed in other ways.

Following the collapse of the UFC's bidding scheme, a new mechanism was set up for the allocation of teaching expenditures amongst universities (Becher and Kogan, 1992; Cave and Weale, 1992). A specified number of students, which varied by university and subject, would be fully funded (at guide price levels) in 1991/92. Monies could be clawed back by the UFC if universities failed to recruit up to their allocated number of fully funded students. Universities would, of course, be free to recruit additional students, if they so wished, on a fees-only basis; that is, the university would receive nothing from the UFC for these additional students, but would receive the fee (normally paid by central government through the student's local authority). The fee falls far short of the average (though not necessarily the marginal) cost of tuition, so extensive new recruitment on this basis would not normally be profitable for the institutions. However, the UFC declared that increases in fully funded numbers in future years would be made on the basis of universities' success, *relative to other universities*, in attracting fees-only students. In so doing, the council provided an incentive for universities to admit such students at low cost to the exchequer. Each institution, therefore, had to weigh up the costs and benefits of enrolling additional students, where the benefits included the possible future increase in fully funded numbers, appropriately discounted. In this model, therefore, it is performance relative to other institutions which matters in securing future resources. For this reason, Cave et al (1992) have likened the system to one of yardstick competition (Shleifer, 1985): each university aims to meet a performance target, but the position of the target - determined as it is by the behaviour of each and every university in the system - is not known.

The 'binary divide' between the (older) universities and the (former) polytechnics was abolished in 1992. This led not only to agonised debate about the renaming of institutions but also resulted in the replacement of the UFC and PCFC by the new higher education funding councils. The system of funding teaching in England in 1993/94 followed a 'core-plus-margin' approach (Higher Education Funding Council for England, 1992, 1993a). The core is awarded on the understanding that the institution will not reduce the numbers of British and other European Community students taught. Across the system as a whole, core funding will match in real value (according to the GDP deflator) the previous year's total funding, *minus* an amount which will be subject to inter-university variation. The amount subtracted will be relatively low for those institutions which currently impose upon the funding council a relatively low cost per British/EC student (possibly by accepting many students on a fees-only basis). The mean reduction in real core funding will be determined by the efficiency gain which government wishes the higher education sector to achieve.

The margin consists of funds, over and above core funds, which became available after the autumn statement on government expenditure. Such monies (£45 million in 1993/94) will be allocated competitively across institutions; again the criterion used will be the level of council funding per British/EC student. The lower the unit cost in the current year, the greater the level of council funding in future. Marginal funding will allow institutions to expand the number of student places available at the institution-specific level of unit cost. With the exception of the new universities, this is an important break from tradition in that it will be the first time that the funding council will be charged such a multiplicity of prices. Monitoring of the quality of tuition will follow in future years and will have an input into the allocation of funds. It should be noted that the HEFCE has not imposed long-term bounds either on the efficiency gain deduction implicit in core funding or on the inter-university differential in this deduction, although it has set figures for 1992/93. Core funding allocated to each institution is, however, guaranteed to be a "very high percentage in real terms of their previous year's funding", and a safety net will operate which ensures that (after summing funding allocations for teaching and research) "no institution is expected to cope with *what the council judges to be* an unmanageable reduction of funding in one year" [Our italics] (Higher Education Funding Council for England, 1993a)

As noted earlier, the new methods of allocating teaching resources amongst universities are designed to replace the old block grant system with a mechanism which mimics the market. Meanwhile, during the early 1990s, the fee per student which universities receive (usually from the students' local authority acting on behalf of central government) has increased substantially. In 1989/90 the full-time undergraduate fee was just over £600. Since then, fees have been increased sharply, and now are determined on a subject-specific basis in a manner which is intended to mirror inter-subject differences in the costs of tuition.

Thus fees for the 1992/93 year (including the college fee which covers examinations) were £1,989 for the arts and social sciences and £2,904 for the sciences.

Fees at such levels, even though they fall below the true cost of provision, have the potential to fund growth in the provision of higher education. From the students' point of view, fees act as vouchers, giving them potential 'buying power' at any institution willing to accept them. From the institution's point of view a fees-only student also lowers average funding council costs per student and (holding other institutions' recruitment constant) abates its annual reduction in funding per student.

In response to the expansion of student numbers in 1992/93 and general pressures on public spending, the government acted in late 1992 to impose a break on growth. This was done by lowering fees by 30% in classroom based courses (notably humanities and social sciences) where expansion had been highest. However, the funding council decided to maintain the earlier fee level for students already enrolled on a fees-only basis in subject areas where fees were cut.

The effect of these changes is that institutions now receive funding for students in each subject area at three rates: a fully-funded institution-specific rate; a new fees-only rate, uniform across each institution; and an intra-marginal fees-only rate 'grandfathered' from 1992/93. The main effect is likely to reduce institutions' expansion plans and maintain or enhance the excess demand for places.

## Price competition

### The former bidding systems

The theoretical model described in this section is a straightforward extension of that developed by Johnes (1992a), and uses auction models of the type usefully surveyed by McAfee and Macmillan (1987), Milgrom (1989) and Wilson (1992). One of the main results of auction and tendering theory concerns the equivalence of revenues or payments irrespective of the particular auctioning procedure adopted. Thus in the simplest case, with independent valuations and no risk aversion, it can be shown that all the principal auction or tendering forms (oral or sealed bid, English or Dutch, first price/discriminatory or second price/non-discriminatory) yield the same expected revenue or payments.

Essentially this is because, in cases where participants cannot observe one another's bids, tenderers are guided in their behaviour by rational conjectures of other tenderers' strategies. To take a simple case, in a multi-object tender, the purchaser would expect on average to pay the same whether the tender was conducted on a discriminatory (each tenderer gets what it bid) or a non-discriminatory basis (each tenderer gets the highest accepted bid). In the former case, each participant conjectures the highest accepted offer and tenders it. Thus with sophisticated and rational bidders, in a discriminatory regime it is differences rather than similarities in bids which require explanation.

To model the bidding processes used in higher education, we adopt a simple model in which each of two institutions is supposed to be risk neutral, and faces an average cost of service provision given by $V_i$, where:

$$V_i = v_i Q_i$$

Here, $Q_i$ denotes the level of service provided by the $i$th institution, and $v_i$ is an institution-specific parameter, $i=1,2$. The $v_i$ are constrained so as to ensure that the $V_i$ are, over time, uniformly distributed over the unit interval. Neither institution has information about the costs facing the other. We assume that the technology which generates this pattern of cost does not admit $x$-inefficiency; this assumption needs to be relaxed in future work.

Now suppose that the two universities bid against each other for the winner-takes-all right to sell $Q$ student places. The $i$th institution ($i=1,2$) offers a bid price, $P_i$, and a bid quantity, $Q_i$. The bidder submitting the lower price bid wins the auction, and the buyer (in this case the funding council which acts on behalf of prospective students) buys all student places offered by the winning bidder.[1] The bidding scheme therefore resembles a first price or discriminatory auction: each bidder gets its own bid price. It is important to note at this stage that, although they are free (if they win) to determine the quantity supplied, quantity bids do not influence the chance of success in the auction: bidders win or lose on the basis only of price bids. Consequently $P_i$ determines the probability of success. The higher $P_i$ is, the greater the probability that the rival institution will undercut the price bid. Given the uniform distribution assumption made above, the *ex ante* probability of success perceived by the $i$th institution must equal $(1-P_i)$.

Suppose that each university tries to maximise, with respect to price and quantity bids, its expected surplus of revenue over costs. This maximand is derived as the product of the *ex ante* success probability, the level of provision, and the difference between price and average cost. Hence the problem is to:

$$\text{Max} \ (1-P_i) \ Q_i \ (P_i - v_i Q_i) \qquad (1)$$
$$P_i, Q_i$$

The first order conditions for a maximum are:

$$Q_i = (2P_i - 1)/v_i \qquad (2)$$

and

$$P_i^2 - P_i(1 + 2v_i Q_i) + 2v_i Q_i = 0 \qquad (3)$$

Simultaneous solution of this last pair of equations yields the result that $P_i = 2/3$ and $Q_i = 1/3v_i$. [2] In other words, the bid price is independent of $v_i$, while the quantity bid varies inversely with $v_i$. Both universities bid the same price. The intuition underlying the above result is simple. Each university sets its bid price to the level which it thinks will win it the auction. Since both universities have similar perceptions about the distribution of costs across institutions, both bid the same price. The universities then adjust the level of provision in order to maximise their expected surplus. So one possible explanation for the failure of the UFC bidding system to generate different bids from different universities is that the mechanics of the council's bidding system were flawed.

However, at least three other explanations have been proposed in the literature. First, Albrecht and Ziderman (1992, p 37) state, without evidence, that the UFC scheme was "abandoned because institutions entered into a cartel arrangement and rigged prices". It is certainly the case that the uncertainties imposed by the bidding process caused certain institutions considerable worry about their financial security. Universities placed in this position had a strong incentive to collude. Moreover, the opportunities for arranging an effective cartel were certainly present. The publication of subject-specific guide prices based upon extant average costs across the university system provided figures upon which bids could converge. The UFC documentation suggested that universities ought to make their bids "competitive with what other universities are offering" - advice which could not be followed without conferring. Indeed, some UFC officials appeared to encourage universities mainly to bid at the guide prices. The Committee of Vice-Chancellors and Principals (CVCP) encouraged the exchange of information between universities. Some professional organisations vociferously opposed the bidding process, implicitly threatening sanctions against departments which bid below the relevant guide price (Cave et al, 1992).

The second possible explanation for the failure of the UFC auction concerns the complexity of the system. In the model described earlier, we abstracted from the two part nature of the pricing system adopted by the council. The transactions costs attached to the submission of a relatively complicated two part bid (implicitly calculating complete cost functions for each department) may have exceeded the related benefits; so might the task of calculating unit costs according to the UFC's somewhat esoteric guidelines. Universities may have taken the easy (costless) option of bidding at guide prices which were known to reflect approximate mean unit costs across the system (measured in Chilver pounds). In other words, the guide prices may have been adopted by unsophisticated bidders as a "focal point" (Kreps, 1990).

Thirdly, in considering reasons for the failure of the UFC bidding scheme, we should note that no bidding scheme could deliver efficiency gains where no such gains remain to be made. So it is possible that all universities bid the same prices because they all deemed unacceptable on pedagogical grounds the notion that efficiencies could be realised by, for example, further increasing class sizes or more intensively using inexperienced and unqualified teaching staff.

There is thus a surfeit of possible explanations in terms of cooperative or non-cooperative behaviour for the uniformity of bids to the UFC. What perhaps is more surprising in the light of auction theory is the divergence of the bids received by the PCFC. In bidding for places in 1991/92, the ratio of highest to lowest bids in the council's seven programmes ranged from 3.7 to 7.7 (see Table 2). In order to examine this issue we first revise the above model so as to incorporate a key feature of the PCFC bidding scheme which was absent from the UFC system: namely the explicit allowance made in the PCFC scheme for teaching quality. Suppose that one university declares its output to be of high quality while the other does not. This raises the former institution's *ex ante* probability of winning the auction, we assume, by an arbitrarily small positive constant; meanwhile, the other university's *ex ante* probability of success at auction is reduced by the same amount. The impact on the *ex ante* probability of success may be denoted by such that $\delta > 0$ for the institution declaring its output to be of high quality, and $\delta < 0$ for the other institution. Thus (1) becomes:

$$\underset{P_i, Q_i}{\text{Max}} \ (1 - P_i + \delta) \ Q_i \ (P_i - v_i Q_i) \qquad (1')$$

and the optimisation problem can be solved as before. The optimal bid price now becomes a function of quality, $\delta$,[3] and it is easily shown that $\partial P_i / \partial \delta > 0$. Put simply, by allowing institutions to claim (and justify) exceptional quality in the teaching of certain courses, the PCFC enabled the providers of such courses to bid a higher price than would otherwise obtain; this goes some way towards explaining the divergence of bids experienced in the PCFC auctions.

**Table 2: Range of bid prices for full-time PCFC places 1991/92**

| Programme | Range of adjusted bid prices 1991/92 (£) | Ratio of highest bid to lowest |
|---|---|---|
| Engineering | 850 - 4,374 | 5.1 |
| Built environment | 250 - 1,195 | 4.8 |
| Science | 495 - 2,700 | 5.4 |
| Mathematics, etc | 265 - 1,426 | 5.4 |
| Business and management | 152 - 900 | 5.9 |
| Health, etc | 295 - 1,090 | 3.7 |
| Humanities | 160 - 928 | 5.8 |
| Arts | 306 - 2,352 | 7.7 |

Source:     London Economics, 1991, p 19

A second reason, not formally modelled here, concerns a particular feature of the PCFC scheme: use of the so-called moderating factors (London Economics, 1991, pp 19-22). In allocating places to institutions, the PCFC did not simply cumulate the bids from the bottom, until available resources were exhausted. Instead, the council bought a proportion of each institution's tendered places, that proportion varying inversely with the tender level. For example, in bidding for one PCFC programme in 1991/92, without a moderating factor 4,222 places would have been bought with a highest successful bid of £1,350; with it, 3,887 places were bought with a highest bid of £2,700. The moderating factor, if correctly foreseen by the institutions, would have confronted them with an even more complex decision procedure. Effectively they would have recognised that they faced not a perfectly elastic demand curve for their places at some unknown level, but a downward sloping demand curve at an institutional level. We conjecture that this would justify differentiated bidding by institutions with different marginal costs.

Finally, we return to possible differences in objectives. If institutions' managements seek to maximise student numbers or revenue, rather than profit or surplus, and face different break-even or quality constraints, then they will bid at different prices.

Thus, as we have seen, the more refined nature of the PCFC scheme - and in particular its emphasis on issues other than price in determining which bids would be successful - lent it an advantage over the UFC's counterpart. A further merit of the PCFC approach was the caution with which it was introduced. The PCFC scheme involved the allocation of relatively small amounts of expenditure. Only 5% of recurrent funds allocated by the PCFC were retained for allocation by the bidding process in the first year, and only 10% in the second year. For institutions funded by the UFC, on the other hand, *all* teaching resources were to be allocated in this way. This means that the incentive for institutions funded by the UFC to oppose the bidding process by all means possible was strong - the survival of some universities might have been at stake. While the PCFC scheme was designed to pressurise institutions into realising efficiencies, in the case of the polytechnics the heat was not intense enough to forge alliances.

## The new funding model

In this section we consider three models. The first focusses upon incentives for the timing of expansion in the system as a whole; the second is a simple model of yardstick competition; while the third examines competitive interactions in a richer framework.

The first concentrates on system-wide issues arising from the newer funding mechanisms, and so assumes a system consisting of a single university. In such a set up, there is obviously no competition between universities, but this simple model does allow us to focus on the growth path pursued by the higher education sector in response to the introduction of the new mechanisms. Later, we consider matters of competition in a framework analogous to that used in the last section.

Interesting features of the new HEFCE funding model can be captured in a simple three period model with just one university in the sector. The output of the university at time $t$ is crudely measured by the number of students, $q_t$, undertaking education at that time. In the initial time period, where $t=0$, the number of students, $q_0$, is given (by historical factors). We assume that the government publishes a target for university output which will be realised in the final time period; hence $q_2$ is also exogenously determined. The problem for the university is to maximize its surplus by judicious choice of $q_1$, subject to the pricing system chosen by the government and subject also to the technology underlying university costs.

Following the HEFCE practice, two different prices are paid by government for the services rendered by the university. It there is no growth in student numbers, then the institution will receive a price, $p$, for educating each student; we assume for the moment that the university automatically receives in the present year core funding which would cover all teaching activities undertaken in the previous year. Any increase from one period to the next in the university's output is, however, funded only by a fee, $f$, for each additional student where $f<p$ and where in general this is a strict inequality. In the present model we assume both $p$ and $f$ to be exogenously fixed. Costs faced by the university are assumed to be made up of two components; the first describes the relationship between costs and the current level of provision, while the second relates costs to the rate of growth of output. The former term may conveniently be thought of as recurrent costs (such as staff time), while the latter reflects the costs associated with capital expansion (for instance, the construction of new buildings). Assuming for simplicity a zero discount rate, the stream of surpluses reaching the university may be written as:

$$\pi = p(q_0+q_1) + f(q_2-q_0) - v(q_1^2+q_2^2) - w[(q_1-q_0)^2+(q_2-q_1)^2] \quad (4)$$

where $v$ and $w$ are exogenously determined parameters.

Differentiating (4) with respect to $q_1$ and setting the result to zero yields, after routine manipulation:

$$q_1 = [p + 2w(q_0+q_2)] / (2v+4w) \qquad (5)$$

Three things should be noted at this stage. First, $f$ is absent from equation (5). This is a direct consequence of the assumption of no time preference, and would not be a feature of more realistic specifications of the model. Secondly, $q_1$ unambiguously falls as $v$ rises. This means that if the institution faces relatively high recurrent expenditures, then it would choose to expand less in period 1 than otherwise. Thirdly, $q_1$ falls as $w$ rises so long as $p > v(q_0+q_2)$; interestingly this is also the condition for expansion in the first period to be faster than expansion in the second period. Moreover, it is also the condition for the institution to make a positive surplus under the restrictive assumptions that $f=p$ and $w=0$. If either $f<p$ or $w>0$ or both, then, *ceteris paribus*, surpluses fall. We may therefore conclude that, so long as the institution's stream of surpluses has a positive value, $q_1$ rises as $w$ falls, and the provision of university places expands more rapidly in the first period than in the second.

Viewed in this light, the recent rapid expansion of the higher education system in the UK is not as surprising as might first appear; it certainly does not, of itself, necessarily imply that rapid growth of the tertiary sector is sustainable beyond the short term. Indeed rapid initial progress to achieving longer term expansion targets is a concomitant of the requirement that, in this system of funding, institutions with relatively high (capital) costs should expand relatively slowly. The model is clearly highly simplified. The assumptions that $p$ and $f$ are given could conceivably be relaxed in order to establish the determinants of the authorities' price setting behaviour.

Our second model, which we do not set out formally, is a version of yardstick competition. The funding authority rations high-priced fully funded places, and attaches a price to them. However, the rate of decline of that price depends upon an institution's overall average revenue for all its places (fully funded and fees-only), compared with the national average. Thus recruitment of an additional fees-only student serves to abate the decline in the price of fully funded students.

In this system, the contribution to profit of an additional unfunded student is thus given by the difference between fees and marginal cost, augmented by the higher proceeds on fully funded students in the following and subsequent periods.

It is easily seen that if this expression is positive, profit-maximising institutions would compete in adding unfunded students. But it is equally clear that it could easily be negative, and is more likely to be (amongst other factors) the lower the fees, the lower the adjustment factor reflecting higher than average or lower than average overall unit costs and the higher the discount rate.

A combination of reduced fees in certain subjects and a very low adjustment coefficient is thus likely to reduce incentives for expansion. As far as the adjustment coefficient is concerned, the HEFCE has decided for 1993/94 to set prices paid to all institutions, whatever their average costs, within a very narrow range. The convergence of costs normally found in models of yardstick competition will therefore take place slowly, if at all.

Our third model incorporates cost differences among institutions, within a competitive framework. It also requires institutions to take fuller account of others' expected behaviour. To throw light upon this aspect, consider the following model. Two institutions face costs given by:

$$V_i(Q_i) = d - v_i Q_i^2 \qquad (6)$$

where $i=1,2$ is an index representing the institutions, d is a constant, and $Q$ denotes student places offered in the current period. We assume that each university supplied $Q_0$ student places in the last period, and that its problem concerns the current period choice of $Q_i$. As before, $p \geq f$, so that the university which imposes lower unit costs on the funding council (and upon itself) is the one which offers the higher number of student places. This university 'wins' the funding council's competition for extra resources. To keep things simple, we assume that the 'winner' receives in the current period a price of $p$ per student, while the 'loser' receives a price of $p$ for each of its first $Q_0$ students, and $f$ for each additional student. Denoting by $\lambda_i$, the probability of 'winning' the competition, the surplus of each university is given by:

$$\pi_i = pQ_0 + [f(1-\lambda_i) + p\lambda_i] (Q_i - Q_0) - d + v_i Q_i^2 \qquad (7)$$

Suppose now that the institution-specific cost parameter $v_i$ determines the *ex ante* probability of winning, such that $\lambda_i = 1 - v_i$ and $0 < v_i < 1$. Assume further that the $v_i$ are uniformly distributed over the unit interval. Substituting into equation (7) and setting $\partial \pi_i / \partial Q_i$ for $Q_i$

$$Q_i = p/2v_i - (p-f)/2 \qquad (8)$$

and it is easily seen that $\partial Q_i / \partial v_i < 0$. This indicates that an institution with relatively high costs (high $v_i$) will choose to expand relatively slowly. By rewarding those institutions which expand relatively rapidly, the funding council encourages the growth of those institutions which can provide their services at comparatively low cost.

The key difference between the scheme described above and the aborted UFC bidding scheme is that the universities now face given prices and can 'bid' only for the quantity supplied. They are, therefore, no longer able to use price as a means of bidding to win, while making quantity adjustments in order to maximise their surplus.

We have not attempted here to incorporate the complexities of the current resource allocation scheme in a single model. Instead, each of the three models which we have described attempt to capture aspects of past or proposed systems. One of the major common strands is the complexity of the arrangement. Even if an institution is clear about its objectives, mastering the implications of the regimes presents very considerable difficulties. However, even though this applies to price competition, the implications of the arrangements for quality of provision are more straightforward. We turn to these in the next section.

## Quality regulation

Any system of price competition in a market exhibiting excess demand or deficient information is vulnerable to quality degradation. In the period before the last decade, when control of institutions of higher education lay primarily with academics and the degree of competition between them was more limited, it was assumed that issues of quality could be dealt with through professional ethics and self-regulation. As government funding has diminished and pressures for growth have increased, that comfortable assumption is no longer widely held.

As a first approximation it is useful to distinguish between investment and consumption outcomes of higher education. Consumption outcomes depend to a considerable degree upon the quality of delivery of service - such matters as teaching and recreational facilities available and the enjoyment gained from the teaching and learning process. These important consumption outcomes can often adequately be judged by students themselves on the basis of currently available information, although difficulties in changing from one institution to another may make direct personal experience hard to attain.

The investment outcomes of higher education, by contrast, present more serious informational problems. It may be several years after students have completed their education that full information relevant to its long-term returns becomes available to them. These problems can be alleviated by the collection of data about rates of return, long-term employability and so forth, but it may not always be appropriate to extrapolate from past data to estimate current returns to higher education.

Thus in important respects, higher education is an 'experience' good, but one lacking some of the obvious mechanisms for dealing with information problems with experience goods, such as repeat buying. Nor, in a highly regulated quasi-market, do institutions have the opportunity to signal their high quality by the standard techniques available in other markets, such as extensive advertising (see, for example, Klein and Leffler, 1981; Shapiro, 1982). Instead, in the light of the general informational poverty surrounding higher education, past reputations are likely to be maintained - possibly unjustifiably - from period to period.

The obvious solutions to this dilemma are regulation of information disclosure, regulation of procedural aspects of quality (quality assurance) and expert inspection of the service itself (quality assessment). Over the past two years, attempts have been made to introduce all three kinds of regulation.

Mandatory information disclosure will soon be required under the Students' Charter in Higher Education. As in the case of secondary schools, institutions will be required to publish information on their performance in respect of a number of key variables, probably including examination outcomes, progression rates and employability of graduates. Although such data are publicly available, relatively few potential entrants into higher education appear to consult them.

Quality assurance has been present in the system since the establishment in 1990 by the institutions themselves of an Academic Audit Unit, since renamed the Division of Quality Audit (DQA) of the Higher Education Quality Council (an independent body set up by the institutions). The DQA visits instititions at what are expected to be intervals of three years or so and examines procedures for such matters as the design and approval of courses, the collection of information concerning student responses to them and internal and external examination procedures.  Following the visits, reports are submitted to the institution's management and normally made public.

The final branch of quality regulation, direct assessment of quality, has only recently been established (HEFCE, 1993b).  The HEFCE has established a Quality Assessment Division (QAD) charged with the task of ensuring that all education for which the funding council provides resources is at least of satisfactory quality, encouraging improvements in quality through the publication of assessment reports and annual reports, and providing information to inform funding decisions.

The QAD will carry out assessments of particular discipline or subject areas, largely undertaken by expert academics from other institutions and by a core of permanent staff.  The assessment method has three main elements: an institutional self-assessment, supported by relevant statistical indicators; examination of the self-assessment indicators by the assessors; and judgement of the quality of education, possibly involving an assessment visit.  It is notable that institutions may choose their own statistical indicators appended to the self-assessment: they should be those used by the institution itself to measure its performance.  In addition, the assessors will have access in all cases to five indicators compiled from national data sets covering entry profiles, expenditure per student, progression and completion rates, student attainment and graduate employment and further study.  It is now well known that caution is needed in intepreting such statistics (see Johnes and Taylor, 1990).

The fact that quality assessment is undertaken by the funding council, and is thus a form of external regulation rather than self-regulation, has attracted much criticism from higher education institutions.  The latter have also objected strenuously to the linking of revenues per student to quality as assessed by the QAD.  It seems that the HEFCE has for the moment moderated some of its earlier intentions in this regard.  At the same time, the institutions have expressed a desire to strengthen certain aspects of their own self-regulatory procedures, including the system of external examiners.

Because the first of the mechanisms described here, the Students' Charter, has not yet been published while the institutions for quality assurance and quality assessment are still at a very early stage of operation, it is not possible to assess the arrangements. On one hand, there is anecdotal evidence that institutions are - reluctantly - committing resources to developing new assurance procedures. On the other hand, the frequency of inspections for both quality assurance and assessment purposes seems rather low and their scale seems limited. Given the likely excess demand in the higher education sector in years to come, the procedures will be hard pressed to provide the same sort of pressures on quality as are present in a market in equilibrium and with well informed consumers. But at present this judgement is little more than a conjecture.

## Conclusions and evaluation

The changes in institutional management arrangements and in the funding system for higher education in the 1980s have had a remarkable effect. Table 3 records changes in real public funding per student over the period. Unfortunately, the series are not comparable, but the general outline is clear. Expansion of student places occurred in the polytechnic and colleges sector several years before the universities. Average costs in the latter thus remained virtually constant throughout the 1980s, while average costs in the polytechnics and colleges fell by about one-quarter. In the beginning of the 1990s, however, the funding mechanisms forced the former universities to expand their numbers considerably, with consequent declines in real public funding. To the extent that the aim of policy has been to expand provision and reduce costs, it has clearly worked.

There are, however, serious reservations about the adequacy of the mechanisms for quality control. Mandatory information disclosure seems a useful step, but given the nature of higher education as a service, by itself it is inadequate.

Moreover, there are well known problems with statistical indicators in higher education, as described in Johnes (1992b). It is clearly desirable that institutions should have proper quality assurance procedures, but inspection of procedures by themselves may not be enough. Under present arrangements, this may impose a burden upon the nascent quality assessment organisation which it is unable to carry.

**Table 3: Changes in real public funding per student**

| | 1980/81 | 1986/87 | 1988/89 | 1989/90 | 1990/91 | 1991/92 | 1992/93 | 1993/94 |
|---|---|---|---|---|---|---|---|---|
| Universities GB (1) | 100 | 100 | 100 | 97 | | | | |
| Polytechnics and colleges (GB) (1) | 100 | 87 | 81 | | | | | |
| Universities (GB) (2) | | | | 100 | 93 | 87 | 83* | |
| Polytechnics and colleges (GB) (2) | | | | 100 | 92 | 85 | 81 | |
| HEFCE (2) | | | | 100 | 92 | 85 | 80 | 78** |

Notes:  * Provisional
 ** Estimate

 (1) *Expenditure White Paper - Old Basis (1980/81 = 100)*
 (2) *Expenditure White Paper - New Basis (1989/90 = 100)*

One notable feature of the existing system is its apparent desire to achieve a broadly uniform (subject-adjusted) price. This has the effect of distorting the operation of the quasi-market in favour of cost equalisation and quality regulation. But we are by no means sure that this traditional approach is the correct one. Several authors (for example Glennerster, 1991) have raised the possibility of a more fully developed, partially publicly funded market in which students themselves exercise choice by taking their buying power to whichever institutions they preferred. Such a system would largely eliminate the role of the funding council as a proxy buyer of services, and enable institutions to deal directly with their clients. The current quasi-market has demonstrated its capacity to reduce costs, but it is quite probable that a fuller market system is required to ensure that the needs of students and employers are satisfied.

## Notes

1. It may be the case that the sellers behave as if they believe that the buyer will buy a maximum of $Q^*$ units, where $Q^*$ may itself be a function of the winning bid price. In other words, the funding councils were not committed to buy the entire quantity bid by the successful bidder. This is what Cave (1990) refers to as a "double auction", since both demand and supply can respond independently to bid price - though, of course, the funding councils do not have competitors bidding against them. The case of the double auction is analysed in Johnes (1992a) and is not therefore, considered further here. Johnes (1992a) also considers the case of a downward sloping unit cost curve.

2. There is also a trivial solution where $P_i = 1$. This assumes that neither player acknowledges the strategic nature of the other's bidding behaviour. Each actor plays as if the other party bids according only to its own costs. In the absence of this assumption a trembling hand or epsilon model would be needed to prevent bids collapsing to zero for both players.

3. Specifically $P_i = \{ 10(1+\delta) + \sqrt{[25(1+\delta) - 24(1+\delta)^2]} \}/6$

## References

Albrecht, D. and Ziderman, A. (1992) *Funding mechanisms for higher education: financing for stability, efficiency and responsiveness*, Discussion Paper 153, Washington DC: World Bank.

Baker, K. (1989) 'Extracts from the Lancaster speech', *Times Higher Education Supplement*, 13 January.

Becher, T. and Kogan, M. (1992) *Process and structure in higher education*, Second edition, London: Routledge.

Cave, M. (1990) 'Tendering trials', *Public Money and Management*, vol 10, no 2, pp 4-5.

Cave, M. and Weale, M. (1992) 'Higher education: the state of play', *Oxford Review of Economic Policy*, vol 8, no 2, pp 1-18.

Cave, M., Dodsworth, R. and Thompson, D. (1992) 'Regulatory reform in higher education in the UK: incentives for efficiency and product quality', *Oxford Review of Economic Policy*, vol 8, no 2, pp 79-102.

Committee of Vice-Chancellors and Principals (1985) *Report of the Steering Committee for Efficiency Studies in Universities (Jarratt Report)*, London: CVCP.

Glennerster, H. (1991) 'Quasi-markets for education?', *The Economic Journal*, vol 101, pp 1268-76.

HMSO (1985) *The development of higher education into the 1990s*, Cmnd 9524, London: HMSO.

Higher Education Funding Council for England (1992) *The funding of teaching by the HEFCE in 1993-94*, Circular 1/92, London: HEFCE.

Higher Education Funding Council for England, (1993a) *Higher education funding 1993/94, Council Decisions*, Circular 12/93, London: HEFCE.

Higher Education Funding Council for England, (1993b) *Assessment of quality of higher education*, Circular 3/93, London: HEFCE.

Howarth, A. (1991) 'Market forces in higher education', *Higher Education Quarterly*, vol 45, pp 5-13.

Johnes, G. (1992a) 'Bidding for students in Britain - why the UFC auction failed', *Higher Education*, vol 23, pp 173-82.

Johnes, G. (1992b) 'Performance indicators in higher education: a survey of recent work', *Oxford Review of Economic Policy*, vol 8, no 2, Summer.

Johnes, J. and Taylor, J. (1990) *Performance indicators in higher education*, Buckingham: Open University Press.

Klein, B. and Leffler, K. B. (1981) 'The role of market forces in ensuring contractual performance', *Journal of Political Economy*, vol 89, pp 615-41.

Kreps, D.M., (1990) *A course in microeconomic theory*, New York: Harvester Wheatsheaf.

London Economics (1991) *The PCFC funding system: a summary report*, London: Polytechnic and College Funding Council.

Marris, R. (1986) 'Higher education and the mixed economy: the concept of competition', *Studies in Higher Education*, vol 11 , pp 131-154.

McAfee, R.P and McMillan, J. (1987) 'Auctions and bidding', *Journal of Economic Literature*, vol 25, pp 699-738.

Milgrom, P. (1989) 'Auctions and bidding: a primer', *Journal of Economic Perspectives*, vol 3, pp 3-22.

Pratt, J. and Hillier, Y. (1991) 'Bidding for PCFC funds: confidentiality or collegiality', *Educational Management and Administration*, vol 19, pp 123-26.

Shapiro, D., (1982), 'Consumer information, product quality and seller reputation', *Bell Journal of Economics and Management Science*, vol 13, pp 20-35.

Shleifer, A. (1985) 'A theory of yardstick competition', *Rand Journal of Economics*, vol 16, pp 319-27.

The Higher (1992) 'The means of growth', *The Higher*, 31 July.

Turner, D. and Pratt, J. (1990) 'Bidding for funds in higher education', *Higher Education Review*, vol 22, no 3, pp 19-33.

Williams, G. (1988) 'The debate about funding mechanisms', *Oxford Review of Education*, vol 14, pp 59-68.

Wilson, R. (1992), 'Strategic analysis of auctions', in R.J. Aumann and S. Hart (eds) *Handbook of game theory with economic applications,* vol 1, Amsterdam: North Holland.

*part two*

# COMMUNITY CARE

*six*

# MARKETS FOR SOCIAL CARE: OPPORTUNITIES, BARRIERS AND IMPLICATIONS

## Martin Knapp, Gerald Wistow, Julien Forder and Brian Hardy

### Community care reform

Community care in the 1980s had many weaknesses. It comprised a relatively narrow range of somewhat inflexible, standardised services. It performed poorly in linking those services to needs, with responses instead dominated by patterns of provision. Users and carers had few opportunities to participate in decision making or to exercise choice. Paradoxically, institutional care became the most readily available option in a period when the policy was community care. Public spending on residential and nursing home care spiralled out of control. Moreover, the combination of (generally) politically marginalised client groups, perverse incentives and a lack of control, accountability and information when it came to the use of social security funds encouraged the shunting of people and costs between agencies and budgets.

The 1989 White Paper, *Caring for people*, and the 1990 NHS and Community Care Act set out reforms designed to overcome these weaknesses. One aim was to move away from supply-led, provider-dominated services to needs-led, purchaser-dominated services, with individual users having more influence. A second objective was to shift the balance away from institutions in favour of community care. Third, there were changes along the spectrum of agency responsibilities, with some alteration to the balance of decision making and funding between the NHS and local government. The other main strategic aim was to encourage a more mixed economy of care.

In this chapter we examine the opportunities for, and barriers to, the development of markets for social care services. It will be some years before the full ramifications of the community care reforms have become clear and we therefore describe the early steps taken by local authorities to develop markets, the reservations they express (many of which would be recognised by economists as familiar symptoms of market failure), and implications for their future roles.

In the next section we briefly describe the mixed economy of care in England prior to *Caring for people*, emphasising that a mixed economy is not a new phenomenon but that the reforms should bring major changes. We then consider the enabling role and local authorities' broad, initial reactions to the community care reforms. Inter alia, local authorities must consider changes to their organisational structures and incentives so as to encourage better planning and delivery, the separation of commissioners from providers being a key requirement. We also examine the government's expectation that market forces will play a greater part in the allocation of social care services, and the characteristics and factors which might impose limitations. Finally, we draw out some broad implications for local authorities as key players in, perhaps even managers of, social care markets.

## The mixed economy of care

A mixed economy has two principal dimensions: alternative modes of provision and sources of funding. Together, they define the broad arrangements for the delivery and purchase of services, ranging from a centrally planned welfare state, with everything provided and funded by the state, to a market 'free-for-all' with users or their relatives buying services from a variety of profit-seeking suppliers. Enthusiastically or otherwise, local authorities are currently following the broad government line in emphasising the development of a mixed economy of provision, with currently little active planning of a mixed economy of funding. Authorities are certainly introducing new funding *mechanisms* (changing some grants into contracts), and some are exploring joint commissioning with health authorities (Knapp and Wistow, 1993), but generally they are not yet actively encouraging the injection of finances from other sources of the kind identified in the otherwise very influential report from Sir Roy Griffiths (1988). Long-term care insurance is only just beginning to be mentioned by Treasury ministers as a possibility.

Of course, the mixed economy is not new (Wistow et al, 1994, Chapter 3). The public sector has never been the sole provider or funder of welfare services. Indeed, most social care is provided by the informal sector (carers), and voluntary and private agencies are major players in certain services and some parts of the country. Market share statistics for residential care for older and younger physically disabled people (Figure 1) show the private sector moving from a position of some insignificance to the provider of more than half of all places in England in less than two decades.

The ready availability of Department of Social Security income support payments was the primary reason for the explosion of private (and to a lesser extent voluntary) residential and nursing home provision. But local authorities themselves have also been long-term funders of the non-statutory sectors. For example, in the year before publication of the community care White Paper, 1.4% of local authority social services department spending went in general contributions to the voluntary sector, and another 4.6% was accounted for by 'contracts' (of one form or another) with non-statutory bodies. The proportions vary for individual client groups, and once again the national figures hide considerable inter-authority differences (see Table 1). To take a third example, the support in the community of people with mental health problems who were previously long-term hospital residents imposes service and funding burdens on a range of local government departments, independent sector agencies and family health service authorities (FHSAs) which bore virtually none of the costs of the hospital provision they are replacing (see Table 2).

Thus community care is already provided within a mixed economy. But the differences introduced by the 1990 Act - which the Audit Commission (1986) heralded as a "cultural revolution" - are matters of scale and orientation. The *scale* of the mixed economy which is being encouraged by government bears no resemblance to anything seen in Britain since 1948 (and has little in common with what preceded the National Assistance Act of that year). Second, the government is actively promoting market forces.

**Figure 1: Percentage by sector and total residential places for older and younger disabled people**

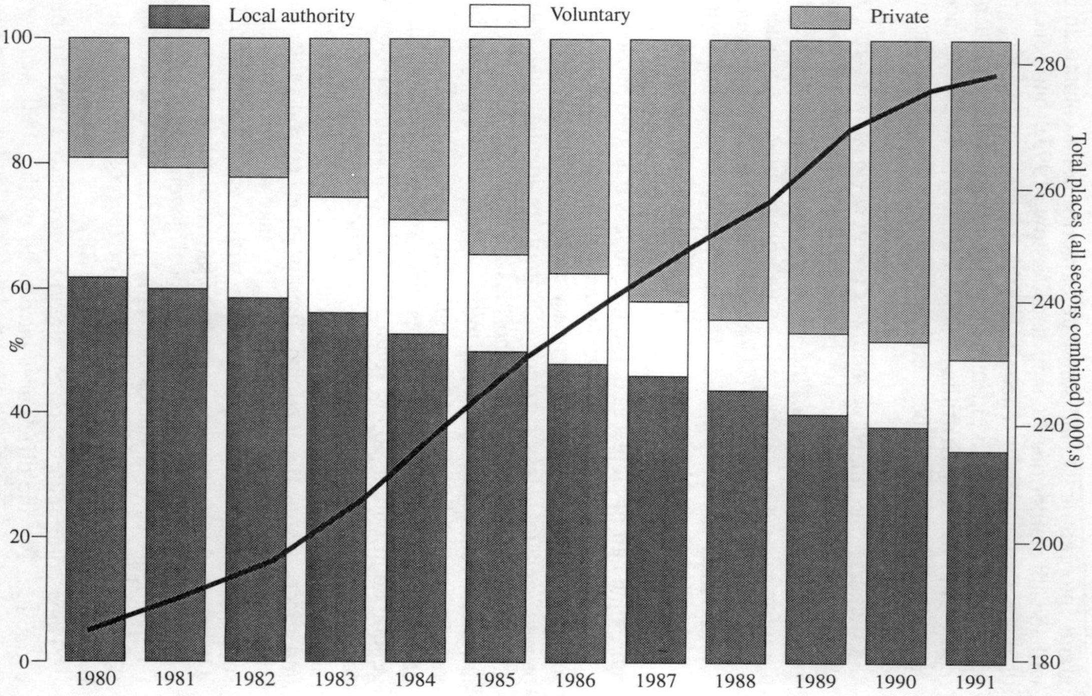

**Table 1:** **Local authority social services department funding of non-statutory organisations as percentage of total expenditure, 1988-89[1]**

| Authority type and statistics | General contributions to voluntary organisations | | | Contracts with private voluntary organisations | | |
|---|---|---|---|---|---|---|
| | A % | B % | C % | A % | B % | C % |
| *Inner London* | | | | | | |
| mean | 2.6 | 1.1 | 3.2 | 7.1 | 27.2 | 8.0 |
| std deviation | 3.4 | 1.5 | 2.5 | 8.6 | 17.0 | 3.4 |
| minimum | 0.0 | 0.0 | 0.0 | 0.0 | 0.0 | 2.5 |
| maximum | 10.2 | 4.9 | 6.9 | 32.1 | 51.7 | 14.7 |
| median | 1.4 | 0.0 | 3.4 | 4.6 | 25.6 | 7.5 |
| *Outer London* | | | | | | |
| mean | 0.6 | 1.0 | 1.1 | 5.0 | 16.9 | 7.1 |
| std deviation | 0.9 | 2.6 | 1.4 | 3.3 | 10.7 | 3.5 |
| minimum | 0.0 | 0.0 | 0.0 | 1.4 | 3.0 | 1.8 |
| maximum | 3.1 | 11.5 | 5.7 | 11.7 | 38.3 | 14.7 |
| median | 0.0 | 0.0 | 0.7 | 3.8 | 14.6 | 6.5 |
| *Metropolitan districts* | | | | | | |
| mean | 0.3 | 0.7 | 1.1 | 1.4 | 4.1 | 3.0 |
| std deviation | 0.6 | 1.8 | 1.2 | 1.4 | 4.3 | 2.2 |
| minimum | 0.0 | 0.0 | 0.0 | 0.0 | 0.0 | 0.0 |
| maximum | 2.7 | 9.4 | 4.2 | 6.8 | 15.7 | 9.2 |
| median | 0.0 | 0.0 | 0.9 | 0.9 | 2.3 | 2.3 |
| *Shire counties* | | | | | | |
| mean | 0.8 | 1.5 | 1.4 | 2.8 | 10.0 | 3.8 |
| std deviation | 1.2 | 3.0 | 1.3 | 2.2 | 9.9 | 2.8 |
| minimum | 0.0 | 0.0 | 0.0 | 0.0 | 0.0 | 0.0 |
| maximum | 5.6 | 12.5 | 4.5 | 9.4 | 35.8 | 13.1 |
| median | 0.1 | 0.0 | 0.9 | 2.0 | 6.9 | 2.8 |
| *All authorities* | | | | | | |
| mean | 0.8 | 1.1 | 1.4 | 3.2 | 11.2 | 4.6 |
| std deviation | 1.6 | 2.5 | 1.6 | 3.9 | 12.0 | 3.4 |
| minimum | 0.0 | 0.0 | 0.0 | 0.0 | 0.0 | 0.0 |
| maximum | 10.2 | 12.5 | 6.9 | 32.1 | 51.7 | 14.7 |
| median | 0.1 | 0.0 | 0.9 | 2.0 | 6.8 | 3.7 |

Notes:  A  Services for elderly people.
B  Services for people with mental health problems or learning disabilities.
C  All PSS services.
1.  Allocations expressed as percentages of relevant total client group expenditure.  Central departmental spending - for example grants to voluntary organisations from central budgets - are not included in these percentages.

Source:  Local authority RO returns to the Department of the Environment.

**Table 2:    Community care for people with mental health problems:
service use and costs[1]**

| Services used[2] | A | B | C |
|---|---|---|---|
| Accommodation facility | Various | 100.0 | 84.9 |
| Hospital in-patient | DHA | 16.4 | 3.4 |
| Hospital out-patient | DHA | 25.2 | 0.4 |
| Hospital day patient | DHA | 24.6 | 3.6 |
| Community psychiatry | DHA | 60.4 | 0.4 |
| Drugs | DHA | 15.5 | 0.2 |
| Nursing services | DHA | 30.5 | 0.5 |
| Chiropody | DHA | 41.3 | 0.1 |
| Psychology | DHA | 16.1 | 0.2 |
| Physiotherapy | DHA | 2.1 | - |
| Occupational therapy | DHA | 10.0 | 0.1 |
| GP | FHSA | 80.4 | 0.4 |
| Dentist | FHSA | 23.8 | - |
| Optician | FHSA | 17.6 | - |
| Pharmacy | DHA | 4.1 | - |
| Social services day care | LA | 22.0 | 1.8 |
| Field social work | LA | 29.0 | 1.3 |
| Voluntary organisation day care | VOL | 19.4 | 1.5 |
| Social club | VOL | 6.2 | 0.2 |
| Volunteer inputs | VOL | 2.6 | 0.1 |
| Education classes | LA | 5.6 | 0.5 |
| Police | LA | 6.2 | - |
| Users' travel | LA | 24.3 | 0.1 |
| Miscellaneous services | Various | 11.4 | 0.1 |

Notes:    A    Agency which organises or delivers the service.
           B    Percentage of people using the service in the year since
               leaving hospital.
           C    Percentage contribution to full costs of community care
               for all cohort members; '-' indicates contribution of less
               than 0.05%.
           1.    Sample size = 341 former long-stay psychiatric hospital
               residents, one year after moving to the community.
           2.    Only services used by more than 2% of the sample are
               listed.

Source:    Knapp et al (1993)

Local authorities will develop purchasing and contracting functions
within what is increasingly being described as a market rather than

simply a mixed economy of care. This can be seen in guidance from central government, where relatively loose formulations and exhortations about promoting a mixed economy have been superceded by more focused requirements to establish and manage a social care market. This, in turn, requires a knowledge and skills base which is generally lacking in the personal social services and which was not immediately compatible with many of the dominant political and professional values that had shaped their organisation and management in local government.

## Opportunities and barriers

Moving England's community care system towards the White Paper vision of a mixed economy without damaging destabilisation requires careful nurturing of provision and new commissioning routes. The 1989 White Paper readily acknowledged that it would take a long time to bring about the proposed supply and funding reforms. The government did not want or expect local authorities to rush these reforms. In contrast to the requirements placed on health authorities to separate the purchasing and providing roles immediately and introduce an internal market, albeit whilst maintaining a steady state in the first year, social services departments were urged to "introduce changes at a pace appropriate to their organisation" (Department of Health, 1990, p 1). More recently, this approach has been followed by an emphasis on securing a "smooth transition", and by treating income support payments to residential and nursing homes as "an implied commitment" in local authority purchasing strategies for 1993/94 (Department of Health, 1992b).

### Enabling

Fundamental to the new organisational framework is the government's emphasis on local authorities as 'enablers'. In our work with 24 English local authorities between 1990 and 1992, we discovered that, while all authorities accepted the legitimacy of adopting an enabling role in response to *Caring for people*, only a handful were supportive of the concept in the terms which the authors of the White Paper had intended it to be understood. As we argued elsewhere, it is possible to disaggregate the notion of the

enabling role into three distinct though potentially related meanings
(Wistow et al, 1992; 1994):

● enabling as *personal* development: maximising individuals'
  potential so that they can participate in 'everyday' lifestyles;

● enabling as *community* development: mobilising and
  supporting community resources, especially those of the
  informal and local voluntary sectors;

● enabling as *market* development: creating a social care market
  based on the purchaser/provider split, service specifications
  and contracts (and frequently the creation of new provider
  organisations).

The first of these meanings not only has long established roots in
the development of social work theory and practice, but also lies at
the heart of the values and outcomes which it seeks to promote for
individual users and carers.   By contrast, the second and third
interpretations of enabling can be viewed, at least in part, as
alternative means for achieving those personal development ends.
Empowerment through the mobilisation of community resources
has an established place in the rhetoric of social work and social
care, though its influence on practice has been less substantial.
Enabling as market development, however, has no such roots.  Yet,
it is this approach which forms the basis of the White Paper's
advocacy of enabling as a means for promoting the values of choice
and independence which the government has defined as among the
ultimate objectives of its policy for community care.  The
differences in interpretation help to explain how different
authorities approached the reforms.

*Initial local responses*

The term 'managing a mixed economy' implies diversity of supply
and a purchasing function capable of specifying requirements in
terms of identified need, together with systematic procedures
through which an appropriate volume, mix and quality of supply
can be purchased and monitored.  Only a small minority of local
authorities were seeking to develop such comprehensive and
coherent arrangements when studied in 1991.  Generally, attitudes
ranged from caution to antagonism, and actions were limited (see
Table 3).  At that time, at least a third of authorities had not yet

decided how to map need, and few were attempting to link individual assessments to authority-wide needs measures. Little work was being undertaken to develop the information base on supply.

There was considerable variation in the extent to which social services departments were developing linkages with independent providers. Only three departments had established a separate purchasing function. Elsewhere, the gradual development of service specification and contracting procedures was largely confined to relationships with the voluntary sector.

On the provider side, almost all of the sample authorities emphasised the valued contribution of public sector provision, although many were beginning to question whether the public sector should or could remain the provider of so comprehensive a range of services. It was not surprising that the most significant interest in diversifying supply surrounded the possibility of establishing not-for-profit trusts providing residential services and, less frequently, day care. These were largely resource-driven initiatives designed to generate income through shunting costs to the social security system or the Housing Corporation; they were generally the subject of single supplier negotiations; and, although they implied a substantial reduction in the social services department's role as a direct provider, they were designed to enable the local authority to retain considerable influence, if not control, over the services so divested.

Few of these early responses to the community care legislation were primarily motivated by a desire to offer greater choice or better targeting of services on needs. Most were prompted by the initial requirements of the implementation timetable: in effect, authorities did what they were required to do. In some cases, however, their responses were prompted by the wish to avoid change in advance of the general election. Our interviews with local authority officers and politicians revealed that political and policy uncertainty were constraining forces in almost half the sample. In addition, financial pressures were cited by almost all as barriers to change (see Table 4).

**Table 3:    Local authorities' attitudes and actions concerning the development of a mixed economy of care, early 1991**

| Component/element in building a mixed economy | positive attitude | action |
|---|---|---|
| Mapping needs | 18 | 6 |
| Purchaser (commissioner)/provider split | 7 | 1 |
| Budgetary devolution | 11 | 2 |
| Residential home trusts | 16 | 6 |
| Management buy-outs (etc) | 7 | 0 |
| Service specifications, contracts | 18 | 12 |
| Joint purchasing | 9 | 6 |
| Market encouragement | 6 | 6 |
| Total number of authorities | 24 | 24 |

**Table 4:    Local authorities' perceived obstacles to change, 1991**

| Perceived obstacle | Number of authorities identifying this obstacle as an important problem |
|---|---|
| Political/policy uncertainty | 10 |
| Money; financial pressures | 22 |
| Inadequate information technology/systems | 11 |
| Social services staff skills shortages | 7 |
| Social services staff resistance | 6 |
| Mistrust of the private sector | 9 |
| Unwillingness to consider some alternative providers | 11 |
| Paucity of alternative suppliers | 9 |
| Changing view of the caring role of families | 3 |
| Labour market changes | 4 |
| Underdevelopment of alternative suppliers | 13 |
| Paucity of volunteers | 8 |
| VAT payments by private and voluntary organisations | 1 |
| High land and property prices facing providers | 2 |
| Rural premium on costs | 4 |
| Voluntary agencies unwilling to develop as providers | 8 |
| Local authority anxiety about loss of control | 4 |
| Disjunction of local authority and NHS reform timetables | 7 |
| Total number of authorities sampled | 24 |

Source:    Wistow et al (1994)

## The purchaser/provider split

A needs-led approach, the Department of Health has argued, "presupposes a progressive separation of assessment from service provision" (Department of Health, 1990, p 25). It was anticipated that separating purchasing and providing would encourage authorities to make more use of the independent sector. Unlike the changes introduced in the NHS, the separation was not immediately mandatory in social care. By early 1991, few authorities had drawn up precise plans for such a split (see Table 4), for reasons described elsewhere (Wistow et al, 1992),[1] but it is unlikely that this remains the position.

There are numerous reasons for making the purchaser/provider split. It provides an opportunity to strengthen functions which otherwise tend to be subordinated to the day-to-day demands of operational management, including: needs analysis; specification of desired outcomes; accurate identification of the costs of decisions; ensuring a match between needs and resources; and evaluation and review. A second reason for separating commissioning and providing is to weaken the influence of provider vested interests in service specifications and hence to strengthen the possibility that service design will reflect user rather than provider needs. Some local authorities have also found that the split makes it easier for senior staff to liaise with their counterparts in the health service. It is also argued to bring the purchaser closer to the user, making them more sensitive and responsive to their needs and preferences. Finally, and the main argument employed by central government, the separation will help to introduce competition into the supply of services and thereby improve responsiveness to need, broaden choice, enhance cost-effectiveness and stimulate innovation. This last argument could mean hiving off existing provider functions and/or creating new provider organisations.

In our 1990-92 study of the mixed economy, we encountered little local authority resistance in principle to the first two objectives - strengthening certain planning functions and responding more flexibly to needs - though this is not to imply that a recognition of the validity of such arguments would necessarily lead authorities to support the introduction of a split between purchasing and providing functions. However, we found considerable resistance to the notion that supply-side competition should be promoted, as we have already indicated in our discussion of enabling as market development. The main objection to markets and the primary source of scepticism about the benefits of competition was summarised in the phrase 'social care is different'. This view transcended political boundaries and meant that authorities which had welcomed competitive tendering for ancillary services were doing little to develop markets in social care.

Moreover, it was not only that the language of competition and the market was seen to be incompatible with the underpinning values of social care, but there was also little conceptual understanding of such matters. Few social services managers, and even fewer frontline professionals, have any formal training in economic analysis and the operation of markets. In this respect therefore, as in a number of others, a very substantial cultural shift is required if social services departments are to take on the role specified for them in the White Paper.

## Market forces and failures

Local authorities show more enthusiasm for a mixed economy when they see clear advantages couched in terms of cost savings, quality and outcome improvements and the enhancement of user choice. In so far as decision making and action are the results of rational processes, most of the local developments which we have observed can be explained in this way. But authorities are less sanguine about the benefits of markets. Is market-style competition therefore a sensible and achievable objective for social care?

There are two basic issues. The first is whether local authorities accept the values and ethics of the market place. Will they engage in hard-nosed price negotiation? Will they draw up detailed contract specifications and conduct the close monitoring which many of these could entail? Will they accept public sector redundancies? Will they let some private sector residential and nursing homes go out of business? Evidence from the USA (see below) is congruent with our observation that local authorities reveal greater enthusiasm for market allocation mechanisms when the fiscal pressures upon them are greater, and of course when their own ideological positions are more attuned to a market culture. The encouragement of markets is also more likely when authorities perceive them as offering significant local quality, cost or choice improvements. This raises the second issue: do local authorities have the expertise to use markets to best advantage?

Under certain conditions, lovingly rehearsed by microeconomics textbook writers, markets will succeed in producing socially efficient allocations of services.[2] But there are also numerous potential sources of market failure. The most likely stumbling blocks in social care can be grouped under the three headings of structural imperfections, the specialised nature and heterogeneity of the 'product', and information imperfections.[3]

## Structural imperfections

The problem of structural imperfections occurs when market power can be wielded by one or more purchaser or provider. A possibility voiced by many people is that few social care markets will contain enough actual or potential purchasers or providers because significant structural imperfections exist.[4] The result could be that price, service orientation, quantity and quality will be determined by one or a small group of incumbent agencies, and that these agencies will select those configurations which better suit them (and their profit margins, or modes of operation, etc), but which may not particularly benefit service users, safe in the knowledge that their position is unlikely to be credibly challenged.

The development of a mixed economy which produces the cost reductions, quality improvements and broadening of choice which the government is seeking thus depends upon an adequate number and range of alternative suppliers of services, or at least the potential for this. But there already appear to be limiting but not mutually exclusive factors:

● the number of alternative suppliers in the short run;

● the ease with which new suppliers can gain entry to the market;

● the ability of current suppliers to assume a different providing role in the longer run;

● the willingness of existing and new suppliers to agree to the contractual links which will be an important part of the new mixed economy.

## Too few suppliers

Though not universal, it was a widely held view among the local authorities in our 1990-92 sample that there is no sizeable, vibrant non-statutory sector ready and willing to take on a larger service providing role.[5] Today's private and voluntary sectors are unable to provide sufficient quantities of services of the requisite standard to replace local authority provision, particularly but not exclusively in relation to domiciliary, day and respite care. It was accepted by many social services directors that they should be stimulating provision.[6] In the longer term, of course, an excess of demand over supply could allow providers to earn greater profits (or greater freedom of manoeuvre in other areas), attracting new providers to the market, particularly private sector operators. As long as the imperfections described below do not exist, an efficient market structure will arise in the long run.

## Barriers to entry

In an ideal and readily contestable market, when there are too few suppliers, or when current suppliers are not meeting the price, quantity or quality demands of purchasers, the frictionless working of the market mechanism would lead one to assert that new suppliers would be attracted in to the market by the reports of high profit margins or comfortably secure positions of current suppliers. (When there are too many suppliers some will go out of business or will be forced to diversify, as happened with residential childcare over the period since 1949.) However entry and exit in social care markets appears to be anything but frictionless. There are a number of sources of entry barriers.

## Underdeveloped suppliers

Two common perceptions among local authorities were that the infrastructures of most small voluntary organisations could not cope with the demands of the new mixed economy, and that private agencies would have neither the skills nor the inclination (because of the likelihood of very small profit margins) to diversify from residential care. Many of our local authority interviewees during our 1991 research questioned the ability of such organisations to develop a major new providing role without considerable investment in training, management and financial accounting systems. Few were as blunt as the director who remarked that "the vast bulk of the voluntary sector is very weak organisationally; it's a shambles", but a number of other officers and members echoed his view that "there are a small number of well-organised voluntary bodies which are primarily run by means of the local authority: every time I go to an AGM of a voluntary body, half my staff are sat on the management committee".[7]

The evidence on not-for-profit child welfare organisations in Massachusetts examined by Lipsky and Smith (1989) emphasises the existence of different types of organisation, some well placed to succeed in the contract market. Unfortunately, some of the voluntary organisations which English local authorities might want to encourage to take new or enhanced roles - such as those serving people from ethnic minorities - are often the least well-prepared (National Council for Voluntary Organisations, 1990; Qaiyoom, 1992).

Private suppliers might be attracted into the market by the prospect of profits, but if local authorities wish to encourage new voluntary suppliers, they may themselves have to provide seed-corn money to recruit and develop the necessary expertise. The 'catch 22' is that the local authority may be reluctant to enter into a contractual relationship with a supplier it regards as managerially unskilled to fulfil the contract, but it may also be reluctant to use its discretionary resources - if it has them - to develop such managerial competencies. The catch for the voluntary organisation is that it may be reluctant to enter into contracts without this expertise, yet be unable to attract the necessary expertise until it has negotiated contracts and the attendant income.

### Absolute cost advantages and sunk costs

New suppliers may not be able to compete on equal terms with existing suppliers for a number of reasons. It may take a long time or prove costly to enter the market. Gronbjerg (1990) describes how proposals for social welfare contracts in Chicago were usually required within three or four weeks of announcement, yet had to include complex specifications and budgets. Smaller non-statutory agencies may find the administrative overheads of contract bidding and negotiation to be excessive, may not have access to national infrastructural support or expertise, and may not easily win the confidence of purchasers. Potential new providers may not have ready access to venture capital, and yet may face considerable 'sunk costs' to be able to operate effectively.  In these circumstances, existing suppliers have clear advantages over potential suppliers. In contracting, short lead times, complex service specifications, acquired knowledge of a local authority's preferences, experience as to one's own best service responses, reputation, visibility and embeddedness within decision-making processes combine to aid the incumbent supplier.  Although one of our sample authorities had tried to organise invitations to tender for domiciliary services so as to create a level playing field, a number of authorities had already decided only to invite bids from extant suppliers. Possession - 'first mover advantage' - may be nine-tenths of the law.

A further disincentive could be fabricated by existing suppliers, who keep profit margins low and inconspicuous by under-pricing their services.  Prices and profits could be hiked up later if there are high transactions costs and low client turnover rates, as is the case in many social care settings.  For example, moving frail older people between different residential care homes endangers their welfare, and perhaps their lives, giving unscrupulous suppliers a wide margin for manoeuvre in the pursuit of larger pecuniary gains. An increase in profits achieved by leaving fees unaltered and cutting expenditure will usually eventually result in poorer quality care, but may go undetected in the short term because many users are not vocal and do not have the power of exit, and because outcomes are hard to measure and monitor.

New or current providers could face resource supply constraints. Some of the resources on which they rely in order to deliver a service which is distinctive are not readily available, or at least not at the same price.  An obvious constraint relates to *volunteers*, both the 'managers' who sit on the committees of voluntary organisations and those who actually deliver the services.  One local authority director remarked that "the idea that the whole world is out there full of enterprising business people who want to run voluntary bodies is rubbish".  There are many possible explanations (see Lynn and Davis Smith, 1991; Knapp, 1990).  In many parts of one shire county, the Women's Royal Voluntary Service "can't get volunteers to do more than two days a week [delivering meals on wheels]". An Age Concern organiser feared that private and not-for-profit domiciliary and day care services might attract volunteers away with the offer of salaried employment.

Private social care providers rely much less on volunteers, but many are dependent on the long hours and low rate of remuneration of proprietor-managers, and the uncosted inputs of family members (Judge and Knapp, 1985; Knapp, 1987). Such low cost resources typical of the small family enterprise are not available in abundance. Because of European Community directives, small private (or voluntary) domiciliary care agencies must pay VAT on carers' wages, as well as on the administration of the services provided, when the VAT registration threshold amount (currently £35,000) is reached (National Council for Voluntary Organisations, 1992). One social services director thought that this "will frustrate any major development of an alternative welfare state in domiciliary and day care". An added complication is that grants, tax exemptions and support in kind from central and local government subsidise the voluntary but not the private sector, which may well help to compensate the former for the difficulties faced in raising venture capital, but which also simply distorts competition (Hansmann, 1987, 1989; Weisbrod, 1989).

### Willingness to accept contracts

A fourth limiting factor could be that voluntary and private agencies may not be willing to take on or increase a service providing role under the contractual arrangements offered by local authorities. Voluntary organisations are particularly concerned about a number of issues.[8] The objectives set out by a local authority's service specification may not be in consonance with an organisation's mission; indeed a charity is bound by the objectives in its trust instrument, constitution or memorandum of association (Gutch, 1991; Warburton and Morris, 1991). The more specific the service specification and contract the better the chances of public sector accountability, but the greater the potential loss of autonomy and the administrative and monitoring costs, and the lower the chances of innovative, efficient service packages emerging.

Voluntary bodies may not be able to pursue their campaigning or advocacy activities with the same energy, either because their energies are diverted to managing contracts or because their contracts forbid it; they may not feel able fully to involve users in decision making (or they may be forced to do so when they would otherwise not have done); and their volunteer management committees may become marginalised as increasingly complex agreements are established. Voluntary organisations may have to compete with one another for contracts, thus straining or even destroying mutual support networks built up over many years.

Even the main benefit often identified for the voluntary and private organisations - greater security of funding - is less a consequence of contracts *per se* than the result simply of thinking seriously about the difficulties that these organisations have always faced, and may anyway have been exaggerated (Gutch, 1992; NCVO, 1991).

## Product heterogeneity and quality competition

Another potential source of market failure is where the product is heterogeneous, specialised and diverse. This heterogeneity can take two forms.

● Differentiation of product quality (*vertical differentiation*) is more feasible when users or purchasers concur on some ranking of service characteristics and on the identification of good and bad quality. This will occur when preferences are fairly similar, and improvements to the quality of the service will raise demand.

● On the other hand, if preferences for product characteristics show more variation, so that different people have preferences for different types of service (*horizontal differentiation*), changing those characteristics may or may not alter the level of demand. If providers can differentiate their products by adjusting their characteristics or quality, and if consumers have heterogeneous preferences for those characteristics or quality, then this strategy allows the provider to establish market niches. Both price and quality then become decision variables for providers. The dimensions of quality could include location, scale, denominational orientation, and the characteristics of care staff and of other users.

Market failure problems occur when there are significant sunk costs in locating in, and hence changing to, particular market niches. Then, a provider would be protected in his/her carved-out niche, and could raise prices for excess gains. Voluntary organisations have often argued to meet the demand for horizontally differentiated products (Weisbrod, 1977; James and Rose-Ackerman, 1986), and may resist attempts to change their product characteristics to those required by local authority purchasers, as this may be seen as distortion of their mission. Unlike private sector providers, increasing the rewards (payments) for these products will not necessarily induce voluntary providers to make product changes (Lipsky and Smith, 1989). Many social services are diverse and localised, and it may be costly for potential providers to enter these specialist niches. This leaves the incumbent in a strong position to influence price, quality and characteristics.

If there are numerous high quality providers of a reasonably homogeneous product, such as residential or basic home care for older people - the classic buyer's market - there will be validity in the government's claim that local authorities will be able to negotiate on favourable price terms, create pressure for efficiency and effectiveness, and lessen the chances of the abuses that come from market power. But in other circumstances, such as in the delivery of the kinds of specialist care for which parts of the voluntary sector are renowned, competition will be limited: the seller's market.

If prices are fixed, or do not enter the purchaser's decisions then competition could be exercised in terms of increases in quality. Indeed, this may generate significant cost inflation. Will this problem arise in social care markets? Nyman (1985, 1989) is explicit about the endogeneity of quality factors in US nursing home markets, and Dusansky (1989) also assumes that both price and quality variables enter the demand for nursing home places. Quality competition is particularly important with third party reimbursement - for example, social security payments or local authority contracts[9] - as evidenced by US health care markets (Joskow, 1983; Maynard, 1991; Robinson and Luft, 1985). There is evidence for English residential childcare services in the early 1980s which suggests that both price and quality were set by voluntary sector providers, but that price competition was more important for the comparatively large number of 'non-specialist' community homes than for the specialist facilities, such as homes with education and facilities for disabled children (Knapp, 1986). There was a degree of price-responsiveness among authorities: a 10% increase of voluntary home fees relative to local authority costs generated, on average, a 6% fall in the proportion of an authority's residential childcare population placed in voluntary homes (Knapp and Forder, forthcoming).

## Information imperfections and deficits

When some or all parties involved in a market transaction are ignorant of the values of key parameters such as price or quality there are information imperfections.  These will distort competition, and could be rife in markets for services with outcomes which are uncertain, technically complex, infrequently produced, of long gestation, and embodied in the characteristics of users.    This describes most social care services, which are "experience goods" because information on quality and characteristics becomes available only after use (Nelson, 1970).[10]  Providers will often start with more information about the service than purchasers, although over time the latter will acquire better information about providers, their products and consequences for users, allowing them to write contracts which embody incentives to good practice, high quality and efficiency.  Transactions costs for purchasers should gradually fall.    Indeed, if the threat of contract termination is credible, if alternative suppliers are available, and if user feedback is reliable, the transactions costs of monitoring could be low.  This might be the case, for example, for residential care services for older people.

The nature and outcome of market interactions could thus be changed fundamentally because providers have an incentive to misrepresent their private information.  The purchaser will have to bear the cost of collecting this information, or the risk of being exploited (Williamson, 1975, 1985; Walsh, 1989; Kendall, 1991). These transactions costs could be high in the future mixed economy of social care, where client purchasers have usually had little relevant 'market' experience, have few opportunities or are less well-positioned to voice their opinions (due to service complexity or individual disabilities), and cannot make a credible threat of 'exit' because they cannot easily move their custom from one provider to another without considerable personal risk (Vladeck, 1980). However, we must not fall prey to selective myopia, for there will always be transactions costs associated with local authority provision, albeit probably somewhat smaller.  When hidden or denied, there can be unfortunate consequences for standards and users.

This could mean that purchasers - whether users, care managers or local authority senior officers - will prefer certain types of provider to others.  In choosing a non-statutory contractor, there are numerous reasons why a local authority might prefer a voluntary supplier to a private organisation (Hansmann, 1980; Krashinsky, 1986).  There is, for example, a common preference for voluntary over private suppliers in circumstances where the monitoring of service quality and outcomes is difficult.  The voluntary body engenders greater trust because it is ruled by the constraint that profits cannot be distributed to owners. Competition also means losers as well as gainers; the fall-out from an insolvent non-statutory provider will damage user welfare. This is a common concern among local authority officers. Other reasons were given for having greater confidence in the voluntary sector. Many voluntary organisations have long track records and good reputations as successful innovators and expert providers, and many have long encouraged user participation in management, helping to ensure that service quality is not impaired. Voluntary sector management boards often appear to share the philosophies of local authorities.

Experience in the USA could stoke local authority anxieties about information imperfections. Contract monitoring which concentrates on inputs or, at best, intermediate outputs, presents providers with the opportunity to obey the letter of the contract but not the incentive to pursue any additional margin of excellence (Flynn and Common, 1990). A study of Wisconsin nursing homes found greater compliance with input and intermediate output regulations by private (for-profit) homes when compared with voluntary (not-for-profit) facilities, but a greater frequency of resident complaints in the former sector (Weisbrod and Schlesinger, 1986). If those complaints reflect final outcomes, albeit imperfectly, we have a good illustration of the reasons for anxiety.

Of course, if the transactions costs of working with the private sector are outweighed by its comparative efficiency, better service quality, or greater willingness to conform to local authority specifications, the private sector could be chosen as the preferred provider. The probability of low transactions costs will be greater for services whose outcomes are more tangible or less complex, are targeted at needs which display less variability across the population, and are not part of a policy to effect substantial redistributions of resources or welfare. The trade-off between efficiency and control will be determined in part by fiscal conditions and political forces.[11]

## Cost, quality, choice and equity

What, then, are the prospects for cost, quality, choice and equity as market forces play an increasingly large part in the developing mixed economy of community care? And what implications are there for local authority roles?

## Costs

The fiscal pressures faced by local authorities will undoubtedly encourage them to seek arrangements for commissioning and provision which maintain or reduce costs. Cost reduction is widely touted by pro-marketeers as a desirable consequence of the reforms, and it is not hard to find evidence of large cost differences between statutory and non-statutory services. However, there are reasons for believing that these cost reductions may not be as large or as simple to obtain as might be hoped.

An obvious difficulty will arise if the new markets for social care are characterised by the kinds of structural imperfections which put power into the hands of profit-seeking suppliers. We identified a number of potential barriers to entry to social care markets, and there is also the danger that local authorities will enter into block contracts with monopsonistic suppliers who might pare their prices to the bone in the short term in confident expectation of the opportunity to widen profit margins in two or three years' time. Authorities should thus be wary of favouring existing providers over new entrants. On the other hand, local authorities which choose to enter into contracts with a multiplicity of providers could lose the opportunity to gain from economies of scale in contract negotiation, monitoring and production. Transactions costs associated with contract drafting, monitoring and enforcement could be especially significant for complex services used by people who have few opportunities or abilities to voice their opinions of quality, or where the user outcomes are intangible or of long gestation. Establishing the necessary information systems for monitoring and to allow case managers the freedom to operate within agreed parameters is a major and expensive challenge.

Contracts between local authorities and independent providers may give the former some influence over the terms of employment offered to their staff by the latter. Thus, some cost inflation may be welcome if it raises salaries and conditions of employment for traditionally poorly remunerated categories of staff or if it promotes equal opportunities. More likely, however, is that salary levels will be forced down in the more fiercely contested social care markets, since staff costs account for a high proportion of expenditure by most agencies.

There is also the simple problem of making like-with-like comparisons, for private and voluntary services may be cheaper by virtue of supporting less disabled, more independent users. This is indeed often the case, but there is evidence that non-statutory services are more cost-effective than statutory when compared on a like-with-like basis.[12] Generally, however, the commonly voiced assumption that markets for social care will introduce the kinds of competitive forces which push costs down is over-simplistic and perhaps over-optimistic. There could certainly be cost savings in time, but local authorities will need to ensure that the benefits accrue to them and not to shareholders.

## Quality

Suitably regulated contracts can enhance product quality and efficiency, but it is far easier to write quality clauses into some contracts than others, and we have seen how most social care services do not lend themselves to unambiguous and readily monitored quality standards. A frequently voiced concern is that, because financial monitoring is considerably easier than quality assurance, because the quality and outcome penalties of skimping on expenditure may not reveal themselves for some long time, and because some groups of users may have difficulty expressing their views (in the absence of the necessary channels, or through disability unsupported by advocacy or communication prostheses), social care services within the new mixed economy may be less beneficial for users and carers than are today's public sector-dominated arrangements. Moreover, the bureaucratisation of provider agencies in response to the burdens of contracting may divert resources away from service delivery to administration.

The new arrangements for community care make it much more likely that users will have a 'voice' in service selection and monitoring, enabling them to register their preferences and perspectives on outcomes in lieu of complex or expensive monitoring procedures. Nevertheless, a careful balance will need to be struck between the cost and inconvenience burdens (for all parties) of quality and outcome monitoring on the one hand, and the risk costs of occasional or superficial monitoring of inputs or basic service levels on the other. A second balance to be struck is between 'tight' and 'loose' specifications, the former possibly creating financial incentives for opportunistic suppliers to exploit loopholes, the latter perhaps leaving too much to chance or taking too much on trust. This may explain why some local authorities prefer to contract with the voluntary rather than the private sector, having more confidence in the quality and orientation of service which they can offer. Other things being equal, lower transactions costs will follow from greater trust, in turn often closely associated with tradition and longevity.

## Choice

The community care White Paper was explicit in its confident assumption that "stimulating the development of non-statutory service providers" will produce "a wider range of choice of services" (Department of Health, 1989), though the point must be made, of course, that the removal of the social security entitlement for many potential residents of residential and nursing homes has narrowed their effective freedom of choice. Rather a lot now depends on whether authorities elect for block contracts with (virtual) monopoly providers. At the moment, a number of issues await resolution. What effective choices will be exercised by users or carers prior to referral or service placement, and how will they be constrained or stimulated by case managers? What range of choice will be offered to purchasers? At the area level, how far will choice of provision be circumscribed by service availability? Will the re-routing of social security funding for residential and nursing homes remove the choice which previously accompanied entitlement, or will it allow local authorities to promote a wider and more appropriate range of service options (especially non-residential services)? Will the Department of Health's directive on choice - which covers *selective* choice over providers but not over service mode - exert an influence?

The inability or unwillingness of private and/or voluntary providers to enter a social care market, or to meet the standards laid down by local authorities, could limit the development of a broad choice range, and the demise of smaller organisations in the face of high transactions costs could remove a distinctive dimension. However, the administrative attractions to the local authority of the large, all encompassing block contract are equally threatening to the choice criterion. It should be remembered that governments often took responsibility for social care in the first place because they were not happy to leave the service to market forces, partly because some users of services were judged not to be able to bring sufficient consumer experience, competence or power to market negotiations. Because users may find it difficult to exercise informed choices, it falls to local authorities to regulate service quantity, characteristics and quality. But the process of regulation may encourage faithful adherence to those practices which are readily subjected to monitoring to the neglect of other objectives or activities. It may also promote the standardisation of product, *reducing* variety as private and voluntary providers are nudged closer to public sector requirements and characteristics (the "coercive isomorphism" problem identified by Di Maggio and Powell, 1983). Innovation may be discouraged by regulators and be financially inadvisable for non-statutory providers. Public authorities will need to work closely and supportively with independent providers to establish contractual links in such a way as not to threaten their diverse and important contributions. They should beware market fragmentation, because of the excessive market power it could give some providers, whilst retaining an ability to respond to the diverse needs of individuals and populations.

## Equity

Very few of our local authority interviewees raised equity or fairness as an explicit concern, yet they were all committed to better targeting of services and financial resources on the needs of the population. In one form or another, equity must, and generally already does, underpin local authority allocations of funds and services. But, as Le Grand and others have pointed out, "a common criticism of conventional markets (and a common justification for their replacement by bureaucracies) is that they foster and maintain inequalities and therefore social injustice" (Le Grand, 1991, p 1266).

A particular difficulty could arise, for example, if non-statutory providers are able to 'cream off' the less dependent and less costly clients, leaving the more costly residual for public sector providers. Market segmentation of this kind may be accompanied by market stratification by income or opportunity: residualisation of the poor may be the price of freedom of choice for the rich (Knapp, 1989; Hoyes et al, 1991). On the other hand, the new mixed economy may offer previously untouched opportunities to disadvantaged groups of clients and their carers, and, by searching out need and making explicit the criteria of allocation of resources, achieve a better match between the two.

## Conclusion

When considering the working of market forces, there is therefore a sense in which social care is different, or at least difficult. The nature of the product and the outcomes it is intended to achieve are themselves sources of distinctiveness and complication when compared with virtually every other local government service. Only in health care are outcomes almost as difficult to measure, but, in contrast to the health reforms which leave purchasing authorities largely operating in markets *internal* to the NHS, local authority social services departments are much more likely to be purchasing in *external* markets, with the voluntary and private sectors as major providers. NHS trusts working in the internal market have very different aims and constraints from those of private, profit-seeking providers in the social care market. The purchaser/provider divide in the NHS separated two groups which were previously part of the same organisation, and therefore presumably sharing at least some of the same values, perspectives and directions. Independent social care providers, by contrast, might approach the new market from utterly different directions and with very different prejudices from commissioners, bringing either the promise of innovation or the threat of conflict.

It is still possible to find some *laissez-faire* reformers "wishing to administer a brisk restorative to the welfare state with a purging dose of market principles" (Taylor-Gooby and Lakeman, 1988, p 23) who set the weaknesses of the old community care system against the unattainable perfection of a perfectly functioning market complete with equality of opportunity or access. And there is no shortage of 'sentimental socialists' keen to ignore many of the inherent problems of a universalist system dominated by historical patterns of public sector provision when opposing the onward march of the market. Both groups will be trying to keep local authorities and markets as far as apart as possible, though for utterly different reasons.

The vast majority of the local authority officers and politicians with whom we are in contact in our various research and other activities hold views which are located some distance from these two ends of the spectrum of opinion. They express concerns about potential market failures, which, combined with financial constraints and political caution (if not opposition), help to explain the widespread support for very slow movement away from the steady state. Markets will emerge by stealth. Consequently, it is very difficult to know what form social care markets will take, or to predict with any confidence whether they will promote cost savings, quality, choice and equity.

## Acknowledgements

Much of the work reported in this chapter has been undertaken with the support of two grants from the Department of Health ('Managing the mixed economy of care', 1990-92, research being undertaken with Caroline Allen, and 'The mixed economy of care programme', 1992-96, research undertaken with Jeremy Kendall and Rob Manning), and in part on research funded by the Economic and Social Research Council ('Voluntary sector activities and public sector support in care in the community', research undertaken with Corinne Thomason).

## Notes

1. Simple logit analyses of attitudes and actions showed that, generally, it was the higher spending authorities (per capita) and those which currently allocated smaller proportions of total personal social services spending to contracts with non-statutory providers which planned to separate commissioners and providers (see Wistow et al, 1994, appendix to Chapter 5).

2. By socially efficient we mean provision which minimises the cost of achieving a given quality of service (or maximises the user benefits or outcomes from a given cost), and which, via allocative efficiency, increases the range of choice. Efficiency will not necessarily produce an equitable allocation of resources, that is one which is fair by the criteria of social justice. In social care debates, social justice is usually defined by reference to judgements about individual needs.

3. Our discussion of market failures, like the comments of our local authority interviewees and others, assume that the public sector will remain the major purchaser of (formal) social care services for the foreseeable future. Were the public sector to shift substantially more of the burden of funding to service users or their relatives, we would need to address two further

and major sources of market failure: externalities and the importance of equity objectives in social care. These issues were discussed at the level of principle in Knapp (1984, Chapter 6), and we consider some of the equity implications of the present reforms in the final section of this chapter. It is important to note, however, that user charges for public social care services remain a neglected research topic, yet are increasingly important sources of revenue to authorities, and that it will surely not be long before privately funded long-term care insurance becomes a government policy objective.

4. The exception, of course, is the market for residential and nursing home care, which is widely believed to contain considerable excess supply in most areas of the country.

5. We must remember that the main providers of community care are not the plethora of voluntary organisations providing residential, domiciliary or day care, nor the private sector, mainly providing residential and nursing home beds (plus an unknown amount of domiciliary support), nor even the statutory services, but informal carers. In this chapter, in so far as we address them as separate agents, we are treating informal carers as 'clients' of local authority action - changes in whose quality of life will be among the salient outcomes of community care reform, and who are therefore potential recipients of support services - rather than as providers. We are therefore assuming an implicit household production function (the "social production of welfare" in the terms and model developed by Netten and Davies, 1990) which embodies the informal care relationship, and markets for 'ex-household' care services. In common with central and local government, we have therefore assumed, in the discussion of social care markets, that the boundary between informal and formal care is exogenously determined, which is equivalent to assuming a given level of need. It is known, however, that payments by local authorities to relatives (for example, via case managers in the original case management experiments in Kent; see Davies and Challis, 1986) can alter the supply of informal care, and thus alter the need and demand for formal care. For the moment, we are not pursuing what would necessarily be a much broader perspective on the economics of social care and its markets.

6. This was not, however, the primary reason for some local authorities transferring residential homes from the public to the not-for-profit sector, or selling them to private agencies. Hardy et al (1993) describe these transfers and examine the motivating forces.

7. This embeddedness of the public and voluntary sectors (Seibel, 1990) places some limitations on the market behaviour of both. Whether or not it is for the good of either party will depend on individual circumstances, and it remains a question in need of empirical research.

8. These can only be considered briefly here. For more detail, see Gutch (1992); Knapp et al (1990); Kramer (1981, 1990).

9. Of course, the change from, on the one hand, a system of social security payments tied to individual residents and paid direct to homes to, on the other, contracts between local authorities and homes is a move from demand-side to supply-side subsidies, and one that lessens, but does not remove altogether, the distorting influences of third party payments.

10. These descriptions relate to the final outcomes of social care - the changes in user welfare. Intermediate outcomes, which are the services themselves (subject to some quality constraint), are more immediate and more readily observed (Davies and Knapp, 1981; Knapp, 1984). However, most social care services are demanded for their expected impacts on the lives of users (the final outcomes). If contracts and regulations are couched in terms of inputs or intermediate outcomes, there will be incentives for suppliers to 'cream' the easiest or most lucrative clients.

11. Public works services, such as refuse collection and bus services, have tangible and easily specified outputs, and have no important distributional goals attached to them, and so are likely to be contracted out, and the contracts are likely to be let to the private sector. By contrast, control difficulties may leave governments more reluctant to contract out social care services, because of their obscure and complex outputs, and because redistribution is an important reason for intervention in the first place. Voluntary contractors are likely to be preferred to private for the same reasons. See Ferris and Graddy (1988, 1989) for an interesting test of these hypotheses with US data.

12. Evidence from almost every local authority area points to the lower costs of private and voluntary providers when compared with public sector provision. There is much less evidence on comparative costs which are standardised for user characteristics, quality of provision or outcomes. What there is suggests a cost-effectiveness advantage for the independent sectors, though one which is sensitive to a number of organisational and market factors (Beecham et al, 1991; Judge and Knapp, 1985; Knapp, 1986; Knapp and Missiakoulis, 1982).

## References

Audit Commission (1986) *Making a reality of community care*, London: HMSO.

Beecham, J.K., Knapp, M.R.J. and Fenyo, A. (1991) 'Costs, needs and outcomes', *Schizophrenia Bulletin*, vol 17, no 3, pp 427-39.

Davies, B.P. and Challis, D.J. (1986) *Matching resources to needs in community care*, Aldershot: Gower.

Davies, B.P. and Knapp, M.R.J. (1981) *Old people's homes and the production of welfare*, London: Routledge and Kegan Paul.

Department of Health (1989) *Caring for people: community care in the next decade and beyond*, London: HMSO.

Department of Health (1990) *Communtity care in the next decade and beyond: policy guidance*, London: HMSO.

Department of Health (1992a) *Priorities and planning ... 1993/94*, EL(92)47, London: NHS Management Executive.

Department of Health (1992b) *Implementing community care*, EL(92)13/C1(92)10, London: Department of Health.

Di Maggio, P. and Powell, W.W. (1983) 'The iron cage revisited: institutional isomorphism and collective rationality in organizational fields', *American Sociological Review*, vol 48, pp 147-60.

Dusansky, R. (1989) 'On the economics of institutional care of the elderly in the US', *Review of Economic Studies*, vol 56, pp 141-50.

Ferris, J.M. and Graddy, E. (1988) 'Production choices for local government services', *Journal of Urban Affairs*, vol 10, pp 273-89.

Ferris, J.M. and Graddy, E. (1989) 'Production costs, transactions costs, and local government contractor choice', mimeograph.

Flynn, N. and Common, R. (1990) *Contracts for community care*, Caring for People Implementation Document, London: Department of Health.

Griffiths, R. (1988) *Community care: agenda for action*, London: HMSO.

Gronbjerg, K.A. (1990) *Managing nonprofit funding relations: case studies of six human service organisations*, Proceedings of the Independent Sector Spring Forum, Washington DC: Independent Sector.

Gutch, R. (1991) *Contracting in or out? The legal context*, London: NCVO.

Gutch, R. (1992) *Contracting lessons from the US*, London: NCVO.

Hansmann, H. (1980) 'The role of nonprofit enterprise', *Yale Law Journal*, vol 89, pp 835-901.

Hansmann, H. (1987) 'The effect of tax exemption and other factors on the market share of nonprofit versus for-profit firms', *National Tax Journal*, vol 40, pp 71-82.

Hansmann, H. (1989) 'The two nonprofit sectors: fee for service versus donative organisations', in V.A. Hodgkinson, R.W. Lyman and Associates, *The future of the nonprofit sector*, San Francisco: Jossey-Bass.

Hardy, B., Wistow, G. and Knapp, M.R.J. (1993) *Residential home transfers*, Nuffield Institute, University of Leeds, and Personal Social Services Research Unit, University of Kent at Canterbury.

House of Commons Social Services Committee (1985) *Community care*, HCP-13-1, Session 1984-85, London: HMSO.

Hoyes, L., Means, R. and Le Grand, J. (1991) *Made to measure? Performance indicators, performance measurement and the reform of community care*, Bristol: School for Advanced Urban Studies, University of Bristol.

James, E. and Rose-Ackerman, S. (1986) *The nonprofit enterprise in market economies*, Fundamentals of Pure and Applied Economics, vol 9, London: Harwood Academic Publishers.

Joskow, P. (1983) 'Reimbursement policy, cost containment and non-price competition', *Journal of Health Economics*, vol 2, pp 167-74.

Judge, K. and Knapp, M. (1985) 'Efficiency in the production of welfare: the public and private sectors compared', in R. Klein and M. O'Higgins (eds), *The future of welfare*, Oxford: Blackwell.

Kendall, J. (1991) 'Is this a transactions costs overview of the role of the voluntary sector in the mixed economy of health and social care', *PSSRU Bulletin*, vol 8, pp 22-23.

Knapp, M.R.J. (1984) *The economics of social care*, London: Macmillan.

Knapp, M.R.J. (1986) 'The relative cost-effectiveness of public, voluntary and private providers of residential child care', in A.J. Culyer and B. Jönsson (eds) *Public and private health services*, Oxford: Blackwell.

Knapp, M.R.J. (1987) 'Private children's homes: an analysis of fee variations and a comparison with public sector costs', *Policy and Politics*, vol 15, no 4, pp 221-34.

Knapp, M.R.J. (1989) 'Private and voluntary welfare', in M. McCarthy (ed) *The new politics of welfare*, London: Macmillan.

Knapp, M.R.J. (1990) *Time is money: the cost of volunteering in Britain today*, Aves Lecture, Berkhamsted: Volunteer Centre UK.

Knapp, M.R.J. and Forder, J. (forthcoming) *Social care markets: forgotten lessons from the recent past*, Discussion Paper 798, Personal Social Services Research Unit, University of Kent at Canterbury.

Knapp, M.R.J., Beecham, J.K., Hallam, A. and Fenyo, A. (1993) 'The costs of community care for former long-stay psychiatric hospital patients', *Health and Social Care in the Community*, vol 1, pp 193-201.

Knapp, M.R.J. and Missiakoulis, S. (1982) 'Inter-sectoral cost comparisons: day care for the elderly', *Journal of Social Policy*, vol 11, no 3, pp 335-54.

Knapp, M.R.J., Robertson, E. and Thomason, C. (1990) 'Public money, voluntary action: whose welfare?', in H. Anheier and W. Seibel (eds) *The third sector: comparative studies of nonprofit organizations*, Berlin: de Gruyter.

Knapp, M.R.J. and Wistow, G. (1993) 'Joint commissioning for community care', in Department of Health, *Implementing community care: a slice through time*, London: Department of Health/Social Services Inspectorate.

Kramer, R.M. (1981) *Voluntary agencies in the welfare state*, Berkeley: University of California Press.

Kramer, R.M. (1988) 'Trends in contracting for the personal social services', unpublished paper, School of Social Welfare, University of California, Berkeley.

Kramer, R.M. (1990) 'Change and continuity in British voluntary organisations, 1976 to 1988', *Voluntas*, vol 1, pp 33-60.

Krashinsky, M. (1986) 'Transactions costs and a theory of the nonprofit organization', in S. Rose-Ackerman (ed) *The economics of nonprofit organizations*, Oxford: Oxford University Press.

Le Grand, J. (1991) 'Quasi-markets and social policy', *The Economic Journal*, vol 101, pp 1256-67.

Lipsky, M. and Smith, S.R. (1989) 'Nonprofit organisations, government and the welfare state', *Political Science Quarterly*, vol 104, pp 626-48.

Lynn, P. and Davis Smith, J. (1991) *The 1991 national survey of voluntary activity in the UK*, Berkhamsted: Volunteer Centre UK.

Maynard, A. (1991) 'Developing the health care market', *Economic Journal*, vol 101, pp 1277-86.

NCVO (1990) *Contracts for care: issues for black and ethnic minority voluntary groups*, London: NCVO.

NCVO (1991) 'Contract used to reverse funding cuts', *Contracting In or Out?*, Autumn, no 6.

NCVO (1992) 'The Vatman cometh', *Contracting In or Out?*, Spring, no 8.

Nelson, P. (1970) 'Information and consumer behaviour', *Journal of Political Economy,* vol 78, pp 311-29.

Netten, A. and Davies, B.P. (1990) 'The social production of welfare and consumption of social services', *Journal of Public Policy*, vol 10, no 3, pp 331-47.

Nyman, J.A. (1985) 'Prospective and cost-plus Medicaid reimbursement, excess Medicaid demand and the quality of nursing home care', *Journal of Health Economics*, vol 4, pp 237-59.

Nyman, J.A. (1989) 'The private demand for nursing home care', *Journal of Health Economics*, vol 8, pp 209-31.

Qaiyoom, R. (1992) 'Contracting: a black perspective', *Contracting In or Out?*, Spring, no 5.

Rhodes, R.A.W. (1992) 'Local government finance', in D. Marsh and R.A.W. Rhodes (eds) *Implementing Thatcherite policies*, Buckingham: Open University Press.

Robinson, J.C. and Luft, H.S. (1985) 'The impact of hospital market structure on patient volume, average length of stay and the cost of care', *Journal of Health Economics*, vol 4, pp 333-56.

Seibel, W. (1990) 'Government/third sector relationship in a comparative perspective: the cases of France and West Germany', *Voluntas*, vol 1, no 1, pp 42-61.

Taylor-Gooby, P. and Lakeman, S. (1988) 'Back to the future: statutory sick pay, citizenship and social class', *Journal of Social Policy*, vol 17, no 1, pp 23-39.

Vladeck, B. (1980) *Unloving care: the nursing home tragedy*, New York: Basic Books.

Walsh, K. (1989) 'Competition and service in local government', in J. Stewart and G. Stoker (eds) *The future of local government*, London: Macmillan.

Warburton, J. and Morris, D. (1991) 'Charities and the contract culture', *The Conveyancer and Property Lawyer*, pp 419-31.

Weisbrod, B.A. (1977) *The voluntary nonprofit sector*, Lexington: D.C. Heath.

Weisbrod, B.A. (1989) 'The complexities of income generation for nonprofits', in V. Hodgkinson, R. Lyman and Associates, *The future of the nonprofit sector*, San Francisco: Jossey-Bass.

Weisbrod, B.A. and Schlesinger, M. (1986) 'Public, private non-profit ownership and the response to asymmetric information', in S. Rose-Ackerman (ed) *The economics of nonprofit institutions*, Oxford: Oxford University Press.

Williamson, O.E. (1975) *Markets and hierarchies: analysis and antitrust organizations*, New York: Free Press.

Williamson, O.E. (1985) *The economic institutions of capitalism*, New York: Free Press.

Wistow, G., Knapp, M.R.J., Hardy, B. and Allen, C. (1992) 'From providing to enabling: local authorities and the mixed economy of social care', *Public Administration*, vol 70, no 1, pp 25-45.

Wistow, G., Knapp, M.R.J., Hardy, B. and Allen, C. (1994) *Social care in a mixed economy*, Buckingham: Open University Press.

*seven*

# QUASI-MARKETS AND COMMUNITY CARE: TOWARDS USER EMPOWERMENT?

**Robin Means, Lesley Hoyes, Rachel Lart and Marilyn Taylor**

## Introduction

This chapter explores the present and likely future impact upon service users of the community care changes which are being introduced as a result of the NHS and Community Care Act 1990. The White Paper on community care claimed that "promoting choice and independence underlies all the government's proposals" (Department of Health, 1989, p 4). Subsequent policy guidance stressed that "the rationale for this reorganisation is the empowerment of users and carers" (Department of Health/Social Services Inspectorate, 1991, p 7). The focus of this chapter is upon the likelihood of such empowerment occurring and how this does or does not relate to the fact that these 'reforms' are driven by the desire to establish what Le Grand (1990) has called a quasi-market in social care.

## Empowerment and the disability movement

One reason why empowerment is now on the community care agenda is because of the growing influence of user groups and the disability movement (Morris, 1991; Oliver, 1990). Indeed, it can be argued that many professionals are now concerned about issues of empowerment primarily because they are under pressure to do so by users and their organisations.

Oliver (1990) has chartered the growth of traditional voluntary organisations such as the Royal National Institute for the Blind who claimed to speak on behalf of disabled people. However, such organisations failed to campaign effectively on behalf of disabled people in terms of resources and appropriate services because of the post-war model of partnership with the state. Disabled people began to appreciate that they would have to take the lead in improving their quality of life through the establishment of politically aware self-help groups. These new groups, such as the British Council of Organisations of Disabled People, criticised the more traditional groups on the grounds that "they operate within a framework which assumes that disabled people cannot take control of their own lives and, therefore, require the 'charitable' assistance of well-meaning professionals, voluntary workers or politicians" (p 114). Overall, the disability movement rejects a medical model of disability which places responsibility for disablement within the individual 'patient' and then gives control over their lives to professionals who are given the power to decide what they are and what they are not capable of. The movement supports a social model of disability in which the emphasis is upon how people with impairments are disabled by society through the prejudices of its non-disabled members and the complete failure to develop the kind of public policies which would ensure the right of disabled people to participate fully in society. Empowerment for many in the disability movement requires a process of 'fighting back' (Morris, 1991, Chapter 7) against the institutions and individuals who oppress them.

Many disabled people are as critical as central government of previous community care provision by local authorities and health care agencies. In her study of disabled recipients of cash grants from the Independent Living Fund, Kestenbaum (1992) found that very disabled individuals were able to put together their own care packages and that:

> The choice and control they valued so highly could not in their experience be provided by statutory authorities. It is not simply a matter of resource levels, though these are very significant. As important are the qualities that any large-scale service-providing organisation would find hard to deliver:

choice of care assistant, flexibility, consistency, control of times and tasks etc. (p 77)

But the rhetoric of the community care reforms is all about delivering these very qualities. This suggests the need to take a more detailed look at these 'reforms' and their background.

## Quasi-markets and the 'reform' of community care

Community care services for older people and those with learning difficulties, physical disabilities and mental health problems were largely neglected in the welfare legislation of the 1940s (Means and Smith, 1985). Care for these groups tended to be institution based, whether provided through the NHS or local government and, partly in consequence, they were often starved of funds relative to resources available for the acute sick or for childrens' services. Despite incremental progress over the next forty years, including some important legislative changes, the fundamental difficulties remained. These included administrative complexity and often hostility between local authorities and the NHS; the failure to shift resources from institutional to domiciliary care; the failure to target and plan resources effectively at a client or authority level; and the failure to empower the consumer.

In the mid 1980s, community care services began to shake off their 'Cinderella' image and to achieve a much higher political profile. Among the factors precipitating this were concerns about the growth in the numbers of 'old old', the explosion in social security payments to support residents in independent residential and nursing home care, and the difficulties associated with the government's 'Care in the community' initiative to close down large mental handicap and psychiatric hospitals (Means and Harrison, 1988). A succession of official and semi-official reports, most significantly those of the Social Services Select Committee in 1985 and the Audit Commission in 1986, criticised existing provision and called for change, culminating in Sir Roy Griffith's report in March 1988 (Griffiths, 1988) and the White Paper, based on Griffith's recommendations, published eighteen months later (Department of Health, 1989).

The White Paper and subsequent act agreed with Griffiths that local authority social services departments should be given the lead role in community care planning. It also confirmed that their role at the client level would increasingly be confined to the assessment of need, the designing of care arrangements to meet that need by appointed 'care managers' and the provision of funds to finance those arrangements. They were to be discouraged from directly providing all care services themselves; instead, services were to be provided increasingly by a 'mixed economy' based largely on the private and voluntary sectors, as discussed in Chapter 6. Local authorities were to become 'enablers' through the allocation of funds; they would have a declining role in direct service provision. Social services were to set out their strategy for achieving all this through a new system of community care plans. Finally, a new funding structure for those seeking public support for residential and nursing home care was proposed with local authorities taking over responsibility for financial support of people in private and voluntary homes, over and above their entitlement to general social security benefits. This was to be funded through a transfer of money from the social security budget to local authorities. However, local authorities would have discretion to use some of this money to fund domiciliary services which might reduce the need for so many people to enter residential care.

## Responding to the reforms: community care in four contrasting local authorities

So what progress are local authorities making in achieving the empowerment of service users, and how does this relate to the fact that 'reforms' are driven by quasi-market assumptions? There are difficulties in attempting to tackle this question: local authorities as lead agents begin from different starting points in terms of service provision and attitudes to the 'reforms'; also, much less is prescribed by central government over what they must do compared with directions to health authorities over the NHS reforms. Local authorities are largely free to decide what are the most appropriate structures for community care planning, what is meant by care management and how best to separate purchaser functions from provider functions. Hence, the social services tradition of organisational variation (Challis, 1990) is being maintained and this makes it very difficult to make overall judgements about the 'reform' package itself, rather than local interpretations of it.

This can best be illustrated by providing a short profile of the overall approach to community care implementation of four local authorities. The situation described relates to Spring 1992 and hence readers need to appreciate that all four of our authorities are now much further down the path of implementing the community care changes than implied by these snapshots.

## County 'A'

County 'A' covers a population of over one million people. It is coterminous with the FHSA, but contains four DHAs and ten separate district councils. The county council is controlled by the Conservatives. The social services department is decentralised to 32 districts, with service planning and budget management responsibilities based on these districts.

The philosophy informing its approach to community care reform was that the centre should set strategic aims and values, but that detailed implementation of these should be carried out at district level in the light of local needs and circumstances. The main emphasis for involvement of users of services and carers was on the individual, at the point of assessment, and through the process of care management.

The 1992 community care plan (CCP) was largely a statement of policy aims and strategic objectives with a much more detailed 'reference file' as background. Consultation on the CCP involved a four month period for comment, during which 10,000 copies were distributed, and the reference file was made available at district offices and other public sites such as libraries.

The commitment to local planning had led to a focus on the need to create systems for the aggregation of individual need, to feed into districts' planning. The intention was that in future years the CCP should be much more the joint product of health and social services. District managers had been required to establish a 'district forum' as a means of ensuring that users and carers had access to the planning process. This central requirement was being interpreted in different ways and with varying degrees of success in the districts. The concept of 'partnership' with the independent sector, in terms of planning service developments, was stressed.

The basic stance of the authority was to accept the idea of the mixed economy and seek to use pluralist provision to create choice for users of services. The size of the private residential sector meant that to a large extent a market already existed and the sector was a significant player within the county, although it did not yet extend to other forms of provision such as day and domiciliary care.

The department was introducing the purchaser/provider separation at district level. This was closely tied to the introduction of care management; the purchasers were the care management teams who would eventually hold the budgets. Care management had been piloted in three parts of the county. Assessment and care management were at the core of how the authority planned to deliver services. The care management teams were the purchasers, with responsibility for a locality or a client group. Care management was a service all users would receive, with different degrees of professional involvement according to the complexity of their needs and care packages.

The contracting process was seen as the key to needs-led services. Although the long-term aim was for individual contracts with all providers, in-house providers would be protected in the transitional period by a gradual move from block contracts to price per case. Independent sector providers would be 'accredited', and contracted with by price per case, for individual services. Strong quality standards and controls would be involved in the accreditation process.

## The London borough

The London borough covers a population of approximately 150,000 people. It is a Labour controlled unitary authority, which had made the implementation of community care a corporate objective. Relationships with the corresponding DHA, which had been good, were being disrupted by radical changes in the configuration of purchasing authorities being made by the regional health authority.

The main focus for involvement of service users and carers was on the collective level of engagement of groups and organisations in the planning process. Joint planning had been strengthened by the creation of a structure of 'networks' of voluntary, community and self-help groups to support the joint planning teams. These networks are underpinned by joint finance money which provides both a small budget and a networks officer who is based at the Association of Community Organisations. The department was now looking at how to make consultation a continuing process, not one based around the publication of the CCP.

Issues like the implementation of care management and the separation of purchasing and providing functions had been approached gradually, with a concern to take all parties within the department along. Care management pilots for most of the community care client groups had been planned, and these would run from April 1992. Many further planning decisions were waiting for the outcome of these pilots.

There was a degree of caution about the idea of the mixed economy and as yet no strategy for development. The authority was not intending to move out of direct provision of existing services and there was a strong feeling amongst the voluntary sector and user groups that the provision of basic services for the main community care groups was a statutory responsibility. As yet there had been no major move to convert existing grants into service agreements. There was very little private residential provision within the borough, although the department did purchase private services on an ad hoc basis.

The quality assurance and planning division was moving towards holding a macro purchasing role. This division contained the HIV Unit, which had already been acting as a macro purchaser, and was widening its role to become the general commissioning unit. Care management would be purchased at this level. The community care division would contain provider services.

The community social services division would have the lead in care management and assessment, and the micro purchase of services for the individual. Care management would be applied to a limited number of people, principally those who were on the verge of entering residential or nursing home care. In a much broader sense, the department saw care management as a way of working which was more client centred.

However, it needs to be stressed that although this structure was already in place, internal and external contracting through service agreements had not yet really started at the time of the interviews, and in-house providers were just beginning to draw up business plans.

## County 'B'

County 'B' is a large, mainly rural county of just under 600,000 people. The county council is virtually coterminous with the DHA and completely coterminous with the FHSA. There are five district councils. Since 1985, a politically balanced council has managed the authority.

The emphasis for the involvement of users and carers in this county was on community care planning based on participation, alongside the empowerment of individuals through needs-led assessment and care management. The participation of users and carers was one of the aims of the community care planning process. There was no rigid framework for consultation and diverse strategies within the divisions reflected the varying commitment and priority given to the process. There was clearly an unprecedented effort in some areas to solicit a wide range of views. Nor were these one-off exercises; structures for continued involvement have been established and are being refined and improved. Issues of resourcing involvement and facilitating the participation of users were beginning to emerge. The importance of advocacy was also gaining acceptance and the significance of carers' support systems was accepted.

At a political level, there was a degree of consensus amongst the three parties that a mixed economy was desirable in principle but, not surprisingly, some divergence about the ideal balance between public and independent sector provision; as well as some concerns over the capacity and reliability of the independent sector. The concept of a vertical purchaser/provider split throughout the social services department was not considered helpful as the need was seen to be the identification of functions rather than their organisational separation. In general, commissioning was carried out at the top of the organisation and providing at the bottom. However, budgets would be devolved to at least team manager level to permit a degree of flexibility and spot purchasing.

Care management functions would be carried out within fieldwork teams by designated social workers, occupational therapists and some home care organisers. Care management would be available to all except those who need specified single services. A number of separate pilot schemes were operating in 1991/92. The assessment process would hinge on a core document approach which would trigger specialised assessments where appropriate.

All social services funding of voluntary organisations was now subject to three year service agreements, negotiated with individual providers. Many of these agreements were for day care services for people with mental health problems and for older people. Contracts existed with voluntary sector care attendant schemes and there were a small number of private domiciliary care agencies, used on a very local basis to supplement the department's home care service. This was seen as a potential area for expansion of independent sector provision, but the implications for the authority's own service staff were a concern of senior managers.

There was not a very large independent residential and nursing home market (although it did account for two-thirds of the total provision), nor was it seen to be a financially attractive service area. There was very little private provision for people with physical and learning disabilities, and over £2 million a year was spent on mainly out-of-county residential placements. The strategy was to replace this provision over time with local services developed through a range of partnerships, including partnerships with housing associations.

## The metropolitan authority

The metropolitan authority has a population of 187,000 people. The council is Labour controlled. The authority has combined its housing and social services provision into a personal services department, although line management remains separate up to assistant director level.

The local authority placed a heavy emphasis upon the role of the elected member in representing the interests of local constituents. However, the community care planning process saw a major engagement with a wide range of organisations and this included a commitment to strengthen the input from users and carers in future years. The need to change practice with regard to assessment and care management was also recognised.

The CCP was drafted by a team of four officers from the personal services department. This group drew upon a number of initiatives, including a care management pilot and a voluntary sector committee on community care. The draft CCP was circulated very widely for comment in early 1992. The process for community care planning involved only limited direct input from users and carers, although the voluntary sector committee did carry out a small survey of user and carer views and its membership did include the parent of a physically disabled child.

The authority has a tradition of local authority provision of services. However, development plans for all services were generated in 1988 soon after the creation of a combined personal services department. These identified the need for new services, and a wider variety of staff and buildings. This helped to open up a more sympathetic view of a mixed economy of welfare. The local authority began to support a limited contracting out of services to the voluntary sector, including a Crossroads Care Attendant Scheme and day centre provision by Age Concern. However, this remains a local authority proud of its investment in its own home care service, and proud of the quality of its own residential homes. A sizeable voluntary sector, based on paid staff, was only just beginning to emerge. A further move to service provision by larger reliable voluntary sector organisations was anticipated, but there was no expectation of a wholesale contracting out of services.

At the time of interviewing, the authority retained a traditional service delivery structure with separate teams in each area involved in assessment and service provision. It had established a care management pilot with a team of seconded staff. Although this team was subsequently disbanded, they did establish some of the key strategic issues requiring resolution. In particular, it was decided to propose a wide definition of who could be a care manager, and referral forms and assessment forms were both piloted.

## Summary

The four authorities expressed different levels of enthusiasm for the emphasis of the White Paper on developing a quasi-market in social care with members of the controlling group in two of the authorities being very uncertain about the appropriateness of encouraging a further growth of service provision by the private sector. Attitudes and strategies towards care management and purchaser/provider splits were quite varied, as were the mechanisms developed for producing the April 1992 CCPs.

However, there were some similarities. All the authorities were keen to develop a needs-led rather than service-led response to users, all were worried about the potential inadequacy of the funding and all were concerned to improve and refine the criteria by which they would decide who could be helped within available resources. And all were struggling to develop mechanisms to facilitate a better dialogue with users and carers. The next section considers the views of local user and carer groups on the implementation 'progress' being made within their localities.

**Progress so far?   User and carer group perspectives**

In each locality, the research team interviewed 30 people: one-third were from social services authorities, just over one-third were from other statutory and independent sector agencies, and just under one-third were from groups of service users and/or carers.  These latter groups ranged from an access group to a local branch of Body Positive, a pensioner action group to a local branch of MENCAP. We were struck by their diversity in terms of who they represented, what activities they engaged in, and what sort of funding they received.  But there was no simple answer to what was meant by a user or carer group.  The majority were of the traditional self-help variety, where people who share a disability or a problem come together for mutual support and information.  These groups might provide some social activities and undertake limited advocacy work, but this was not the reason for their existence.  Not all members will necessarily be in receipt of community care services and some groups admit local professionals and lay enthusiasts as members.

*Community care planning*

At the time of the interviews (Spring 1992), the CCPs had just been published.  Local authorities had been required to consult widely with users and carers in their preparation.   Many of the organisations we visited, particularly the voluntary agencies and the larger user and carer groups, had indeed been invited to local consultation or planning meetings or asked to comment on drafts. A marked increase in opportunities to participate in service planning was reported and welcomed.  Some organisations felt that they had at last been recognised and accepted by the local authorities.  Nor were these one-off exercises; in some areas, new local planning groups were set up which have now become part of the mainstream service planning systems.

Having said that, we were struck by the extent to which local authorities relied on well-established networks of voluntary organisations for their consultation procedures.  Many smaller user groups were not reached; nor were users and carers who were not members of such groups.  Whole sections of service users, notably frail older people, were excluded from the process in most areas.

Also, those who had been invited to join local planning groups sometimes felt that important decisions were taken elsewhere, and that the results of consultations seemed to have been ignored (all unattributed quotes are from interviewees):

> The current community care plan doesn't reflect the consultations.

There was a common suspicion that the authorities had already made up their minds before consultation:

> The whole thing was signed, sealed and delivered before it went out. The social services department is in a position to pick out the bits that suit them.

In one area, there was a feeling that the real agenda had been to produce a CCP rather than to plan services. One person commented:

> They use us when they think we can help them. When you feel used, you don't want to participate.

Methods of consultation came in for some criticism. The distribution of draft CCPs was often felt to have been badly handled. Timescales sometimes allowed as little as four or six weeks, so that most group members could not be involved. Documents were sometimes too long and professional. Language and jargon were major factors in dissatisfaction:

> The plans aren't user-friendly - they should run seminars to explain them.

> They send you bumph which is not very easy to read or understand, so it's no use to you.

Public meetings were sometimes poorly attended because of timing, location and means of notifying people:

> The local authority's approach is to leave things until the last moment and then invite the same faces.

To those attending, meetings often appeared unfocused and disorganised with no clear understanding of follow-up arrangements. In one area, meetings were used simply for explaining what services would be available, managers were "telling, not listening".

Some user groups stressed the need for training for users and carers so as not to feel intimidated and gain the confidence to participate. One local authority had included a facilitator on a local planning group to support two user members who have learning difficulties:

> Having users on the group is difficult for professionals - they don't have the same capabilities as the rest. The facilitator needs to spend time with them outside the group.

Efforts to involve users and carers also assume that they have the time, resources and means to attend meetings. Carers often did not have much time to become involved; many users and carers may not have easy access to transport. One respondent pointed out:

> People from social services are paid to attend meetings. Carers are doubly exploited, expected to provide care for nothing and attend meetings free of charge.

## The mixed economy

The mixed economy is intended to give service users more choice, with local authorities purchasing services from a wide range of private and voluntary agencies. People we talked to had difficulty relating that idea to the reality of their experience of services. Many said that while choice was important, a guaranteed minimum level of service delivery was more of a priority.

One respondent, when asked about the importance of choice in provision of meals, as an example, said she was more interested in who decided how many meals a week she needed than in where they came from. Many saw the changes as being ways for social services to avoid providing services.

Voluntary organisations were having to respond to the opportunities and risks of the mixed economy. Some were willing and able to take on a provider role, either extending their existing services or developing new ones. This was clearest in specialist alcohol and drugs services, which had been established principally as service providers rather than campaigning organisations.

Others were more wary about their independence and advocacy role being compromised by moving into service provision:

> We were set up to provide a consumer voice to statutory agencies.

User and carer organisations which had taken on services were, in general, wary of taking on more:

> We don't have the resources to take on further contracts.

> It changes the nature of the organisation. Alzheimer's was a very small self-help group until it got itself a day centre.

## Care management

Care management became a reality in April 1993 when new assessment and funding systems came into operation. In all the local authorities we visited, pilot schemes had given many users and carers an understanding of what care management was meant to achieve. For most of these people, the possibility of a package of care, tailored to individual needs and preferences will be limited by the flexibility available to care managers. And this flexibility will be constrained by factors like the size of the budget and the range of providers to purchase from:

> The theory of a package is bunkum - there is a set list and if what you want is not there, it is not available.

Most groups expressed doubts as to where there would be adequate finance to put plans into effect. Scepticism about the feasibility of care management at times bordered on derision, since its success was seen to hinge on the issue of resources:

> It's lovely in theory but what if the resources aren't there?

> There won't be the money to produce packages of care for any but a small number of people. For everyone else, things will be the same.

The issue of information about what services are available also emerged as important. If neither users nor care managers have full details of all the options, meaningful choices cannot be made. Some users and carers felt that access to information depended on belonging to an organisation or having a good GP or social worker; the information was there but publicity about how to get it was poor.

### An overall judgement

Overall, the user and carer groups expressed very mixed views. Most were highly critical of the progress being made towards empowering users and carers through the community care reforms. Most of the groups we visited certainly took the view that the real choices would not be theirs to make. Some saw local authorities' unwillingness to give up control as the major obstacle.

But many saw progress within the context that local authorities are operating in and were encouraged by their commitment to increasing user involvement, if not empowerment. Most felt that the real constraint to good community care lay outside the control of local government; no-one was convinced that adequate resources would be made available, in which case the reforms would just "limp along and lose credibility".

## No money?  No empowerment?

This last point raises a fundamental dilemma faced in writing this chapter. Should the message be that quasi-markets fail to deliver on empowerment or that any system of social care is bound to fail by this criterion if hopelessly under-resourced?

Elsewhere, we have pointed out that any 'policy failure' by quasi-markets in community care would be open to several alternative interpretations (Hoyes and Means, 1993). These include:

- quasi-markets are no better, and possibly worse, than conventional markets or bureaucratic systems;

- quasi-markets were a good idea but one that received little understanding or commitment from the supposed lead authority;

- the missionary zeal of the local authority was undermined by vested interests, low quality staff or the service legacy of the last forty years;

- a major opportunity was lost through chronic under-funding by central government;

- quasi-markets are a good idea, and the research has only identified implementation disruption which will settle down over time.

The community care 'reforms' are under-resourced despite the transfer of money to local authorities from the social security budget as a result of the new funding regime for those in institutional care. And it is too early to make judgements about what is going to be achieved within the money available. However, these longer term judgements require us to be clear about the effective preconditions for empowering users and the preconditions for effective quasi-markets.

## What is empowerment?

There is no simple answer as to what does and what does not represent user empowerment since it is a contested concept (Taylor et al, 1992). However, most would probably agree that it involves users taking or being given more power over decisions affecting their welfare and hence it probably involves taking at least some power away from service providers.

But how might this be achieved? Power shifts can relate to very different degrees of authority and this can be expressed in the form of a 'ladder' which outlines the degrees of power that can be conferred on users or taken by them (Taylor et al, 1992):

HIGH    Users have the authority to take decisions
        Users have the authority to take some decisions
        Users have an opportunity to influence decisions
        User views are sought before making decisions
        Decisions are publicised and explained before
        implementation
LOW     Information is given about decisions made

There are very different views about how best to achieve progress up this 'ladder' and not all would agree about the importance of all the steps. For example, the inclination of Ramon (1991) is to reserve the term empowerment for situations where real power and control is taken by users. She complains of "the use of the concept of empowerment by politicians, who are constantly cutting back in services and benefits available to people with disabilities" since they confuse "buying power with empowerment" (p 17). This underlines the need to look at the main strategic approaches to empowerment and the different assumptions that they make. These are:

- empowerment through 'rights';

- empowerment through 'exit';

- empowerment through 'voice'.

## Empowerment and 'rights'

The clear preference of the disability movement and many user groups is for a rights-based system of empowerment, based upon a right to a reasonable income, appropriate services and protection from the prejudiced behaviour of the non-disabled. Such a perspective is consistent with broader debates within the UK left about the need to develop new social rights in order to ensure the welfare of all citizens. This is justified on the following grounds:

> Citizenship entails being able to participate in society, to enjoy its fruits and to fulfil one's own potential, and it follows that each individual citizen must be equally able (or 'empowered') to do so. This suggests two things: first, that all individuals must have equal access to education, health care and other services necessary to give them an equal chance in life. Second, no-one should be subject to unfair discrimination. (Coote, 1992, p 4)

The difficulty of this perspective lies in moving away from generalities about social rights to the specification of what these might be. Authors such as Cranston (1976) have long argued social rights can never be enforceable in the same way as civil rights because they are not universal. For example, the meaning of any right to medical care would vary enormously according to which society one was in or what time period one was talking about. No society could possibly manage to meet every medical need of every single citizen at all times. Social rights are expensive and have to be rationed even if, unlike new right theorists, you believe in high public expenditure.

Plant (1992) feels it is easy to exaggerate such difficulties since many of the same issues exist with regard to the enforcement of civil and political rights. He points out that "there must be a right to the protection of civil and political rights, but there cannot be a right to the services of a policeman, as these are subject to the same problems of scrutiny as doctors and teachers" (p 21). He goes on to argue:

> The idea of rights in the public sector provides a new way forward between the market and democracy as two models of empowerment. This is not to decry either markets or democracy, only to say that there is a case for looking at a new way and seeing how far we can get with it. If these rights can work and be made clear and enforceable, whether they are rights to have certain procedures followed, or actual rights to resources, then this would clearly be a more direct way of empowering the citizen than either the market, or bureaucratic regulation, or greater democratic accountability. (p 28)

With regard to community care services and disability benefits, the Disability Manifesto Group (1991) has produced detailed proposals on what such a rights-based package would need to look like.

However, the community care 'reforms' are not driven by a rights-based perspective even if they did include a strengthening of the right of users and their carers to make complaints. Nevertheless, attempts are being made by specialist lawyers working with user groups to establish that a disabled person has a right to a service once assessed by a local authority as having a need. This is based on their interpretation of the Chronically Sick and Disabled Persons Act 1970 and emerging case law. And it seems to be causing concern to central government. Recent advice to local authorities from the chief social services inspector has been interpreted by some local authorities as asking them not to record information about unmet needs because of the danger of being taken to court under the judicial review element of the complaints procedures introduced by the 1990 Act (*Community Care*, 7 January 1992). Perhaps one of the dilemmas of a rights-based approach to empowerment in a hostile climate is that it risks provoking resource holders to limit the information they make available to service users and to curtail their use of discretion.

## 'Exit' and 'voice'

The community care 'reforms' were based on a narrower vision of empowerment and consumer control than that embodied in the rights perspective. Hoyes et al (1993) have followed others in drawing on the work of Hirschman (1970) to differentiate between two further models of consumer control: 'exit' and 'voice'. The exit approach emphasises the central importance of being able to switch services and move on to alternative providers. Hirschman argues that voice comes into operation when consumers wish to remain with a particular provider but wish to change its nature, and this suggests that user participation and representation must be at the centre of service evaluation and development. Our present research project is centrally concerned with the implications of exit approaches (and their assumptions about markets) and voice approaches (and their assumptions about democracy) for user empowerment in community care. These differ markedly in their assumptions.

The market approach seeks to empower consumers by giving them choice between alternatives and the option of exit from a service and/or provider if dissatisfied. Here the total pattern of provision is dictated by the sum of consumer choices - those services which are not chosen will go to the wall. In other words, if you do not like your day centre, you move to another one. Day centres which are unpopular will cease to trade.

The democratic approach would keep more services in the public sector but seeks to empower users by giving them a voice in services and therefore the chance to transform their existing service or service organisation. In other words, if you do not like your day centre, you join the user committee and change it to your liking.

The next question is to consider the prerequisites for successfully implementing empowerment strategies. Le Grand (1992) argues that all the quasi-market reforms need to be judged in terms of whether they deliver efficient equitable services in a way which generates choice. Drawing on the theory of markets, he has identified five conditions which have to be met before this is likely to happen.

- *Market structure* - for a conventional market to be efficient and offer genuine choice, there must be competition or the potential for competition. That is there should be many providers and many purchasers, or the opportunity for new providers to enter and existing providers to exit from the market relatively costlessly.

- *Information* - both sides of a market must have access to cheap and accurate information about the costs and quality of the service provided. Monitoring of quality is an essential part of any quasi-market system.

- *Transactions costs* - the costs involved in drafting, negotiating and safeguarding contracts, and also the costs of monitoring compliance and resolving disputes after transactions are agreed, must be less than the costs of the administrative systems that contracts are replacing.

- *Motivation* - for markets to work appropriately, providers need to be motivated at least in part by profit making, whilst purchasers must be motivated to maximise the welfare of users.

- *Cream-skimming* - in order to achieve equity, markets must restrict opportunities for discrimination, by either purchasers or providers, in favour of the cheaper or less troublesome users (the cream) - the relatively healthy, the less needy, the more self-sufficient.

As Le Grand argues, the division between purchaser and user in the quasi-markets operating in public services like community care poses a number of problems. Competition in the market may be reduced by the existence of monopoly or near-monopoly purchasers and cosy relationships with dominant providers. Do users have the sanctions to upset these cosy relationships and demand that the authority exit to another contractor? Quality in welfare is notoriously difficult to monitor; if it is defined by purchasers and providers, there is no guarantee it will fulfil user needs. Information flow is constrained by the fact that many choices are made under duress (mental health) or in crisis. Many welfare providers are not commercially motivated and may find it difficult to make the shift from considering the welfare of their users to the financial state of their provider units. Why should purchasers (indirect consumers) have the direct consumer's interest at heart? And how will they know what the consumer's interests are?

Finally, welfare services are particularly vulnerable to cream-skimming.

Le Grand provides a useful framework for beginning the process of judging the capacity of the community 'reforms' to empower from a market perspective. However, it leaves a number of issues unresolved. First, some users are in a position to provide for themselves or to buy directly all their own services but most are not (Oldman, 1991), and this situation is unlikely to change dramatically in the rest of the decade (Bosanquet and Propper, 1991). The reforms of central government in community care are essentially about creating quasi rather than pure markets. Indeed, at the individual level, the user is dependent upon their care manager for empowerment. In future years, some users may be given the chance to change or reject care managers (an exit strategy) but for the vast majority, the user and the care manager will be 'locked' in a relationship in which the user is trying to make his/her voice heard. To facilitate this, the care manager has to do far more than just impart information. The ironic situation exists wherein quasi-markets in community care will be unable to work effectively unless a user-centred approach to care management is developed, based upon giving the user a clear voice during assessment, care package creation and care package review. Even when the service user is given a voice during review and major service deficiencies are identified, exit may well not be the choice of the user. Exit can be a blunt instrument, when the overall service may be what the consumer wants, but there are aspects of it which he/she would like changed, such as the time at which a home help arrives or the range of tasks he or she is willing to do.

Second, as illustrated by the profiles, authorities are tackling the reforms from very different starting points in terms of previous patterns of provision and in terms of their assumptions about how best to move forward. Even an authority which tried to contract out all its services would still have a legal obligation to pursue the voice strategy of a community care plan after consultation with others, including user and carer groups. In other words, each authority will end up with a complex pattern of voice and exit strategies for empowerment, but the exact mix will vary considerably from authority to authority.

All this underlines the importance of the voice components of the quasi-market reforms in community care if they are to make a contribution to the empowerment of service users. The degree of empowerment available through voice will depend on the extent to which purchasers, providers and, crucially, care managers are willing to share power and at what stage. But it will also depend on the extent to which service users are able to take power. Users of community care are often faced with crucial decisions at times of extreme stress (when illness forces decisions about residential care, for example, or when the loss or departure of a carer leaves them without essential services). They are more likely than other sections of the population to be in poverty, and people who are struggling for day-to-day survival are unlikely to get involved in abstract decision-making processes. Those who are may find these processes too difficult to understand.

The profiles underlined how local authorities vary in their preference for exit and voice strategies, and Hoyes et al (1993) link this to preferences for different models of welfare. There are three models of welfare which might operate in community care at the local level:

● The *welfare state model*, where the state both finances and provides care.

● A *pure market model* which makes the consumer or client the purchaser of care from independent providers. The consumer would have a contract directly with the provider, services would need to conform to a British standard and there would be a system of redress in the event of a faulty service.

● The *quasi-market model* which is embodied in current policy, where the state is the purchaser of care from independent providers, but where the choices of the consumer are mediated through a care manager, with a system of redress related to quality standards set (usually) by the purchaser. The user may have a contract, mediated by the care manager with access to redress via the purchaser, but also with a voice through the democratic system.

If the combination of exit and voice that the third model above represents is to operate to the best advantage of the user, this requires that authorities, whether they identify more closely with the welfare state or market aspects of the model, should:

● stimulate a market of diverse providers which offers choice to users and carers, through funding and other powers;

● ensure the provision of advice, information and advocacy to help service users and carers through this range of services and to help them assert their claims to a quality service;

● develop service standards and definitions of quality in conjunction with users and carers through which standards can be regulated;

● promote and encourage organisations which give disadvantaged citizens and service users the opportunity both to develop their own services and to have a say in existing services, whoever provides them;

● provide accessible channels for them to express their views and negotiate with other users.

## Conclusion

It is our view that the introduction of quasi-markets into social care has a contribution to make to the empowerment of service users and their carers, especially if the above five conditions can be met. However, a number of caveats needs to be made about this statement.

First, it is clear that local authorities have made only limited progress so far, although it is still very early on in what is bound to be a long, complex and disruptive implementation process.

Second, the potential of quasi-markets will be undermined if provision is under-funded by central government - a growing concern of many commentators and practitioners (Cervi et al, 1992; Harding, 1992). At present, overall resource levels mean that many people in severe need will not be empowered because they will not receive a service. There are also more specific areas where local authorities need more support. For example, they need increased help with the development of information systems which are appropriate to decentralised budgets and care management systems. Our present research and previous work (Hoyes, Means and Le Grand, 1992) emphasises the inadequacy of many of the systems which exist and we have argued that central government needs to fund a specific initiative to address this crucial issue (Hoyes and Means, 1992).

Third, even a well-funded quasi-market system of social care is no more a panacea than a social rights system. We would argue for an approach which draws on the strengths of a 'rights' strategy as well as the 'exit' and 'voice' perspectives. The main contribution of the 'rights' approach needs to be on ensuring adequate incomes for disabled people because people on very low incomes experience poverty not empowerment (Chappell, 1992; Disability Manifesto Group, 1991). More specifically, the Independent Living Fund experience shows that many disabled people wish to organise their own care packages with money received because of their disability (Kestenbaum, 1992).

Finally, we need to stop thinking in terms of structures as the main route to empowerment for many service users. Service users are dependent upon the skills and commitment of the professionals who assess their needs and then develop care packages on their behalf (Phillips, 1992). The critical point is the quality of those relationships. Quasi-markets may increase options for both the professional and the user. The delivery and maintenance of those options will depend upon whether the professionals oppress or attempt to empower the users by creating a relationship in which users can explore their own needs and the various ways in which they might be met (Gomm et al, 1993). Whether care managers can perform this brokerage/advocacy role while also performing a rationing/budgetary role is one of the unresolved dilemmas of the quasi-market 'reform' of community care in the UK.

## References

Audit Commission (1986) *Making a reality of community care*, London: HMSO.

Bosanquet, N. and Propper, C. (1991) 'Charting the grey economy in the 1990s', *Policy and Politics*, vol 19, no 4, pp 269-82.

Cervi, B. et al (1992) 'Facing a trickle or a flood', *Community Care*, pp 14-15.

Challis, L. (1990) *Organising public social services*, London: Longman.

Chappell, A. (1992) 'Towards a sociological critique of the normalisation principle', *Disability, Handicap and Society*, vol 7, no 1, pp 35-52.

Coote, A. (1992) 'Introduction', in A. Coote (ed) *The welfare of citizens: developing new social rights*, London: IPPR/Rivers Oram Press, pp 1-14.

Cranston, M. (1976) 'Human rights: real and supposed', in N. Timms and D. Watson (eds) *Talking about welfare*, London: Routledge and Kegan Paul.

Department of Health (1989) *Caring for people: community care in the next decade and beyond*, London: HMSO.

Department of Health/Social Services Inspectorate (1991) *Care management and assessment: summary of practice guidance*, London: HMSO.

Disability Manifesto Group (1991) *An agenda for the 1990s*, Disability Manifesto Group.

Gomm, R., Cathles-Hagen, A., Rudge, D. and Smith, R. (1993) 'User-controlled self-determination of need: a care management pilot project in Cheltenham', in R. Smith et al, *Working together for better community care*, Bristol: SAUS Publications, School for Advanced Urban Studies, University of Bristol, pp 86-117.

Griffiths Report (1988) *Community care: agenda for action*, London: HMSO.

Harding, T. (1992) *Great expectations - and spending on social services*, London: NISW.

Hirschman, A. (1970) *Exit, voice and loyalty: responses to decline in firms, organisations and states*, Harvard: Harvard University Press.

Hoyes, L., Jeffers, S., Lart, R., Means, R. and Taylor, M. (1993), *User empowerment and the reform of community care*, Bristol: SAUS Publications, School for Advanced Urban Studies, University of Bristol.

Hoyes, L. and Means, R. (1993) 'Quasi-markets and the reform of community care', in J. Le Grand and W. Bartlett (eds) *Quasi-markets and social policy*, London: Macmillan.

Hoyes, L. and Means, R. (1992) 'Needs in the lead', *Social Work Today*, 3 December, p 19.

Hoyes, L., Means, R. and Le Grand, J. (1992) *Made to measure?*, Bristol: SAUS Publications, School for Advanced Urban Studies, University of Bristol.

Hudson, B. (1990) 'Social policy and the new right - the strange case of the community care White Paper', *Local Government Studies*, vol 16, no 6, pp 15-34.

Kestenbaum, A. (1992) *Cash for care*, Nottingham: Independent Living Fund.

Langan, M. (1990) 'Community care in the 1990s', *Critical Social Policy*, issue 29, pp 58-70.

Le Grand, J. (1990) *Quasi-markets and social policy*, Studies in Decentralisation and Quasi-Markets no 1, Bristol: SAUS Publications, School for Advanced Urban Studies, University of Bristol.

Le Grand, J. (1992) *Paying or providing for welfare?*, Studies in Decentralisation and Quasi-Markets no 15, Bristol: SAUS Publications, School for Advanced Urban Studies, University of Bristol.

Means, R. and Harrison, L. (1988) *Community care before and after the Griffiths Report*, London: ALA.

Means, R. and Smith, R. (1985) *The development of welfare services for elderly people*, London: Croom Helm.

Morris, J. (1991) *Pride against prejudice*, London: The Women's Press.

Oldman, C. (1991) *Paying for care*, York: Joseph Rowntree Foundation.

Oliver, M. (1990) *The politics of disablement*, London: Macmillan.

Phillips, J. (1992) 'The future of social work with elderly people', *Generations Review*, vol 2, no 4, pp 12-14.

Plant, R. (1992) 'Citizenship, rights and welfare', in A. Coote (ed) *The welfare of citizens: developing new social rights*, London: IPPR/Rivers Oram Press, pp 15-30.

Ramon, S. (1991) 'Principles and conceptual knowledge', in S. Ramon (ed) *Beyond community care: normalisation and integration work*, London: Macmillan, pp 6-34.

Taylor, M., Hoyes, L., Lart, R. and Means, R. (1992) *User empowerment in community care: unravelling the issues*, Studies in Decentralisation and Quasi-Markets no 11, Bristol: SAUS Publications, School for Advanced Urban Studies, University of Bristol.

*eight*

# QUASI-MARKETS AND THE TRANSFORMATION OF THE INDEPENDENT SECTOR

## Marilyn Taylor and Paul Hoggett

### Inconsistent policies?

This chapter seeks to examine to what extent policies which seek to develop a mixed economy of care are providing the conditions under which such an economy can develop. On the one hand, the present government has expressed its commitment to policies which will give the independent sector a far more important role in service provision than in the past. For instance the current community care guidelines demand that 85% of money transferred from the social security budget (and thus 63% of the money which is ring-fenced for expenditure by the local 'lead' authorities) be spent on care provided through non-statutory organisations in the private and voluntary sectors. Yet simultaneously the survival of many local organisations in the voluntary and community sector is in doubt as a result of local authority expenditure cuts, while a period of recession has provided an unpromising environment for the development of private care, with private residential care homes going out of business. These apparent contradictions raise questions about the extent to which policy makers have understood the way in which non-statutory organisations operate and the motivations which fuel them. The end result is that the choices available to managers and policy shapers within local government, and ultimately to service users, may not be those promised by the rhetoric surrounding the community care legislation. We need to go beyond concepts of the market if such choices are to be available.


## A mixed economy of care

Current policies in the field of community care seek to develop a mixed economy of care through the introduction of quasi-markets. Although part of the language underlying these reforms has been that of efficiency, there has also been frequent reference to pluralism and increased choice for the consumer. The opportunity exists to develop a diversity of provision catering for a range of different needs and preferences. Voluntary and private organisations as well as the consumers they serve should be in a position to gain a great deal from such a move. Indeed these are the kinds of policies which key thinkers on the voluntary sector were advocating back in the 1970s (Wolfenden, 1978; Hadley and Hatch, 1981).

Provision under the welfare state was criticised by them and others for being too uniform and unresponsive to consumer needs and preferences, with power too strongly focused in the hands of monopoly providers and producers. Opportunities to use the energies of a diversity of non-statutory organisations were ignored. But two questions must be addressed:

● Will current policies produce a genuine mixed economy with diversity at a premium or will financial stringency and the particular features of the community care environment pull in the opposite direction?

● Will provision in this market be different in kind to that which prevailed under conditions of 'public sector monopoly' and if it is, what is the role - if any - required of government?

To answer these questions we need to understand the character of the independent sector and the range of organisations within it. How far will current policies allow the present variety of organisations to be maintained or even expanded and how far will a quasi-market allow the organisations within it to maintain the characteristics which distinguish them from the state and from each other, thus catering for the diversity of need? This chapter addresses these questions drawing on research which we are carrying out in the field of community care.[1]

## What is the independent sector?

The independent sector in community care contains within it a wide range of organisations, among them: the independent care firm; the family-run residential home; the joint initiative with statutory representatives or co-optees on the board; the independent organisation set up by the local or health authority; the small good neighbour scheme or self-help group; larger local organisations employing staff and running day centres or hostels; campaigning and self-advocacy organisations; the big 'household name' charities; and the community association based in a locality or around ethnic identity.  There is no doubt that, even against a background of state welfare provision, a rich diversity of organisations has developed over time to help people to meet their welfare needs and promote different approaches to welfare.

Normally organisations in this territory are described as private, for-profit or voluntary, not-for-profit.  Our research suggests that the voluntary sector is generally seen as flexible, close to the consumer, and relatively cheap (because it can call on voluntary effort).  But it is also seen as unaccountable and amateur.  Private organisations may be seen as untrustworthy, interested only in profit.  But they are also seen as efficient and business-like, responsive to consumer demand.

Our own research suggests that there is a far greater variety of organisations in this territory than the usual distinction between the 'voluntary' and 'private' sectors suggests.  There are differences in size (small, medium and large organisations face different pressures); funding (grants, donations, voucher-type subsidies - fees from government, independent donors, individual customers); and ownership (the ultimate responsibility may lie with shareholders, private owners, staff in cooperatives, trustees for charitable gifts, community associations, user groups, or even government appointees).

Thus it is possible to argue that smaller voluntary organisations may have more in common with small family businesses than they do with large national charities.  In relation to ownership, beneficiary-owned or community organisations stress their differences from the 'traditional' voluntary sector as they see it, while staff in cooperatives are quite explicitly different in their organisational form from private organisations which are owned by sole traders or which have outside shareholders.

These distinctions are important for a number of reasons. Firstly, pluralism and choice have been among the driving forces behind the rhetoric of current reforms and their supposed absence one of the major criticisms of public sector provision. If the reforms are not to be seen as a cynical cost-cutting exercise, it is important that they deliver diversity in provision and doubly important that they do not reduce the diversity that already exists.

Secondly, a positive notion of the 'enabling authority' would give local government a role in encouraging a market that can meet the diversity of need. If public service managers are to do this, they need to understand the potential range of organisations that exist, what they deliver and how different values and management styles determine what is delivered. They also need to manage relationships with this diverse range of organisations in a way which respects and reinforces their distinctive qualities.

It is also possible to argue that diversity is necessary so that we do not tie up 'all our eggs in one basket'. Should policies change, it is important that we have a range of different institutional choices to call on in the future.

## What kind of market, what kind of players?

Government guidance (Department of Health/Social Services Inspectorate, 1991, paragraph 4.2.15, as cited in Lewis, 1993) encourages authorities to be active in stimulating a mixed economy of care. How far will the quasi-market stimulate a variety of provision and develop a diverse range of provision in community care?

Le Grand (1992) suggests that it is possible to identify five requirements for a successful quasi-market in social care, as mentioned in Chapter 7. To recap, these are:

- *market structure* - the potential for competition requires that there is the opportunity and incentive for new providers to enter the market with relatively few costs;

- *minimal transactions costs* - ie the costs involved in drafting, negotiating and safeguarding transactions;

- *motivation* - providers need to be motivated at least in part by profit making;

- *information* - both sides of a market must have access to cheap and accurate information about the costs and quality of the service provided;

- *no cream-skimming* - to achieve equity, markets must restrict opportunities for discrimination in favour of the cheaper or less demanding user.

## Market structure

Where authorities are moving into quasi-markets, they tend to go for the bigger, more 'trusted' providers, those that are, in any case, the best-equipped to enter the market. Small is not yet beautiful. Large well known organisations have the contacts and public profile to initiate discussions. The same is true of the growing number of statutory/voluntary hybrids that are being set up and of ex-statutory workers forming not-for-profit or even private organisations. If contracts are widely drawn, these may well be the only organisations in the market; US research suggests that there is a limited number of potential suppliers in the care market (Kramer, 1992). It is, in any case, the bigger organisations (whatever their ownership) that can afford the transactions costs of tendering for contracts. They can afford to have loss leaders, to cut and run if the terms and conditions do not suit.

Research in the USA suggests that once organisations get a contract, they are unlikely to lose it (Kramer and Grossman, 1987). Smith and Lipsky (1992, p 244) argue that: "major shocks to the provider system tend to be avoided, and this is more the case the more government depends on particular providers for delivery". They suggest also that those providers are likely to become implicated in determining the future shape of the market. It could certainly be argued that such organisations are more likely to have access to consultation procedures that determine community care plans and through them the pattern of delivery, although some authorities are now questioning the legitimacy of consulting with organisations who could be potential contractors.

In these circumstances the prospect for smaller, newer or non-traditional providers is uncertain. There is a fear of large organisations parachuting into areas without consideration for local networks (and maybe out again), something that was a feature of the special employment programmes of the mid 1970s and early 1980s. Small organisations in the private sector fear that "if the big operators come in we will fold" (research respondent).

Many potential providers are very fragile and at the fringes of survival. Our research suggests, for example, that rising insurance costs could represent another barrier to entry where, for example, black and minority ethnic organisations in 'high risk' areas are concerned. Private organisations are having to expand to remain viable, which raises questions about the extent to which care in the community policies will really have the effect of getting people out of institutional settings.

In the voluntary and community sector, anecdotal evidence suggests that the funding situation for small organisations is grim, especially in authorities subject to capping. Many authorities are consulting the sector on how to make cuts rather than how to develop capacity within the sector to take on new services. Statistics on local authority funding need to be treated with caution, but initial surveys (Taylor, Kendall and Fenyo, 1993; Mabbott, 1993) suggest that grant aid from this source (as opposed to fees) is decreasing, especially in metropolitan authorities which have in the past been significant funders of the sector. Fees are rising, once organisations enter the market, but the retreat from grants will affect investment in development, advocacy and ancillary activities. Under these circumstances, the ideal of the local authority developing a market of potential providers seems unlikely to be realised.

A system of 'spot purchase', ie buying a specified service for an individual service user, could work against some, at least, of these trends. The rhetoric of care in the community suggests the creation of a consumer market which will enable those in need to construct packages of specific services as appropriate. If authorities go for spot purchase related to individual packages of care rather than block purchase, then the smaller organisations have more of a chance of entry. But the flexibility that spot purchase brings has the disadvantage that it is a very unstable basis for organisations in vulnerable areas to plan ahead. For providers, block purchase of services will create more stability but restrict entry to the market.

In reality, producer markets (ie markets between agencies as opposed to markets between the consumer and the supplier) are more likely to be formed on the basis of block contracts, even in authorities who are committed to a market approach. Our research suggests that some 'flagship' Conservative local authorities are contracting out considerable portions of provision but doing very little to develop a strategy to introduce individually tailored care plans.

## Motivation

The assumption prevails that the market will only work if providers are motivated by profit.    But voluntary and community organisations are, by definition, not-for-profit.  If motivation is to apply to the quasi-market, a new criterion must be found.  One possibility is market share which, it can be argued, has been a motivation in the fund-raising market for years and may well become one in the contracts market.  Perhaps behind both the motivation for profit and that for market share is the urge to survive, ie the need to race in order to stand still.  But even market share has its limitations when applied to the majority of voluntary and community organisations, which have traditionally been motivated by 'welfare making' not 'profit making', although some may wish to see their values and models of care being adopted on a wider scale (for example, those concerned with evangelism or empowerment).   Does the Le Grand model mean that they must either change their motivation (and hence their character) or keep out of the market?

   Perhaps what is more surprising is to find that many small businesses exhibit similar characteristics.   Moreover, it has long been known that the bulk of the small business sector in western type economies has only a limited potential for growth and development. The vast majority of small businesses are in fact very small (involving less than five employees) and are run on either a 'family' or sole-proprietor basis.   Summarising recent research Marceau (1990) suggests the usefulness of distinguishing between the "craftsman entrepreneur" and the "opportunistic entrepreneur". The former "usually has few or no long-term plans for product development. ... Empirical evidence suggests that while the companies so formed may persist for very long periods of time they will not grow much" (p 364). According to Marceau their primary motivation is not capital accumulation but "independence, the chance to take one's own decisions and be one's own boss - to which some added a closely related set of motivations, expressed as 'job satisfaction', 'self-satisfaction' or 'flexibility' by some and by others as challenge, achievement, opportunity and security for the family or financial reward" (p 365). This is supported by our research and by a separate study of the development of entrepreneurialism in small businesses in Hungary, where the desire for 'independence' is also emerging as a primary motivational factor (Hoggett and Kallay, 1993). As social work job descriptions change towards assessment and care management in the public sector, it is possible that private enterprise may offer the only alternative to professionals seeking to continue to practice their face-to-face support skills.

In the context of community care many small businesses involved in day and residential care appear to be of this traditional form. There are a few 'opportunistic entrepreneurs' (mostly larger firms such as the one which was successful in winning the contract for the bulk of residential service provision in one of our study areas) but many would appear to be primarily concerned either with immediate survival or 'remaining as we are'. Interestingly many small family businesses also bring a 'family ethic' to their work. The residents of many homes, for example, are seen and treated as part of a kind of extended family (with all the positives and negatives associated with family life). For many such organisations growth would threaten both to destroy this ethic and the need to maintain a sense of personal control.

Small community or beneficiary run organisations are also concerned that growth will destroy the 'face-to-face' and democratic ways in which they try to operate. Will a move into contracts or service agreements take them away from their associational roots and alienate their members, forfeit the very things that 'make them tick'? (Taylor and Lewis, 1993).

The larger voluntary and not-for-profit organisations also display a variety of forms of ownership and motivation. However, they may be above the watershed where growth changes the face-to-face nature of an organisation, though there is a need for further research to establish where this watershed is and what structures are needed to maintain it. Our research suggests that some of the medium-sized private care firms that are now emerging are planning to expand as they see new gaps opening up. Other private residential homes argue that growth is the only way of maintaining viability.

There are also questions about the continuing motivation of board or management committee members in the voluntary and community sector as the market orientation develops. The voluntary nature of board membership is a significant distinguishing characteristic of this sector (Salamon and Anheier, 1992), but board members are now snowed under with new responsibilities, which is going to make it hard for a variety of organisations to find willing volunteers at this level. It could also shift the balance of membership away from people based in local communities or service users towards professionals from other agencies. As it is, our research suggests that with the most recent legislation, trustees are concerned about issues of liability as well as the implication of contracts for their trust deeds.

A lot will depend on the way in which contracts are managed. The shift from grants to contracts suggests a move away from relationships based on trust and discretion towards impersonal mechanistic transactions (Fox, 1974). If so, it could be argued that this would destroy the very things which have traditionally motivated individuals to give up their time on a voluntary basis in order to work on boards or management committees. Smith and Lipsky (1992, p 242) suggest that the attractiveness of working in private agencies may diminish as they become more regulated and lose their quasi-voluntary character.

## The independent sector is not just about service provision

The quasi-market analysis tends to focus mainly on those services which were provided by the public sector in the welfare state. But this does not cover all the formal organisations through which people seek to further their welfare. Many smaller organisations are not in the market for contracts, for some of the very reasons outlined above. But they perform functions on which mainstream services and choice depend (advocacy) or which may prevent people from having to call on mainstream services (self-help). As we noted earlier in this chapter it is ironic that at the very time when current legislation envisages the transfer of service provision to non-statutory organisations, local authority cutbacks may be having a devastating impact upon the grant aid available to organisations which engage in advocacy, self-help, campaigning and research or the provision of support services to other local voluntary/community organisations. Their disappearance could have an enormous knock-on effect. Some may require very little support from government. But the support they get is crucial to their survival. Or the participation of their unpaid leaders may depend on other services and benefits which are also under pressure (childcare provision, community transport, environmental safety, training, voluntary sector infrastructure). Public authorities need to consider their policies towards this wider support system as well as the contracts market if the whole structure of community care is to survive.

## Entry to the market: summary

These findings suggest that the answer to our first question - how far will current policies stimulate a variety of provision and develop a diverse market in community care - is that without active policies to develop diversity, it may well go by the board. Without such policies (Taylor, Hoggett and Bartlett, 1993), while the government's objective of substituting private for public provision may be met, there is no guarantee that the service user will have a greater choice. Meanwhile the less formal organisations through which they seek to further their welfare beyond the definitions adopted by the state may well have difficulty in surviving.

## New kinds of providers?

But what about the second question? Will provision through quasi-markets be different in kind from that which prevailed under conditions of a public monopoly? Di Maggio and Powell (1983) have alerted us to the problem of what they call "institutional isomorphism", whereby organisations facing common institutional pressures begin to adopt similar organisational forms. The quasi-market would seem particularly vulnerable to this tendency, especially if it becomes the dominant form of funding.

The evidence already presented suggests that new providers may be those closest in form to the purchaser, insofar as purchase of service favours the more familiar, larger provider. There is a further twist on this situation insofar as, where there is no independent provider geared up to take over, local and health authorities are floating off parts of their provision as independent not-for-profit organisations. This is happening particularly in relation to residential accommodation for people leaving institutional care. How far they increase diversity or choice within the market has yet to be seen.

But there are other forces that drive voluntary organisations to become more like the statutory organisations that purchase their services, which relate to the information criterion specified by the Le Grand model.

If diversity is to be sustained, then government purchasers must find a way of holding independent organisations accountable without controlling them. At the most basic level, this requires devolution. The drive for targets to be met from central government runs counter to the recognition of the need for local solutions.

But local solutions need local imagination and risk taking. At present, a lot of purchaser energy is going into monitoring, standard setting and regulation, not to mention service charters. Contracts are specifying outcomes and in that sense they are taking control by reducing discretion. Many private and voluntary organisations welcome inspections, monitoring and standards. But there is no guarantee that the investment in regulation actually results in improved services. It is arguable that mechanistic and procedural standards such as the British Standards model have more to do with consistency than excellence and may eclipse a drive to real quality. Regulation may not represent investment in service improvement so much as an investment in organisational (purchaser) safety - insurance rather than a drive to improve services. There is a question mark in parts of the sector over the extent to which the information required is actually used by the service managers who demand it. Do straitened public authorities have the resources to process all this information? And if they pull resources into these areas, what else will have to make way?

Some organisations in our research were particularly concerned that they would lose control over admissions or referrals and that it would be public purchasers who would dictate whom they can serve. This, as well as an increased emphasis on professional standards of assessment, management and evaluation can have a knock-on effect on the motivation and skill requirements of volunteers (Lewis, 1993). There is also a time cost. Lewis' research suggests that it can take up to 75% of a manager's time to administer a contract, of which a significant proportion is providing information in relation to the contract, either for the bid or for monitoring.

Wider measures initiated from beyond the authority are also impacting on the regulations which public service managers may have to police. Volunteers who used to help out in serving teas in clubs or parents helping out in a parents and toddlers group are suddenly finding that their premises are no longer adequate because of environmental heath and safety measures originating from the European Community, or that they have to go on a training course and 'qualify' if they are to continue to be seen as helpful. This may well take out of the resource pool many people on whom services have so far depended. Regulations (eg on lifting) may also demand the employment of more paid staff or a sophisticated hoist, which organisations on a shoestring can ill afford.

There are genuine dilemmas here. It is, of course, essential that standards of service are maintained and that users of services are not put at unnecessary risk. In a related research project, service users and carers have expressed concern at the standards that could be expected of voluntary and private organisations (Hoyes et al, 1993). But the difficulty of regulating many complex service areas and highly diverse organisations can lead to the danger of overkill. And, by their nature, the voluntary and private sectors reflect that thriving diversity which the statutory sector has tried to reduce to manageable proportions.

*To summarise*, one could argue that transactions between the statutory and 'third' sectors have progressively shifted over the last decade from what Fox (1974) terms "high discretion/high trust" relationships towards "low trust/low discretion" relationships. In this sense the leap from grant aid to contracts can be seen as consistent with the general trend towards much greater monitoring and regulation of all sectors which began in the early 1980s. If this is the case, even the move towards markets based on "an ethical ideal of persuasion between individuals who are legally equal and free" seems to have been pulled back into the hierarchical straitjacket (Ring and van de Ven, 1992), surely the very straitjacket that current policies are seeking to escape. If this is so, the move to a quasi-market may be more concerned with the appearance of choice than its reality. Indeed, some US scholars suggest that contracting and other forms of purchase of service are simply a means of hiding the growth of government from public scrutiny, and that the penetration of government through contracting "has resulted in an unprecedented growth and involvement of government in the affairs of private organisations" (Smith and Lipsky, 1992, p 249).

Smith and Lipsky (1992) seem resistant to the idea of government involvement with the independent sector. We would not share this view. Indeed, it can be argued that the growth of a diverse sector in the 1980s has owed much to government funding, a significant part of which has been fairly loosely controlled. And, as Fox (1974) and others since him have pointed out, the use of contracts does not have to be rigid. Ring and van de Ven (1992) argue that in "high risk" exchanges, organisations may engage in "relational" contracts based on trust rather than markets or hierarchies. Relational contracts with "welfare maximisers" as opposed to "impersonal contracting" for profit maximisers (see de St Croix, 1992) overcome the need for detailed scrutiny. Ring and van de Ven (1992) go on to argue that transactions cost economics theories ignore "the crucial role that informal, socially embedded personal relationships have in producing stable relations of trust, obligation and custom among formally independent firms". Though originating in relations between private firms in the market, this argument could be applied to funding relationships between government and independent organisations. It would certainly be consistent with economic theories of the existence of the voluntary sector at least, which explain it in terms of "contract failure" (Hansmann, 1987), ie that donors invest in not-for-profit organisations where there is information asymmetry and donors need to be assured that their funds will not be syphoned off into personal profit or gain.

The concept of a quasi-market fails to distinguish adequately between two quite different kinds of market: *producer markets* (which are essentially inter-organisational systems) and *consumer markets* (where the individual purchaser engages directly in a transaction with a provider of services). Writers on the Japanese experience suggest that if the West wishes to emulate their success they could do no better than explore the possibility of combining conditions of impersonal and free competition for final consumer goods with a highly collaborative, network-based forms of producer-goods market (Dore, 1983). Indeed the more one looks at existing producer-goods markets within the private sector the more hard-pressed one is to find any examples of impersonal free competition prevailing. In the 'real world' (something public sector managers are being increasingly exhorted to take cognisance of) personal ties, social norms and conventions play an inevitable role in the development of inter-organisational relations (Granovetter 1985). In community care, we are dealing largely with a producer market and one which is concerned with the kind of 'high risk' exchanges for which, Fox (1974) and Ring and van de Ven (1992) argue, relational contracts are needed. Certainly, government guidance envisages close ongoing relationships with providers rather than short-term contracts (Department of Health and Price

Waterhouse, 1991, p 11 as cited in Lewis, 1993). This is some way from a pure market, even in the quasi-market form.

But this still runs the danger of taking us back to the first problem that we have identified, whereby entry to the market is more and more restricted to those who are known. If relational contracts are too cosy, this may lead to what Propper (1992) has called "regulator capture".

There is a need for a trade-off between quality and regulation that will focus on *building quality in* rather than *testing quality out* (ie quality assurance and management rather than quality control). We would contend that regulation needs to be balanced with development. Accreditation systems can be used to support the development of good practice. Monitoring forms without training and support will achieve little. But training cannot be injected into small voluntary and private organisations without an understanding of their capacity. There is sometimes a limited recognition of the value of training, especially when pressure of work is high. It is hard to make funding for training explicit in voluntary organisations and it is readily cut when budgets are tight. Also there is a strong likelihood that trained staff will not stay with the organisation that invests in their training. Smaller organisations can ill afford the investment if it will mean that staff move on to statutory organisations or larger organisations who can pay more and offer career prospects.

Networks can provide smaller organisations with access to training. But questions then arise as to how to assure standards within the sort of federated structure that is common to many national organisations with autonomous local branches, like Age Concern England. Values and priorities differ from area to area.

## A continued role for government

The move towards a mixed economy of care is one which has the support of politicians from the opposition benches as well as government. But the introduction of markets into social care can be supported for very different reasons and thus have very different outcomes. The outcome hinges upon the kind of market that is to be created and the impact this has upon the 'independent sector'.

In the social services field, as in many others, policies which demand that public services are increasingly delivered by 'third-party' non-statutory organisations are changing the nature of the public management task. As Salamon (1989) argues, instead of command and control, public managers must increasingly rely on bargaining and persuasion. This point is echoed in the UK by de St Croix (1992) who talks of "influence rather than authority". Here, much has been said in recent years about the 'enabling authority'. Local government in particular is being expected to move from a position where its major concern is with the direct delivery of services to one where it encourages others to deliver.

There are, of course, many ways of encouraging people to deliver, which will depend on the values and assumptions of those empowered to do so. In a 'Ridleyesque' model, this can mean an authority which meets once a year to let contracts. But, as we have seen, a number of authors have stressed the variety of ways in which contracts or independent services can be managed (Ring and van de Ven, 1992) along a spectrum from rigid specification and control to relationships which depend on trust and integration. An alternative and still wider notion of the public management task is one which would shift the centre of gravity of the authority to the community which surrounds it, rather than its own organisation and systems. In a recent publication, Stewart and Taylor (1993) have coined the term "orchestration" to describe a new strategy for local government, which would place the emphasis on its relations with the outside world rather than a preoccupation with internal structures and procedures. This would highlight the development roles we have identified in both creating a market and developing quality services which reflect the diversity of need. But crucially, it would be based on relationships mediated through the network principle as much as through either markets or hierarchies. The role of government is thus to 'orchestrate' networks of independent organisations according to a set of themes (eg quality, choice, user empowerment) which reflect its core values.

If the current diversity is to be maintained and extended in community care, there is a role for government as a 'social entrepreneur', whose task is to stimulate through funding and other powers a market of alternative providers which offers choice to the user and carer. This would include ensuring the provision of information; advice and advocacy to help users through this range of provision, to ensure their rights to a quality service, and to help providers to meet these requirements; and stimulating and encouraging the formation of organisations which give a voice to disadvantaged citizens and users (Taylor et al, 1992). But its credentials for playing this entrepreneurial role need to rest on the accountability and debate that should arise from local democratic control. And there are many pressures in the opposite direction. Local social services departments are facing a "cascade of change" (Audit Commission, 1992) and a climate of severe financial restraint which combine to force attention back to internal operations and agendas.

## Markets or participatory networks?

Much of our thinking about current changes within the welfare state has been influenced by the transactions costs economics associated with Williamson (1975, 1985). However the markets and hierarchies framework has encountered great difficulty in satisfactorily explaining many contemporary forms of economic governance such as those found in Japan. In the last few years a number of writers (Lincoln, 1990; Powell, 1990; Larson, 1992) have argued that 'network' or 'clan' (Ouchi, 1980) based models should be seen as a distinctive third form of governance, one relying upon a high degree of reciprocity and collaboration. Networks are built upon and reproduce high trust/high discretion relationships. They commonly occur within milieux where common value systems or high degrees of social familiarity based upon previous interaction prevail. As Lincoln (1990, pp 280-81) notes, a strong definition of social networks within the sociological and anthropological literature "views such ties as generally informal, diffuse, and personalistic relations of trust, obligation and affect which emerge through natural evolutionary processes, not the formal designs of rational decision makers".

It is immediately apparent that 'networks' describe the mode of governance which has prevailed within the voluntary and community sectors, although they are not confined to this sector (this argument is further developed in Taylor, Hoggett and Bartlett, 1993). They also describe the type of relationship which is needed to promote effective cooperative relationships between purchasers and providers (the 'relational contracts' we have referred to) and the other organisations through which people seek to further their welfare. They further describe the relationship that government, at least at local level, will need to develop in the new institutional environment that the quasi-market has created. But if too narrow a concept of the market is adopted, it is precisely this mode of governance which may now be under threat.

For there is considerable debate as to the role of government in the market.   On the one hand, developments towards a mixed economy could provide the opportunity to draw a richer variety of providers into the public sphere by encouraging forms of local democracy which enable diversity within a framework of public accountability, support and discussion.   On the other hand, they can be seen as an attempt to undermine the public sphere by taking services out of local democratic control and exposing them much more directly to the disciplines of the open market.   Given the political philosophy of the present government and the present climate of resource constraint, there are dangers that the second line of development is more likely to occur.   For the citizenship that goes with the market is essentially the citizenship which Lowery et al (1992) define as the classical liberal form of citizenship, "founded on individual and property rights that enable citizens to address problems of interdependence via exchange".   This citizenship entails "contracting to establish a civic entity to provide agreed-upon public goods and services and to enforce the contractual arrangement", with "a sharp delineation of public and private spheres, with the latter having priority".   We need a wider analysis which goes beyond the market and the tools of the economist to achieve optimal patterns of welfare, one which recognises the other motivating factors that lead people to form and use organisations which may not be optimally efficient in the economists' terms and which draws on sociological, psychological and political explanations.   For the remainder of this chapter, our concern is with the need for a political analysis which takes the concept of citizenship beyond that of the market.

The concept of the public sphere refers to the existence of a space in our social world in which issues are open to debate, reflection and moral argument. This space partly coincides with the exercise of government within the system of representative democracy, but it is much more than this.   Crucially the public sphere also coincides with the extent of participatory democracy existing within a given society - the autonomous activities of clubs, associations, voluntary and philanthropic organisations, campaign groups, cultural associations, self-help and advocacy organisations, and so on. For this is the seed-bed from which new needs spring, new visions of social relations are constructed and new concepts of social justice are demanded.

Many authors have stressed the importance of plural institutions to a democratic society, from de Tocqueville onwards.   Voluntary and community organisations are not just service providers. A number of organisations in the voluntary sector have been set up to empower their members - service users, usually excluded groups and communities - by giving them a voice in the way services are provided, whoever may provide them, and in entitlement for service. Others, though primarily service providers, have increasingly seen the need to advocate for those they serve (NCVO, 1991). As Anheier and Seibel point out (1990) they "combine aspects of social and political integration with economic objectives" and any analysis which tries to separate out these functions fails to appreciate the nature of the sector (Taylor and Lewis, 1993). In a system which is increasingly fragmented it may be argued that their social and political roles are as important as they have ever been and have a crucial role alongside government in holding diverse systems of provision accountable.

The kinds of organisation we are discussing have in the past been funded by local authorities and are often the channels through which much of the consultation required by government (eg in community care planning) takes place. In budgets which are increasingly defined by service provision, it is increasingly difficult to find space for them, while other larger organisations find their advocacy role prejudiced by the role they are taking on as contractors for the state. And, crucially, the erosion of local government powers means that the channels for influence themselves may give way increasingly to more individual mechanisms, based on consumer charters. While the latter are important, they do not replace the need for a wider democratic accountability for service planning, purchasing policies and decisions about entitlement. The danger is that by thinking only of the service providing function of community organisations, their contribution to the maintenance of a vibrant public sphere is overlooked and subsequently undermined. This could be seen as part of that wider trend within the public sector in which democracy is seen primarily as a 'cost' rather than a 'benefit' (CIPFA, 1988)

## Conclusion

It is our contention in this chapter that pluralism and choice will best be served by policies which encourage and stimulate a variety of provision and develop a diverse market in community care. We suggest, however, that the introduction of quasi-markets in their present form could be leading away from choice not towards it. There are a number of perverse incentives in current policy, which could prejudice the potential for a wide range of organisations to enter the care market, whether it is defined in the narrow quasi-market sense or in our broader sense of all organisations through which people seek to further their welfare. They also run the risk of extending government ownership into the independent sector rather than the reverse so that the transfer of services from government to independent organisations will be symbolic rather than real.

If this tendency is to be countered we need to learn more about patterns of provision and how they can be optimalised. What is the healthiest range of organisations? What encourages the formation and survival of such organisations in the real world? How can a diversity of organisational forms and sizes be woven into a reliable system of provision? To do this we need to supplement the market analysis with a political and sociological understanding of the new institutional environment and how it can be generated and regenerated.

Quasi-market models recognise that the advantages of the market cannot work without a role for government in the distribution of welfare. But we would go further than this. We have argued for an interventive role for government which goes beyond handing out contracts or even policing the operation of the market. Instead we would see for it an active development role, but one which is based on an active democratic involvement which goes beyond the paternalism of the post-war era. This will marry the concern for customers which has sprung from the market with a concern for citizens, which is a peculiarly misunderstood word in the UK. In this respect, the current erosion of local government powers and undermining of the autonomy of the community sector is a transformation in precisely the wrong direction.

But if we are to avoid the mistakes of the post-war welfare state, government's role must be based on its ability to negotiate the participative democracy to which independent organisations themselves contribute. Thus the culture of government and of democracy itself needs to be transformed. Such an approach would move us away from the markets and hierarchies of past analysis to an approach which focuses on value-led networks and relationships between organisations.

## Note

1. *Values and management in community care* is mapping the range of non-statutory organisations in community care in three localities and developing frameworks for understanding the complex network of players in this territory, the different forms they take and the different pressures they face.

## References

Anheier, H. and Seibel, W. (1990) *The third sector: comparative studies of nonprofit organisations*, Berlin: de Gruyter.

Audit Commission (1992) *Community care: managing the cascade of change*, London: HMSO.

CIPFA (1988) *Accounting for support services*, London: Chartered Institute of Public and Financial Accountants.

de St Croix, R. (1992) *Can quality be assured in an uncertain world?*, Studies in Decentralisation and Quasi-Markets no 10, Bristol: SAUS Publications, School for Advanced Urban Studies, University of Bristol.

Di Maggio, P. and Powell, W.W. (1983) 'The iron cage revisited: institutional isomorphism and collective rationality in organisational fields', *American Sociological Review*, vol 48, pp 147-60.

Dore, R. (1983) 'Goodwill and the spirit of market capitalism', *British Journal of Sociology*, vol 34, pp 459-82.

Fox, A. (1974) *Beyond contract: work, power and trust relations*, London: Faber.

Granovetter, M. (1985) 'Economic action and social structure: the problem of embeddedness', *American Journal of Sociology*, vol 91, no 3, pp 481-510.

Hadley, R. and Hatch, S. (1981) *Social welfare and the failure of the state: centralised social services and participatory alternatives*, London: Allen and Unwin.

Hansmann, H. (1987) 'Economic theories of nonprofit organisation', in W.W. Powell (ed) *The nonprofit sector: a research handbook*, Yale: Yale University Press.

Hoggett, P. and Kallay, L. (1993) *The development of the small business sector in Hungary*, Working Paper no 117, Bristol: SAUS Publication, School for Advanced Urban Studies, University of Bristol.

Hoyes, L., Jeffers, S., Means, R., Lart, R. and Taylor, M. (1993) *User empowerment and the reform of community care*, Studies in Decentralisation and Quasi-Markets no 16, Bristol: SAUS Publications, School for Advanced Urban Studies, University of Bristol.

Kramer, R. (1992) 'Voluntary agencies and the contract culture: dream or nightnmare?', Paper presented to the Annual Conference of ARNOVA, Yale University, November.

Kramer, R. and Grossman, B. (1987) 'Contracting for social services: process management and resource dependencies', *Social Services Review*, pp 32-35.

Larson, A. (1992) 'Network dyads in entrepreneurial settings: a study of the governance of exchange processes', *Administrative Science Quarterly*, vol 37, no 1, pp 76-104.

Le Grand, J. (1992) *Paying for or providing welfare*, Studies in Decentralisation and Quasi-Markets no 16, Bristol: SAUS Publications, School for Advanced Urban Studies, University of Bristol.

Lewis, J. (1993) 'Developing the mixed economy of care: emerging issues for voluntary organisations', *Journal of Social Policy*, vol 22, no 2, pp 173-92.

Lincoln, J. (1990) 'Japanese organisation theory and organisation theory', *Research in Organisational Behaviour*, vol 12, pp 255-94.

Lowery, D., de Hoog, R. and Lyons, W.E. (1992) 'Citizenship in the empowered locality', *Urban Affairs Quarterly*, vol 28, no 1, pp 69-103.

Mabbott, J. (1993) *Local authority funding for voluntary organisations*, London: NCVO Policy Department.

Marceau, J. (1990) 'The dwarves of capitalism: the structure of production and the economic culture of the small manufacturing firm', in G. Redding and S. Clegg (eds) *Capitalism in contracting cultures*, Berlin: de Gruyter.

NCVO (1991) *Cause and effect: a survey of campaigning in the voluntary sector*, London: NCVO.

Ouchi, W. (1980) 'Markets, bureaucracies and clans', *Administrative Science Quarterly*, vol 25, pp 120-42.

Powell, W. (1990) 'Neither market nor hierarchy: network forms of organisation', *Research in Organisational Behaviour*, vol 12, pp 295-336.

Propper, C. (1992) *Is further regulation of quasi-markets in welfare necessary?*, Studies in Decentralisation and Quasi-Markets no 14, Bristol: SAUS Publications, School for Advanced Urban Studies, University of Bristol.

Ring, P.S. and van de Ven, A.H. (1992) 'Structuring cooperative relationships between organisations', *Strategic Management Journal*, vol 13, pp 483-98.

Salamon, L.M. and Anheier, H.K. (1992) 'In search of the non-profit sector I: the question of definitions', *Voluntas*, vol 3, no 2, pp 125-52.

Salamon, L.M. (1989) *Beyond privatisation: the tools of government action*, Washington DC: The Urban Institute Press.

Smith, S.R. and Lipsky, M. (1992) 'Privatisation in health and human services', *Journal of Health Politics, Policy and Law*, vol 17, no 2.

Stewart, M. and Taylor, M. (1993) *Local government community leadership: the strategic role of the local authority,* Luton: Local Government Management Board.

Taylor, M., Kendall, J. and Fenyo, A. (1993) 'The survey of local authority payments to voluntary and charitable organsiation', in Charities Aid Foundation, *Charity Trends*, 16th edition, Tonbridge: Charities Aid Foundation.

Taylor, M. Hoggett, P. and Bartlett, W. (1993) 'How does the ant shift the rubber tree plant: networks, hierarchies and markets in modern democracy', Paper presented at the Well-being in Europe by Strengthening the Third Sector Conference, Barcelona, May.

Taylor, M and Lewis, J. (1993) 'Contracting: what does it do to voluntary and non-profit organisations', Paper presented at the Contracting: Selling or Shrinking Conference, South Bank University and NCVO, July.

Taylor, M., Means, R., Hoyes, L. and Lart, R. (1992) *User empowerment in community care: unravelling the issues*, Studies in Decentralisation and Quasi-Markets no 11, Bristol: SAUS Publications, School for Advanced Urban Studies, University of Bristol.

Williamson, O.E. (1975) *Markets and hierarchies: analysis and antitrust implications*, New York: Free Press.

Williamson, O.E. (1985) *The economic institutions of capitalism*, New York: Free Press.

Wolfenden Commission (1978) *The future of voluntary organisations*, London: Croom Helm.

*part three*

# HEALTH

*nine*

# THE EVOLUTION OF QUASI-MARKETS IN THE NHS: EARLY EVIDENCE

## Ewan Ferlie

## Introduction

Throughout the UK public sector, we see the legislatively driven introduction of quasi-markets in settings where previously resources were allocated through planning based mechanisms. Alongside this top-down restructuring lie important changes to control strategies as traditional management by hierarchy is giving way to new style management by contract.

It is true that these are still 'inward facing' rather than 'outward facing' markets given the range of regulatory controls that the government has retained (see Chapter 1). However the present situation may represent an unstable transitionary phase and elsewhere it has been argued that overall the pace of change - at least in health care - is accelerating and that real "organisational transformation" may occur (Ashburner and Ferlie, 1993). This is a counter intuitive finding given the common view that reorganisations in the public sector are little more than 'relabelling' exercises.

Scholars working in the field of public sector management - as in other fields - need to generate a new discourse better to describe and analyse these phenomena that are arising. Some macro level consequences of the changes have been well explored (Le Grand, 1991; Maynard, 1991). Useful in some ways, from the point of view of one who is interested in questions of organisational behaviour, these accounts are over abstract and removed from the phenomena under observation.  Cause effect relationships (eg the effect of monetary incentives on behaviour) may be attributed rather than demonstrated.  A major theme in this chapter is therefore to tilt the analysis further towards the study of organisational behaviour at local level.  The analytic focus should shift towards the micro politics of the public sector organisation and indeed of the interorganisational network.

This switch of focus should not, however, pave the way to endless and purely descriptive case studies.  This would be to reinforce the atheoretical empiricism characteristic of much British social science.  The redeeming feature of highly abstract models lies in the explicit nature of their assumptions or propositions and the ability to test these propositions against data.  A second theme in this chapter is therefore the development of a theoretical base which can generate propositions which are then testable against case study data.  There is a need in any case to undertake some theoretical groundclearing in the new landscape.  This should also help to generate a more grounded theory which takes into account changing patterns of organisational behaviour in a way that is beyond the capacity of more schematic approaches.

## Methodology

The introductory section argued that our theoretical focus now needs to move towards a greater concern with the micro politics of the organisation and indeed of the interorganisational network.  This reformulation also has implications for preferred methodology, shifting us towards longitudinal case study work and away from econometric modelling.

However, in order to help generate grounded theory, it is helpful to undertake comparative case study work where there is likely to be variability in outcomes (in the organisational rather than clinical sense) between the sites in the sample.  We can then begin to ask such questions as: why was *this* the organisational outcome in site A, but *that* the organisational outcome in site B?  This approach was found to be useful in an earlier analysis of variation in the rate and pace of strategic service change between DHAs (Pettigrew et al, 1992) in which a more general model was derived inductively from the cross case data.

## Research design

This chapter reports data from a NHS based longitudinal research project which examined the role of the new health authorities and trusts from 1990 to 1993 following the introduction of reforms to their membership in 1990. This project was funded by the National Health Service Training Directorate (NHSTD) with support from the National Association of Health Authorities and Trusts (NAHAT). A key strategic issue facing these boards was the creation and evolution of the quasi-market in health care in their localities.

An intensive approach necessarily results in an ability to undertake only a limited number of case studies making it difficult to generalise from the sample to the population. In this study - which was planned as national in character - we responded to this criticism by making provision for a postal survey as well as intensive case analysis (see Ashburner and Cairncross, 1993).

The qualitative module consisted of eleven comparative and longitudinal case studies. The sample took the form of two 'nested hierarchies' of interlinking health care organisations: two RHAs; three DHAs; two FHSAs; and four acute NHS trusts. These sites were divided between a team of four researchers.

Methods included the analysis of written material, attendance at board meetings over a considerable period of time and semi-structured interviews with board members and other key respondents. About 20 interviews were undertaken in each site, with material gathered from non-executives, executives and chairs.

We believe that the degree of access obtained to board meetings is an unusual feature of this study, giving us a rare opportunity to observe 'boards in action'. This chapter will report qualitative data from two sites (a DHA and interlinked trust) where the author undertook the fieldwork personally.

## Literature review

If we analyse the theoretic base of much recent writing about quasi-markets, much of it derives either from standard microeconomics (eg Brazier et al, 1990) or from the 'new institutional economics' or the transactions costs perspective based on the work of Williamson (1975, 1985; also in Aoki et al, 1990) which claims to be more open to organisation theory. New modes of organisation arise because they are 'efficient' in the light of changed circumstances. Applications of this approach to the substantive field of health care include Bartlett (1991) and Burke and Goddard (1990). There are indeed signs of a transactions costs 'boom' emerging which may sweep all before it.

However, the transactions costs perspective has come under longstanding attack from organisational sociology for its neglect of such factors as power, ideology and culture (Perrow, 1981; Bauer and Cohen, 1983). This chapter will try to generate an alternative way of conceiving of quasi-markets (see also Ferlie, 1993, for a more sustained theoretical piece), accessing some of the new work emerging from the rising field of economic sociology.

## Relational markets

We have considered the relational view of markets elsewhere at greater length (Ferlie et al, 1993). This model of markets developed out of the concerns of marketeers and is associated with the Scandinavian work of the 1980s (Ford, 1990). It was felt that the conventional view of an active marketeer, passive consumers and an atomistic market restricted understanding of what actually happened in markets. The neo-classical model of markets assumes that markets are populated by individuals or simple firms, yet economic life is often dominated by a small number of large and complex firms which behave in a different way.

A number of important implications follow from seeing markets in more relational terms. Unlike individual consumers, corporate buyers might often interact with sellers. The relationship between companies might display a complex history of adaptation, commitment, trust and conflict. Buyer-seller relationships are but one example of sets of relations which may shape a market, as buyer-buyer and seller-seller relations may also be important.

The interaction process is not seen as solely revolving product/service exchange, but also includes important processes of social exchange, undertaken so as to reduce uncertainty and to build trust. The result may be a common value system which emphasises source loyalty. There is a tendency to 'keep things in the family', so that buyers - once locked into a set of relationships - may be relatively inert in seeking new sources of supply.

A relational market might display the following 'signs and symptoms'. A relatively small number of well established buyers and sellers could be locked into long-run contracts or repeat buying. Buying decisions can be made on the basis of soft data (eg trust) as well as hard information. It may even be impossible to generate the hard information ideally required. The result is that 'reputation' is a key intangible asset on which providers trade.

## Social embeddedness

An attack on the assumptions of the 'new institutional economics' was apparent in an important paper by Granovetter (1985). Economic transactions needed to be seen as much more socially embedded than in the transactions costs framework. The focal unit of analysis was less the transactions and more the social relationship.

Granovetter (1985) argued that Williamson's work overstated the role of governance systems and of hierarchy in regulating transactions rather than the trust so necessary for economic life to continue. For Granovetter, the research problem becomes one of tracing the actual, concrete, interactions of individuals and groups and considering how these networks influence trading and the formation of prices within the market (Granovetter and Swedberg, 1992). Others may feel that the continued development of a grounded theory is also of key importance.

A further question is whether such embeddedness of economic behaviour is changing over time. One view might be that economic behaviour was heavily embedded in social relations in pre-market societies, but becomes much more autonomous with modernisation. Instead of economic life being submerged in the market, these relations become an epiphenomenon of the market. Modernisation is thus associated with marketisation and the reduction of social ties (Polanyi, 1957). This view has been questioned by Granovetter and Swedberg (1992) who argue that even in modern markets patterns of social relations still shape trading. In professional services (eg medicine), information on reputation transmitted through organisational and occupational networks is critical in establishing market position.

A key issue of quasi-markets concerns the long-term effects of the introduction of contracts on patterns of organisational and interorganisational behaviour. Will contracting lead to the atomisation of social relations? Socio-legal scholars such as MacNeil (1974, 1978, 1983) have distinguished between various types of contracts: commonly classical, neo-classical and relational forms of contracts.

The development of a 'relational contract' is seen as resulting from the increased duration and complexity of contracts. The contract becomes increasingly embedded in a social relation with its own history and norms. Sociological purists might argue that the term 'relational contract' is almost a contradiction in terms, because in close relationships diffuse social norms of trust and reciprocity replace contracting as a means for restructuring recurring transactions. MacNeil (1983), however, contends that law facilitates the construction of relations because it fosters cooperation through internal and external values of contract behaviour based on pointless past contacts.

Professional networks in particular may well prove influential in shaping the relational market. Classically the uncertainty facing consumers in health care and their need to trust the producer could result in a continuing willingness to hand over responsibility to professionals who speak with great authority in decision making. The managerial bloc - although increasing in importance and more willing to confront professionals in some areas - can be expected in general to work in alliance with professionals. Most managers continue to be recruited from within the NHS and attempts to break the mould by bringing in managers from the private sector have generally failed.

In addition proxy consumers (themselves often medical personnel such as GP fundholders) will often have more power than individual consumers. As a result, professional and managerial control will continue to prove more powerful than radical consumerism and will work to restrain any market based solutions.

One might expect well established local cliques and networks to continue to dominate decision making. Within the quasi-market there will be continuing barriers to market entry and exit; inherited contracting patterns may be rolled forward and there may be little reletting of contracts.

## Institutional embeddedness

Markets may not only be socially embedded, but also institutionally embedded. This shifts us away from the micro level analysis of social networks and towards the more macro level of economic (and indeed social and legal) institutions. While in his most recent work Granovetter (1992) retains his network perspective, there is now more focus on an institutional level. However, he argues that existing networks of personal and political relations in turn shape economic institutions which act in effect as "congealed social networks". Institutions are to be seen as socially constructed by cliques of actors.

This view still has its roots in social network theory and is very different from those theorists who see institutions more as forces in their own right, independent of individuals' motives and actions. In these accounts, notions of organisational fields, legitimating myths and institutional discourses assume greater prominence. This is a major area of debate between macro and micro theorists which can only be briefly touched upon in the space available in this chapter (see Powell and Di Maggio, 1991, for a fine review of the field; also Dingwall and Strong, 1985, for a critique).

While there is no consensus within the field, at least some theorists draw attention to the importance of the institutional context. For instance, Meyer and Rowan (1977) see modern formal organisations as operating in highly institutionalised contexts. Organisations are driven to incorporate the practices and procedures defined by prevailing rationalised concepts of legitimate work (eg 'hospitals should be business like'). Organisations that do so increase their legitimacy and their survival prospects, independent of the immediate efficacy of the acquired practices and procedures.

New organisational forms (Di Maggio and Powell, 1983) may arise not because of efficiency considerations but because of strong fads and fashions in organisational design and strong pressures to conform to centrally mandated templates. The state and the professions are seen as particularly important sources for structuring such organisational fields, with these pressures being particularly strong in public sector organisations which relate to powerful professions or which are dependent upon state finance.

This perspective draws attention to the role of government, of NHS higher tiers, of the professions and of national associations (eg NAHAT) in structuring the health care field.

Our three central propositions derived from this review of theoretical literature are thus as follows:

● that quasi-markets in the health care sector can be best seen in 'relational' terms;

● that quasi-markets in the health care sector are - and will continue to be - socially embedded;

●    that quasi-markets in the health care sector are - and will
      continue to be - institutionally embedded.

**Early evidence from the NHS**

Some case study evidence is now drawn from two localities: a
DHA and its previous acute unit, which subsequently achieved
second wave trust status.  Retrospective analysis was carried out
back to 1982, and real time observation of board meetings took
place between Summer 1991 and April 1993.  At this point the
DHA formally merged with neighbouring authorities to form a
larger purchasing organisation.

*The DHA, now a purchasing authority*

> [The district] has become more innovative than most ... it is
> better at managing change than most ... very much middle of
> the road in terms of service provision, service development
> issues, all those kinds of things because its profile very much
> has been as a district which has relied in service provision
> terms quite heavily on the London teaching hospitals ... we've
> got good managers, we've done a lot of good work on
> management development and organisational development.
> (Executive Director, DHA)

This DHA has been moving towards a new purchasing role since
1989 and can be seen as a rapid mover in this shift.  For instance,
the public health function has developed rapidly.  It is located in a
semi-rural area, with a mainly white, middle class population.  The
DHA moved from its old boundaries (1982-Autumn 1991), through
a transitional purchasing consortium stage (Autumn 1991 - Spring
1993) to full merger with two neighbouring DHAs to form a new
purchasing organisation (Spring 1993 onwards).  These shifts are
consistent with national trends.
     The district is regarded as a well managed authority.  It has long
been trying to rationalise and redevelop its acute sector facilities
onto one site, and this agenda has now been picked up by the acute
trust.  There was no loss of financial control in the 1980s and the
district achieved considerable efficiency savings.  A distinctive
approach to general management was evident as early as 1986 with
an  emphasis  on  teamwork,  devolution  and  organisational

development. There have been a number of strong authority chairpersons in this locality.

Perhaps because of this past track record of success, the note is one of very substantial continuity at senior management level and many of the officers in the authority went on to achieve new posts in the new consortium and authority. The chief executive officer (CEO) and director of finance, for instance, both go back ten years. There is little evidence of appointments of 'outsiders' to senior posts. Many of the non-executive members were personally known to the chairperson and so also could been seen as a coherent social grouping. A senior doctor continued to serve as advisor on the new DHA until he became medical director for the new trust, and then withdrew from the DHA.

Between 1989 and 1991, the pace of development of the purchasing function seemed modest at DHA level. The chairperson and all but one of the non-executive members, for instance, were continuing members, as were all the executive members. Much time was spent on national initiatives (eg reducing waiting list times) and some on continuing management responsibilities for directly managed units. However with the formation of the purchasing consortium, and as the acute unit prepared to go out to trust status in Spring 1992, the pace of change began to accelerate.

The district agreed to full merger from April 1993, under a firm steer from the CEO and RHA, and the non-executives in truth seemed to exercise only a minor role in making these key decisions. With the formation of the new authority in 1993, although most of the executive directors won the new posts, only one non-executive from this locality continued onto the new authority. The perception was that the authority was now rapidly developing its purchasing role, for example, paying much more attention to liaison with GPs than previously.

## The previous acute unit, now a NHS trust

> Trust status is not an end in itself, it is a way of helping us to do what we were going to do anyway. (Executive Director, NHS trust)

The other case study has taken place within an acute hospital group which had previously been the DHA's acute unit, but which achieved second wave trust status in April 1992. The pattern in this area is for large towns about twenty miles apart each to have their general hospitals, so there is little 'natural' competition for general services. This hospital is also well placed to benefit by the movement of services out of London.

The main site is set in spacious grounds and the plan is to move services presently provided in peripheral hospitals onto the main site. It must also be said that this agenda is longstanding and has proved intractable in the past (due to constraints on capital). The potential for greater freedom over capital was seen as a significant benefit of trust status. The case for becoming a trust was not presented in terms of the market, but in terms of autonomy: 'you are the master of your own ship'. Consultant opinion moved behind the application for trust status following the collapse of the regional capital programme in 1990.

While general management had proved influential at district level from 1986, there was a view that it 'never really happened' at hospital level, at least until the appointment of a new unit general manager (UGM) (with a human resources background) from outside the locality in 1990. From very early on he maintained a distant relationship with the DHA (usually not attending DHA meetings). There was also a clearout at middle management level. At the same time, there was much more emphasis on building an organisation based on principles of learning and development, rather than competing solely on price. The trust was therefore developing a strong personality which was rather different from many other trusts.

All the executive directors appointed to the board were internal appointments. The CEO had previously been the UGM and had steered the successful trust application. Both the medical director and the director of nursing, for example, were long serving and highly respected. The chairperson had a long record of service in charitable work with the hospital. However, the non-executives represented a mixture of continuity and change. There were two strong appointments from outside the service who were seen as influential in contributing to the significant changes in culture that were apparent at least at the top of the organisation:

> I think what we as executive directors who are basically health service professionals have done is start thinking of ourselves as a business, and that, probably, would not have come about so quickly if we had non-executive directors who had come from a similar background to ourselves. (CEO, NHS trust)

However, expectations of increased autonomy were not always fulfilled. While the trust managed to escape the control of region, it was monitored by the new Management Executive Outpost which took a keen interest in financial control. At the end of its first financial year the trust curbed elective work in order to restore its financial control.

## The purchaser/provider relationship

Initially, there was pressure from higher tiers to restrain the pace of change and to ensure 'no surprises'. In terms of local market structure, the DHA was overwhelmingly the prime purchaser of the trust's services. Extra contractual referral (ECR) income was relatively small. There was no sign of an expanding private sector and no expressed desire by the prime purchaser to switch basic services between general hospitals. In effect, here was a monopoly purchaser relating to a monopoly provider. By 1993, however, the local market was beginning to develop as more GP fundholders came on stream and a greater plurality of purchasers was apparent.

The traditional district/unit relationship has been evolving into a purchaser/provider relationship in which the hospital (now NHS trust) can be seen as a full and equal partner. More and more, the key issues centre on the setting, monitoring and financing of the contract. So far, one year block contracts have remained the preferred form of contract locally.

The relationship between purchaser and provider can (in the judgement of the researcher) best be described as *negotiative*. For example, the loading of contract risk between purchaser and provider is a recurrent concern. This relationship is not fixed, but changes its character subtly through time - 1992, for example, was seen as more difficult than 1993.

There are many areas where the interests of both parties coincide (eg repatriation of work from London). Networks (eg the clinical network) continue to cross the two bodies. By contrast, contact between the two groups of non-executives seems much weaker. It would thus be erroneous to see the relationship between the two parties as simply conflictual.

However it cannot be seen as fully cooperative either. The trust very quickly developed its own identity, based on an ideology of autonomy. There was a feeling within the purchasing authority that as a consequence traditional informal flows of information were drying up. Continuing negotiations were evident in relation to contract setting and the parties went to arbitration two years running.  For example, there were long negotiations between the two CEOs in relation to the signing of the 1992/93 contract where issues included:

- how to fund the higher than expected increase in activity;

- whether an allowance should be made for backlog maintenance;

- the level of detail of any quality specifications in the contract.


## Concluding discussion

### Empirical findings

So far the pace of development of the local health care market has been slow.  It remains very much an 'inward facing' and regulated market.   There have been as yet few changes to services.  Contracting is still based on block contracts rather than cost and volume contracts.  However, there are the first signs that the pace of change is now beginning to accelerate, with the expansion of GP fundholding and the liberalisation of regulations concerning the use of private capital.

We are still at the early stages of a long-term change process.  However, the changes so far to forms of organisation and management have been very significant.  We are seeing much more than the conventional interpretation of public sector reorganisation as no more than a 'relabelling' process and could be in the first stages of an "organisational transformation" (Ashburner and Ferlie, 1993).  The case study evidence suggested that the DHA has made a major transition to its new purchasing role, and that the NHS trust is significantly more 'business like' and autonomous than the old acute unit.


### Theoretical implications

The theoretical purpose of this paper has been to conceptualise the internal market on the basis of a framework rooted in the 'new economic sociology' rather than from the conventional viewpoints of microeconomic theory or the 'new institutional economics'.

These ideas can be used to interrogate the early case study evidence presented so as to stimulate a dialogue between theory and data. Three core ideas were advanced.

1.  That the internal market must be seen as a *relational* market. Clearly, the case study evidence suggested that this was not an atomised market but rather one in which a monopoly purchaser was in more or less continuing negotiation with a monopoly provider. The negotiations between the two CEOs around the contract represented the core of this process. The relationship between the two parties was seen as continuing, perhaps even as indefinite.

    However, the view that the interaction process would include important processes of social exchange, undertaken so as to reduce uncertainty and to build trust was not confirmed. If anything, traditional informal flows of information seemed to be drying up. Different cultures and value systems could be seen as emerging in the trust and in the purchasing organisation, with very little staff movement between the two. This is consistent with a negotiative, rather than fully cooperative, approach to contracting.

2.  That the internal market is *socially embedded*. There was found to be a high degree of continuity in the personnel staffing at the upper reaches of both health care organisations. There is then a small health care elite (containing clinical, managerial and quasi-political components) which displays considerable stability at the apex of these organisations. Long-term careers emerge and continue despite reorganisation.

    Although the general picture is one of stability, there was also some change. Change to the composition of the board was more in evidence at trust level where influential outsiders were brought in as non-executives. Nevertheless, a number of different social networks continued to link the two bodies. In the judgement of the researcher, the professional network was the strongest, followed by the managerial network with (perhaps surprisingly) the links between non-executives being the weakest form of network.

3.  That the internal market is *institutionally embedded*. Much evidence was found to support this proposition and a social network approach by itself can be seen as too 'micro'. The

market is still very much 'inward facing', regulated by the higher tiers (region, the ME outpost). The practical expression of this can be seen in the regional/outpost based arbitration mechanism which was used two years running to resolve disputes between the purchaser and provider. Rules concerning 'prices', rates of financial return and productivity targets are all set centrally and transmitted downwards. There is in fact a potential contradiction between the rhetoric of free markets and the heavy weight of a continuing regulatory apparatus.

We conclude that this is a theoretical approach which is worthy of further exploration. This early case study is interesting, but more examples are needed before a pattern can be said to emerge. By linking theory and data in this way, it should be possible to produce a grounded theory which is sensitive to patterns of social and organisational behaviour.

## Note

Thanks are due to Dr David Hughes, University College of Swansea, for acting as discussant at the SAUS Conference and for his helpful comments on an earlier draft.

## References

Aoki, M., Gustaffson, B. and Williamson, O.E. (1990) *The firm as a nexus of treaties*, London: Sage.

Ashburner, L. and Cairncross, L. (1993) 'Membership of the 'new style' health authorities: continuity or change?' *Public Administration*, vol 71.

Ashburner, L. and Ferlie, E. (1993) *Organisational transformation and top down change - the case of the NHS*, Coventry: Centre for Corporate Strategy and Change, University of Warwick.

Bartlett, W. (1991) *Quasi-markets and contracts: a markets and hierarchies perspective on NHS reform*, Studies in Decentralisation and Quasi-Markets no 3, Bristol: SAUS Publications, School for Advanced Urban Studies, University of Bristol.

Bauer, M. and Cohen, E. (1983) 'The invisibility of power and economics: beyond markets and hierarchies', in A. Francis, J. Turk and P. Williams, *Power, efficiency and institutions*, London: Heinemann Educational Books.

Brazier, J., Hutton, J. and Jeavons, R. (1990) *Analysing health care systems: the economic context of NHS White Paper proposals*, York: Centre for Health Economics, University of York.

Burke, C. and Goddard, A. (1990) 'Internal markets - the road to inefficiency', *Public Administration,* vol 68, pp 389-96.

Di Maggio, P. and Powell, W.W (1983) 'The iron cage revisited - institutional isomorphism and collective rationality on organisational fields', *American Sociological Review*, vol 48, pp 147-60.

Dingwall, R. and Strong, P. (1985) 'The interactional study of organisations: a critique and reformulation', *Urban Life,* vol 14, no 2, pp 205-31.

Ferlie, E.B.(1993) 'The creation and evolution of quasi markets in the public sector', *Strategic Management Journal*, vol 13, Winter, pp 79-98.

Ferlie, E.B., Cairncross, L. and Pettigrew, A. (1993) 'Understanding internal markets in the NHS', in I. Tilly (ed) *Managing the internal market*, London: Paul Chapman.

Ford, D. (ed) (1990) *Understanding business markets*, London: Academic Press.

Granovetter, M. (1985) 'Economic action and social structure: the problem of embeddedness', *American Journal of Sociology*, vol 91, no 3, pp 481-510.

Granovetter, M. (1992) 'Economic institutions as social constructions: a framework for analysis', *Acta Sociologica*, vol 35, pp 3-11.

Granovetter, M. and Swedberg, R. (1992) *The sociology of economic life*, Oxford: Westview Press.

Le Grand, J. (1991) 'Quasi-markets and social policy', *Economic Journal*, vol 101, September, pp 1256-67.

MacNeil, I. (1974) 'The many futures of contracts', *Southern California Law Review*, vol 47, pp 691-816.

MacNeil, I. (1978) 'Contracts: adjustments of long-term economic relations under conditions of classical, neo-classical and relational contract law', *Northwestern University Law Review*, vol 72, pp 854-906.

MacNeil, I.(1983) 'Values in contract: internal and external', *Northwestern University Law Review*, vol 77, p 340.

Maynard, A. (1991) 'Developing the health care market', *Economic Journal*, vol 101, September, pp 1277-86.

Meyer, J.W. and Rowan, B. (1977) 'Institutionalised organisations: formal structure as myth and ceremony', *American Journal of Sociology*, vol 83, no 2, pp 340-63.

Perrow, C.(1981) 'Markets, hierarchies and hegemony', in A. van de Ven and W. Joyce (eds) *Perspectives on organisational design and behaviour*, Chichester: John Wiley.

Pettigrew, A.M., Ferlie, E.B. and McKee, L. (1992) *Shaping strategic change*, London: Sage.

Polanyi, K. (1957) 'The economy as instituted process', in K. Polanyi, C. Arensberg and C.M. Pearson (eds) *Trade and markets in the early empires*, New York: Free Press.

Powell, W.W. and Di Maggio, P.J. (1991) *The new institutionalism and organisational analysis*, London: University of Chicago Press.

Williamson, O.E. (1975) *Markets and hierarchies and anti-trust implications*, New York: Macmillan.

Williamson, O.E. (1985) *The economic institutions of capitalism*, New York: Free Press.

*ten*

---

# PLANNING AND MARKETS IN THE NHS

## Calum Paton

### Theoretical perspectives

It is important to analyse developments within the NHS from the perspective of policy analysis. From the present author's viewpoint, policy analysis draws primarily upon political science and microeconomics in order to understand both the rationale for quasi-markets and possible limitations upon the effective operation of quasi-markets within an NHS where an agenda which is both centralist and 'political' remains strong.

Microeconomics allows us to spell out the necessary conditions for a successful market. Some of these have been recently documented as a theoretical underpinning to the SAUS work on markets and quasi-markets (Le Grand and Bartlett, 1993) and have been mentioned in earlier chapters of this book. They comprise: appropriate market structures, such as competing providers and *possibly* competing purchasers; adequate information whereby providers can be monitored as to desired outcomes; appropriate motivation on the part of providers on the principle that, through the invisible hand, 'private vice produces public good'; a situation whereby the transactions costs of running markets rather than directly managing providers are under control and less in aggregate than the benefits of running markets; and - possibly - attention to equity (in a public sector market) such that patients/users/consumers are not disadvantaged as a result of inadequate finance or excessive need for healthcare by comparison with population averages.

The four fundamental characteristics of the NHS quasi-market can also be enumerated. They are as follows (again, a selective but salient list):

1.   the nature of regulation of providers;

2.   the fact that the purchaser and user are distinct (respectively the agent and principal);

3.   the fact that the service is globally cash limited;

4.   the fact that publicly defined rights must be incorporated into agreements between purchasers and providers.

Taking these in turn, characteristic 1 implies that, if the regulation of providers prevents them operating as profit maximising or quasi-profit maximising institutions, then the benefits of market behaviour may ironically be lost.  That is, the more 'altruistic' hospitals and other self-governing trusts are, the less they may fulfil the criteria of the market's 'invisible hand'.  In essence, one may be left with neither the advantages of the market nor the advantages of coherent planning.  A rationalised system may be impossible, and a comparison with the duplication and yet omission inherent in the US 'private but not-for-profit' hospital sector may well be an instructive one.

Furthermore, the nature of regulation of providers in the NHS - primarily of self-governing trusts in the near future - may effect the composition and nature of those trusts.  It may be efficient for trusts to comprise both hospital and community units together; that is, to be comprehensive, all-embracing trusts, perhaps even embracing all the services of what was previously a health district.  This would be 'efficient' if the total packages of patient care (for example, enabling 'seamless care' for particular clients who require both hospital and community services) can best be organised by a provider unit which maximises its cost-effectiveness ratio by taking responsibility for all services.

Furthermore, a comprehensive trust will tend to avoid the problems of 'cost shifting' between autonomous hospital trusts and autonomous community trusts.  Otherwise these might seek to maximise contract income and minimise expenditure, possibly with the adverse effect that hospitals seek to 'dump' patients onto the community and vice versa.

On the other hand, in the pre-reform NHS, it often became a truism that hospital services swallowed-up the budgets of community services whenever hospital resources were stretched. Separate hospital community trusts may be the best means of avoiding this. Ironically directly accountable hospital and community services - but self-managed in an operational sense as separate provider units - may be the best means of ensuring the benefits of separation without the costs of separation.

From the present perspective it should be noted that the US Health Maintenance Organisation (HMO) operates through direct control of providers and integration of both hospital and non-hospital services into one organisation. That is, the purchaser/provider split is diminished rather than increased by the operation of the HMO (although admittedly choice of purchaser - of HMO financed either by individuals, their employers or by government finance for the poor - exists as a counterweight to directly managed provision *within* the HMO).

The moot point for the purpose of the present argument is that the regulation of provision, according to political as well as economic criteria in the NHS, may mitigate the ability of trusts to be 'red in tooth and claw' and therefore to provide 'the public good from private vice'.

Regarding characteristic 2 of the quasi-market, the fact that the purchaser and user are distinct may have a number of consequences. Firstly, providers may market themselves directly to users/consumers and to GPs (non-fundholding as well as fundholding) such that a 'political head of steam' is built up to mandate the provision of certain types of services. Purchasers may be then constrained in their choices, in the real world of a political NHS where local pressures may still be strong (although mediated now through national politicians and members of Parliament rather than through quasi-representative local health authorities).

If the politics of Britain - as in so much of the 'advanced West' - is now governed by what Galbraith (1992) has called the values of the 'contented majority' and the 'culture of contentment', then such purchasing priorities, if so determined, may be those of the contented majority rather than the truly needy in society. That is, the discontented minority may have a raw deal if this dynamic operates in the reformed NHS. Another way of putting this is to say that the traditional argument that the NHS 'benefits the middle classes rather than the poor' may be enhanced by a dynamic of provider power rather than purchaser power, ironically as a result of both the purchaser/provider split and the purchaser/user split in the new NHS.

Secondly, where this does not apply, purchasers may not reflect users' wishes unless a particular incentive is created for them to reflect local wishes rather than either central criteria or their own autonomous criteria. Again, the nature of regulation rather than the dictates of microeconomic theory may determine outcomes in this area.

Regarding characteristic 3, a cash-limited NHS may mean that competition by providers is competition 'to do more for the same money', or indeed to do the same for less money, if public expenditure reviews and cuts bite in the future. That is, provider competition is a zero sum game. One provider's gain is another's loss. While this may still enable competition, it is difficult to see much of an incentive for maximising income as a result of provision of innovative services as a result. In practice, 'squeezing providers' in this way may simply lead to greater technical productivity or efficiency at the expense of either more appropriate services or what economists would call allocative efficiency. At the very least, allocative efficiency will only be achieved in the context of greater exploitation of the NHS's workers.

It might be argued that this is an argument opposite in direction to that of my previous argument, concerning the 'autonomous provider' ironically empowered more in the post-reform NHS than in the pre-reform NHS when providers *allegedly* 'did their own thing'. It is, however, possible to reconcile the two arguments. Providers can call the tune as regards priorities yet be forced to offer these priorities in a market place through greater productivity, due to limited finance. A further way of making the point is to say that money cannot follow the patient, but the patient must follow the contract and the money in order to ensure that referrals are kept within the NHS's available expenditure.

Regarding characteristic 4, one can distinguish between process rights and substantive rights. The Patients' Charter is an example of fairly minor 'process' rights whereby citizens are guaranteed certain types of treatment and providers. Purchasers, therefore, must be quite interventionist in dealing with providers, normally at the behest of central government's priorities. The purchaser/provider split may be something of a myth in such circumstances. More importantly, substantive rights involve rights to specific forms of health care in specific locations. In order to guarantee these, again central regulation in alliance with local purchaser wishes (or rather a rendering compatible of the two by whatever means) may ensure that a social or political agenda prevents provider competition according to market principles. If certain services, for example, must be available and must be available in a certain locale, then the scope for provider competition is reduced to something considerably more marginal. The result of such regulation might be a series of local monopolies which would have to be heavily controlled by purchasers to prevent excessive provider power.

A number of specific consequences are likely to flow from such theoretical considerations, comprising the necessary conditions for markets and the specific characteristics of the NHS quasi-market. The rest of this chapter discusses some of these consequences.

## Background

The Prime Minister's review of the NHS was instituted in January 1988 by the then Prime Minister, Margaret Thatcher, during a television interview on Panorama. The motivation was to take issue with the persistent claim that the NHS was underfunded, and attempt to turn attention instead to efficiency in the provision of health services (Paton, 1992). An additional interpretation has stressed the role of the medical profession in challenging the overall amount of money going to the NHS. It has been argued that as long as leading representative bodies of the medical profession were willing to work within whatever allocation was provided, the government was willing to leave them largely to determine the cutting up of the cake in a role which was fairly autonomous of management. Nevertheless, this 'quid pro quo' broke down, it is argued, as doctors began to challenge NHS financing at a political level and Mrs Thatcher in particular decided that if the informal bargain had been broken, then 'leaving the medical profession alone' would no longer apply either.

The story of how the Prime Minister's review reported in the form of the White Paper *Working for patients*, which was then translated into the NHS (and Community Care) Act of 1990, is now a familiar one. The main planks of policy - at the political and strategic levels - flowing from the 1990 Act have included: the purchaser/provider split; the creation of self-governing trusts (opted out units); the encouragement to a certain level (still undetermined) of fundholding by GPs; the agreeing of formal contracts (although not legal ones) between purchasers and providers; and a raft of less 'political' initiatives concerning areas such as medical audit, consultants' contracts and so forth (Department of Health, 1989).

A question worth asking is to what extent did the recommendations of the Prime Minister's review represent 'policy learning' from other countries or indeed from theories in the social sciences about either public management or the organisation and provision of health services? The most obvious answer is that Professor Alain Enthoven from Stanford University had some considerable influence on the idea known as the 'internal market'. Enthoven had, in 1985, published a short book entitled *Reflections on the management of the National Health Service*, in which he identified a number of barriers to efficiency in provision, which he termed "gridlock" (Enthoven, 1985). The answer was to institute a system of direct charging between health authorities to ensure that money followed the patient when they were exported or imported. At a more grandiose level, Enthoven considered that such a scheme might involve importing the idea of the HMO to the UK. Therefore, both in the theory of the internal market (internal because it did not *necessarily* involve privatisation and was internal to the public sector) and in the practice of the HMO, there was policy learning both from simple economic theory and from US practice.

This is in truth the extent of the influence of significant ideas or institutions from outside prevailing British practice. Earlier reviews (in 1981/82) had looked at the health care systems of France and other West European countries in an attempt to ask whether a form of national health insurance would be either more efficient or more effective, and it had been unequivocally decided that it would not be. At the time of the Prime Minister's review in 1988/89, systematic reconnaissance of other health care systems was not undertaken. This was quite deliberate, in that the Prime Minister's review was *intended* to be a cryptic exercise reporting by Summer 1988 (it did in fact report at the beginning of February 1989.) In line with government practice of the day, it was less an exercise in widespread consultation than a mobilisation of a quasi-practical agenda to conform with the prevailing ideology of the government of the day. Those consulted were therefore people who were sympathetic to the Thatcher administration, and included those located in the 'right wing think tanks' such as the Adam Smith Institute, the Institute of Economic Affairs (Health Unit) and Centre for Policy Studies. More formally, the Prime Minister's review committee included some advisers from business and the private insurance industry, as well as civil servants and ministers (Paton, 1992).

In terms of the new health authority and management relationships established following the NHS Act of 1990, the main trends were a move to more direct business-style health authorities rather than loosely quasi-representative health authorities, on the one hand, and to a strengthening of general management as had been instituted after the Griffiths inquiry of 1983, on the other hand. In this regard, some policy learning took place from New Zealand, where more radical ideas concerning the private management of the public service had been under consideration and had subsequently been instituted. Indeed in New Zealand's health care system generally, more thoroughgoing privatisation has subsequently occurred than in Britain.

Overall then the changes instituted in the British NHS followed a certain amount of market theory, although the extent to which this has survived the implementation of the reforms and the succession of the Thatcher administration by the Major administration is very much a question for debate (Paton, 1991). In essence, providers (whether hospitals or otherwise) were to 'market' themselves to purchasers, including health authorities, GP fundholders and (possibly) private purchasers as well.

It was understood at the time that an end to the 'localism' of the NHS whereby most populations received their service 'on the doorstep' would be replaced by a system whereby travel to the most efficient (and possibly effective) form of care would occur. In practice, however, *more* localism has probably been stimulated by the NHS reforms, rather than less. Referrals now have to be sanctioned by managers from a purchasing budget, and providing services locally is generally considered more attractive. In the old system, referrals were made by GPs (without their own budgets) and a complicated formula reimbursed the care, although often there was not enough money to allow money to follow the patient quickly or adequately. In the new system, such referrals have to be sanctioned and the consequence has been that, for example, purchasing health authorities from the shire counties around London will contract with local providers rather than sanctioning referrals to Central London.

Part of the financial crisis confronting London's health services flows from this, although the movement of monies out of London due to the resource allocation formula is also significant, indeed probably more so.

## The purchaser/provider split: insights from abroad?

The essence of a purchaser/provider spilt is to institute a system whereby the financing of health care is separated from the provision. Obviously at one level this is an unavoidable truism. All health care systems (whether public or private) consist of money to pay for services, on the one hand, and providers of services, on the other hand. In Britain, due to both financing and provision being broadly public, the conflation of the two under the responsibility of the old-style health authority was a practical feature. In the early days of the implementation of the NHS reforms, it was believed that purchasers would be divorced from providers, and of course - to the extent that self-governing trusts are autonomous providers - this may be true. It is, however, interesting to note, on the theme of policy learning from abroad, that the essence of the US HMO is to *end* the split between the financier and the provider, not accentuate it. The HMO in the USA has been a response to what economists would call 'the problem of the third party payer'. This is the so-called problem which results from agreements being made between a provider and a consumer with a third party being left to pick up the bill. In the USA the third party is of course the insurance company or in some cases the employer acting as 'in-house' insurer. The essence of the HMO is that a special type of insurance company is created whereby the financier directly employs or tightly contracts with the provider. In consequence, it is argued, both managerial and financial control can take place, and both providers and significant professionals (primarily doctors) can be given financial incentives to stay within the budget of the HMO or to help create a surplus (or a profit if the HMO is for-profit).

Thus in Britain a HMO would in theory consist of a health authority directly employing its providers: the antithesis of what has happened under the NHS reforms, indeed arguably this was a feature of the pre-reform NHS. What of course is true is that, in the USA, HMOs compete with traditional fee for service providers - where there is competition - in order to attract consumers. Thus, although there is not much scope for providers within (or contracting with) the HMO to compete for finance, or very little, there is competition to choose the purchaser/financier. In Britain this is not the case.

In the Netherlands, health service reforms have been proposed and partly implemented which involve the creation both of provider markets and of purchaser markets (Dekker, 1987). In other words, providers are allegedly to compete for income from purchasers - insurance companies, merging with the not-for-profit sick funds - on the basis of contracts similar to those in Britain. Additionally, however, purchasers are to compete for enrolment from the population, which is financed mostly through the government national health insurance system (or more accurately the health tax system, organised through the payroll).

In Britain, if the consumer/patient does not like the decisions made by his or her purchasing health authority, there is nothing much to be done about it. In other words, any provider competition is to suit the desires of purchasing managers at purchasing health authority level, and the extent to which this is the result of democratic consultation with the local population is a matter for the future. Some interesting experiments have already taken place. In the Netherlands, on the other hand, consumers can arguably move to a different purchaser if they are unhappy with their purchasers' practices or contracts. In practice this is still limited, and the reforms have not been implemented fully as proposed, on the grounds that an all party coalition government has been developing - and reflecting the need for - political consensus. In Britain, on the other hand, the NHS reforms were the partisan creature of the Conservative government. Nevertheless a pointer to the future in the Netherlands would argue that consumer choice of purchaser as well as purchaser choice of provider will be important.

In Britain, to the extent that GP fundholders develop as the linchpin of the new system rather than an optional extra wild card, it could be argued that choice by consumer/patient of GP fundholding practice is an exercise of consumer choice of purchaser. However, the development of GP fundholding has gone hand in hand with the development of large consortia of GP fundholders, and local choice amongst rival purchasers - even were this model to become the linchpin of the system - would be the exception rather than the rule.

Furthermore it can be argued that in a tightly funded NHS as opposed to a more generously funded Dutch (public) health insurance system, choice of purchaser by consumer might in practice become choice of consumer by purchaser, whether at the margin or more generally. In other words, purchasers would seek to enrol those consumers less likely to make untenable financial demands on the system. HMOs in the USA, as well as conventional insurers, have indulged in practices such as excluding medically or financially 'unviable' enrolees, subject to state law which varies throughout the USA as well as federal law which has in fact been loosened throughout the 1980s to allow such discrimination to a greater extent than envisaged in the 1970s when the HMO was less common but more widely discussed as a reforming element of the system.

## The NHS reforms in the future

The main problems and challenges which have emerged from the implementation of the NHS reforms may be summarised as follows.

### The purchaser/provider split

To what extent should a rigid or significant purchaser/provider split be institutionalised, with minimal contact between purchasers and providers? This would be the rationale of creating an internal market whereby providers were free to market themselves without being regulated by either purchasers or 'the centre'. The other extreme position, somewhat against the original ideology behind the NHS reforms, is that purchasers and providers 'live very closely together'. A phrase which has evolved in semi-official documents is that the relationship between purchaser and provider ought to be 'cosy'. Here, the conflict is between market logic, on the one hand, and the logic of a regulated public service, on the other hand. The question is not just one at the level of theory or even of ideology. Taking a specific example: when it comes to quality assurance, or its sub-component medical audit, should the purchaser be responsible for detailed regulation of the provider? It might be argued that only outcomes are of interest to the purchaser, and that it is the provider's business how quality assurance is done. On the other hand, one can look at private sector examples such as that of Marks and Spencer, which is very interventionist in terms of quality criteria relating to process as well as outcome for its suppliers. It can be argued that Marks and Spencer is a provider in the market place and the relationship with its subcontractors or subproviders is different to the relationship between a *purchaser* and provider. However the provider/subprovider link may have the same logic as the purchaser/provider link, especially in the NHS, where the purchaser is in a sense a provider to the public. Admittedly the purchaser is using public money to buy on behalf of the public and is therefore a purchaser fair and square. The point however stands.

In practice, both DHA purchasers and GP fundholders are being encouraged to set up stable relationships with providers. Otherwise the transactions costs of permanent renegotiation of contracts would be very high indeed. This is one of the areas which was relatively ignored in devising the logic of the NHS reforms. As a result, given the general nature of the prescriptions underlying the NHS reforms, the implementation process is in fact a policy-making process as well.

## Regional authority

At a higher tier also, the degree of purchaser/provider split to be allowed or encouraged is a moot point. Regions - which are now formally to be abolished yet replaced with 'regional offices' which will be strengthened strategically - are responsible for the overall coordination of purchasing and resource allocation to purchasers (districts, consortia and GP fundholders). The institutions known as 'zonal outposts' which were developed to regulate self-governing trusts on the provider side will also have their functions taken over by the new regional offices, and the question therefore arises: how self-governing are trusts? The purchaser/provider split may in fact be closed somewhat at the strategic level, just below the national level. This is not the theory but it may be the practice. In consequence, purchasing decisions may be taken closely in coordination with provision decisions, and the purchaser/provider split may be an operational policy for encouraging efficient management by providers and thoughtful commissioning by local purchasers, rather than a significant strategic plank of the NHS reforms. This is of course a grey area, and the final answer is not yet available. It is increasingly being realised that, in a supposedly 'anti-bureaucratic' reform, to strengthen regions in certain ways may in fact make a nonsense of the original pretensions of the White Paper *Working for patients*. What this does to the purchaser/provider split remains to be seen, if it happens.

## Rationing

Rationing decisions - or in some cases decisions to deny care - have to be taken to some extent at a central level. Otherwise a series of 'mini NHSs' emerges, and this is unacceptable in a political culture where a publicly funded health service is responsible to ministers, who in turn are responsible to Parliament and in particular to the Public Accounts Committee, which has often been the most interventionist of the Commons committees supervising and planning new developments in the NHS.   Niceties about purchaser/provider splits and devolution to agencies, as the NHS Management Executive is often seen as being (in part), often do not interest members of Parliament, as the theology to which they have to subscribe is rather different from the theology of devolved and discrete management in a public sector reorganised due to insights from the private sector.

Naturally there is scope for rationing decisions to be taken at the local level, as districts and other commissioners undertake needs assessment and seek to form local priorities.  Again this is an area where resolution of the key issues will have to be made, but it seems at the moment that the national role will continue to be important.

### Purchaser coordination

The coordination of different purchasers - in particular GP fundholders with DHA and consortia purchasers - poses a major challenge.  The original ethos behind the purchaser/provider split was that the DHA would undertake global needs assessment on behalf of its resident population and commission services accordingly.  GP fundholders have developed as a wild card - and a wilder and larger card than originally envisaged - and in many cases are making decisions as to priorities which are not in line with the decisions of DHAs.  This can have serious knock-on effects for providers, who may be denied their marginal source of income which makes all the difference between financial viability and financial failure, at an extreme.  In other words, one may be talking 'marginally' in the language of economics, but the margin may be very wide indeed in the real world.  This is especially the case if GP fundholding becomes more salient.  One option is for GP fundholding to become the linchpin of the system.  This would mean that, eventually, GP fundholders would be likely to become large consortia, and would in effect then become the DHA under another name.  In other words the poacher would have become the gamekeeper.  The advantage of GP fundholding - promoting 'micro' innovation based on their 'nuisance value' to providers - would then be removed. On purely economic (as opposed to political or ideological) grounds, there seems little logic in such a move.

More likely - under any political party - is the increasing coordination of purchasing involving DHAs, GP fundholders and FHSAs. It might be that these could be merged formally. If not, informal working relationships, including local authorities' social services departments for the purposes of community care, will develop.

## Management

Concerning the constitutional and managerial relationships created under the aegis of the NHS reforms, policy learning has primarily been from the private sector. 'Private style' boards now run health authorities and trusts. The management structures of health providers - and indeed purchasing health authorities - often mirror (in name at the very least) the structures of either private companies or public enterprises traditionally considered distinct from public services.

The latter change is one which is likely to be fairly long-lasting. Operational efficiency is the main goal. While adjustments may be made to the particular structures developed over time, there will be no return to the pre-general management 'public administration' ethos, it seems. What does require to be done, however, is to incorporate a greater democracy into the management of commissioning, and arguably into the management of provision as well. Currently the NHS is widely believed to suffer from a 'democratic deficit'. Health authorities are no longer quasi-representative bodies, and the paradox for any government is that a removal of a democratic safety valve at the local level is likely to lead to greater centralisation, as public unrest is focused at the centre in that local democratic institutions do not exist to handle or channel such issues.

## Reinventing planning?

There is a view frequently expressed in some health service circles to the effect that 'planning is dead' and that those who advocate it are somehow embracing or retaining a philosophy or approach which has been rejected worldwide, not least in the former Eastern Europe. To the present author, simple assertion of such a view is naive. It fails to differentiate between many different types of planning. Furthermore it would be ironic if the NHS were to adopt the orthodoxy of the 1980s just as it is falling into disrepute elsewhere in the economy. It would, however, be familiar for the NHS to be 'one step behind' in enthusiastically embracing yesterday's answer whether in the realm of political economy or managerial doctrine.

Let us distinguish between the following types of planning:

- *comprehensive planning*, including central determination of capital programmes and both mode and location of provision of health care;

- *indicative planning*, which seeks to identify needs, identify trends in demand and supply and then seek to regulate or intervene to ensure that objectives are met (analogous to economy-wide indicative planning);

- *'social market' planning* which seems to the present author to mean (given that it is a very loose and ambiguous phrase) one of the following three (not mutually exclusive) phenomena:

  a)  use of market mechanisms in provision yet public purchasing;

  b)  combination of market mechanisms and either regulation or planning;

  c)  the co-existence of a market economy generally with a relatively high-tax, high-welfare social sector, possibly including comprehensive planning in the health sector;

- *planning of new developments* such that, for example, central and regional responsibility for new hospitals co-exists with the so-called 'internal market';

- *incremental planning*, whereby planning exists but is limited in its pretensions;

- *planning of resource allocation*, whereby purchasers in the NHS are given specific allocations for a range of purposes, some of which are stipulated by 'planners';

- relatively close *coordination between purchasers and providers* in the post-reform NHS, for example, such that performance of providers is regulated or policed by both purchasers and possible government (for example, through the House of Commons Public Accounts Committee as well as the Department of Health) to ensure that objectives are met.

This list is by no means exhaustive and is indeed illustrative rather than comprehensive. The aim is to point to the complexity of any debate about planning. To say that planning is dead is pretty meaningless, as well as potentially dangerous.

Some of the main challenges for the planning system (in whatever institutional form) include the following.

- *Mechanisms for deciding priorities generally.* For example, some see the purchaser/provider split as a means for moving away from both 'provider capture' and an alleged bias to acute clinical care. Others, however, see the purchaser/provider split as a means of ensuring that the NHS concentrates on its alleged 'core business' which is defined as acute clinical care rather than social care. It cannot be a means of doing both, and in a public NHS it is reasonable to expect the planners (whomsoever they may be) to make such strategic decisions prior to the placing of specific contracts by local purchasers.

- *A decision as to which tier of the NHS ought to be regulating purchasing, and with what degree of specificity.* For example, it now seems likely that regions (albeit a fewer number) will be preserved and indeed strengthened to undertake this role. 'Zonal outposts' created to be responsible to the NHS Management Executive will regulate providers (self-governing trusts in particular) to a certain degree at least. Providers' business plans have to be created in the context of purchasing decisions. A rigid purchaser/provider split in this arena is not likely to be very helpful, at the level of efficiency let alone ideology.

- *The coordination of purchasing* to ensure that priorities for health are tackled coherently within already tight budgets is a major planning challenge. Currently DHAs (or consortia formed from merged authorities), GP fundholders and FHSAs all have a purchasing role. Various proposals for coordinating these purchasers exist, both for formal mergers and for informal 'joint planning' (also including local authority purchasers in the case community care).

- *Ensuring compatibility between GP fundholders' priorities and overall global health needs* (again, defined by whomever) is a major priority for Britain.

- *The planning, or at least regulation, of the care mix* to be offered by self-governing trusts is an important challenge, as is the need to ensure that hospital trusts do not 'cost-shift' in order to unload a burden of care onto community trusts and indeed vice versa. In this connection, the creation of unified hospital and community trusts has recently been discouraged, if not forbidden wholly; and this task is therefore rendered all the more necessary.

## Rationing?

The phrase rationing is currently much in vogue, not least because of the debate around the 'quality adjusted life year' in both the USA and Britain and the debate around the 'Oregon formula' (Strosberg et al, 1992) which provides a framework for making so-called tough decisions in the realm of public funding for Medicaid patients in the state of Oregon in the USA. Used in its pure sense, rationing would imply central decision making as to priorities and their allocation through a public process to the whole citizenry. If 'rationing' is simply the making of choices within constrained public budgets yet the co-existence with the public health care sector of a flourishing private health care sector, then 'rationing' may mean denial of care to the poor.

Whether we talk of rationing or simply the making of priorities, however, the key questions seem to be:

- determination of the health care budget;

- priorities within that budget;

- specific modes of provision within those priorities;

- which categories of patients to receive such services;

- mechanisms for denying care where this is necessary, in a manner which is possible within the prevailing political system and political culture and also within the planning and management framework of the health service in question.

These various levels of rationing have to be taken at correspondingly various levels of planning and or management within any public health care system. Some of the key questions arising must therefore be as follows.

- How centralist should rationing decisions be?

- Is rationing to be done according to criteria of need as defined by experts (for example taking into account experts definitions of 'health gain' defined as quantified improvements in health status for individuals classes or the nation as a whole)?

- Should such decisions be taken centrally or locally?

- Are citizens' or consumers' preferences to be taken into account, and if so what about any incompatibilities between such preferences and experts' definitions of health gain?

- Are consumers preferences coherent in any case?

- How is formal rationing (for example by purchasers) to be reconciled with informal rationing by providers and indeed mechanisms for ensuring that those denied care are 'squeezed in' through extra-contractual referrals (in the new British system) or simply by joining informal waiting lists decided by doctors who are not necessarily prepared to go along with purchasers' or indeed providers' managers' decisions?

- What if local variation in services provided (due to different decisions taken by different purchasers in different localities) occurs to such an extent that the concept of a 'national' health service breaks down? Will this be acceptable to the citizenry? Will citizens in one locality accept that they are denied service X (while admittedly, perhaps, having access to service Y unavailable elsewhere)? In other words, is it possible to ration by service as opposed to by person? Again, is local variation as opposed to centralism possible?

- If there is to be a significant rationing role for local purchasers, how acceptable is the current undemocratic constitution of purchasing health authorities?

It can quickly be seen that reconciling rationing (conceivable defined broadly as priority setting within available resources, as well as determination of the level of resource) with different options for giving the public a say in rationing decisions is an important challenge. There are different means by which the public can be given power in this realm, and these range from democratic representation through more informal consultation through local audit of desired priorities through formal mechanisms for consulting the public such as that undertaken in the Oregon formula. Furthermore detailed mechanisms for what are almost iterative forms of negotiating with the public can be devised, drawing on insights from service agreements developed by a number of local authorities. Other approaches naturally aim to establish a set of specific 'rights' to health care. The Patients' Charter in Britain allegedly does this, but in a somewhat vacuous form. The rights established are not enforceable. Furthermore the Patients' Charter deals by and large with rights to specific forms of quality in support service rather than establishing rights to specific forms of clinical care.

## Conclusion

The main challenges confronting the NHS involve some policy learning. The word 'market' has increasingly been used in European as well as British health care, and specific lessons of relevance to Britain may be learned from the Netherlands (where competition between purchasers for clients and between providers for contracts from purchasers are both major objectives, although not guaranteed to be realised, in the evolving Dutch health care system); and from Sweden where "health care markets" (Saltman and von Otter, 1992) tend to refer simply to money following the patient rather than competitive or private sector-style markets; and from various other countries seeking to control costs while increasing consumer choice. The hey-day of the market in the USA was the early and mid 1980s when it was alleged that rationalisation of the health care system through market discipline was an alternative to the allegedly discredited planning of the 1970s.

With the election of President Clinton, however, a mix of market and regulatory approaches is likely to be forged in a considerably more interventionist manner than, for example, in the early years of the Reagan administration. Clinton has campaigned specifically on the need for 'managed competition' drawing on the ideas of Enthoven which point to the need for 'cash-limited' purchasing budgets and the coordination of purchasing (to allow consumers meaningful choice in both choosing purchasers and knowing what services are likely to be available as a result of that choice) but also involving regulatory approaches involving global budgeting and (possibly) rate regulation in order to make a national health care system affordable for all Americans (White House, 1993). That, of course, is the objective, as it has been since the late 1960s, when the political attempt to establish national health insurance was resumed after the compromise represented by the enactment of Medicare and Medicaid in 1965 had been established.

On the other hand, many of the challenges confronting the post-reform British NHS, and indeed any critiques and amendments of the reforms, consist in dabbling in new waters, in that the combination of a centrally directed, publicly funded NHS and limited market mechanisms is occurring in Britain for the first time significantly in the world. Other countries which have had a similar structure are also moving towards the market (for example New Zealand). Nevertheless, the challenges outlined in this chapter - at a very sketchy level - require both original policy analysis and *critical* policy learning from the international scene.

## References

Butler, J. (1992) *Patients, policies and politics,* Buckingham: Open University Press.

Dekker, (1987) *Commissie struktuur en financiering*, The Hague: Staatsdrukkerij.

Department of Health (1989) *Working for patients*, Cmnd 555, London: HMSO.

Enthoven, A. (1985) *Reflections on the management of the National Health Service*, London: NPHT.

Galbraith, J.K. (1992) *The culture of contentment*, London: Sinclair-Stevenson.

Le Grand, J. and Bartlett, W. (1993) *Quasi-markets and social policy*, London: Macmillan.

Paton, C. (1991) 'Myths of competition', *Health Service Journal*, 6 May.

Paton, C. (1992) *Competition and planning in the NHS*, London: Chapman and Hall.

Saltman, R. and von Otter, C. (1992) *Planned markets and public competition*, Buckingham: Open University Press.

Strosberg, M. et al (eds) (1992) *Rationing America's medical care : the Oregon plan and beyond*, Washington, DC: Brookings Institution.

White House (1993) *Health security: preliminary plan*, September.

*eleven*

# CREAM-SKIMMING AND FUNDHOLDING

## Manos Matsaganis and Howard Glennerster

Le Grand (1991) has identified one of the central dangers of quasi-markets as the potential they create for cream-skimming. The extent of that danger depends, however, on the particular structure of the market. Where purchasers compete for the custom of patients or clients on whose behalf they then purchase services, there may be an incentive, in certain circumstances, for the purchasers to seek 'cheap' clients. They will then be able to offer their services as a purchaser at a cheap premium. This incentive will be strong where each purchaser receives the same flat sum of money per client and where the risks or potential costs of purchasing for clients differs systematically for one or more kinds of client. No such incentives exist, however, if clients are simply allocated to the purchaser or if there is competition between providers of services but not between purchasers.

The NHS reforms (Department of Health, 1989) provide an interesting case because they incorporated two kinds of purchaser. DHAs were to purchase on behalf of their populations (following Enthoven, 1985). They were to be monopsonist purchasers. Maynard (1986) objected that this gave too little say to the consumer. This view won support from the then Secretary of State, Kenneth Clarke, and others associated with the reforms (Glennerster et al, 1992). Alongside the district purchasing model, therefore, the government introduced the GP fundholder. They competed for custom - patients have always been able to choose their GP - but they also received a sum of money with which they could purchase services for their patients from hospitals.

The reforms were, therefore, based on a combination of the two models, with budget-holding GP practices purchasing alongside DHAs. Any practice could now opt for 'fundholding' status, provided it had the necessary skills and equipment to cope with managing the scheme, and a patient list of no less than 7,000. The budget covers non-emergency elective surgical procedures, all laboratory tests and out-patient visits, drugs prescribed by the practice, and staff costs. Community health services have been included in the scheme from April 1993.

The shift in financial power to the family doctors and away from hospitals has been shown to have salutary effects in terms of efficiency and consumer responsiveness (Glennerster and Matsaganis, 1993). Nevertheless, concern has been voiced over the possibility of increased administrative and transactions costs, interference with planning, and the equity implications of fundholding (Bartlett, 1991; Maynard, 1993; Ham, 1993). We concentrate here on the possibilities that this form of purchasing may give rise to the cream-skimming phenomenon. Because those who designed the reforms were well aware of the dangers of cream-skimming they introduced a 'stop loss' provision so that the costs of any patient that amounted to over £5,000 a year in hospital expenditure would be met by the district. A similar provision covered drug expenditure. The reformers also hoped that they would be able to develop a formula-based budget that would counteract any cream-skimming effects by paying GPs more for potentially costly patients. In the early years of the scheme this defeated the Department of Health. Instead it relied on setting fundholders' budgets on a historic cost basis. Practices were given enough to be able to pay for last year's levels of referrals. This got around the cream-skimming problem, in theory at least, because a practice with a high referral rate got a high budget. But it did so at the cost of encouraging high referral rates or rewarding high referrals whether for good or bad reasons. This was, of course, incompatible with the declared aim of the scheme to increase efficiency, while it also reinforced pre-existing inequalities in the use of resources in general practice (Glennerster et al, 1992).

The Department of Health therefore decided to move towards its original intention of using a weighted capitation formula to fix fundholders budgets in 1993-94. It was only a tentative move because it was agreed to use the formula merely as a negotiating tool or guide to regions and FHSAs in setting the budgets of individual practices. For the most part in 1993-94 the budgets of fundholders still reflected their historic levels of referrals and the costs of the providers they used. Nevertheless, in this chapter we explore how far the intended Department of Health formula would, if applied, counteract the incentives to cream-skimming.

## Biased selection in pre-paid remuneration systems

The concept of biased selection has been explored extensively in the literature of the economics of imperfect information (Akerlof, 1970; Rothschild and Stiglitz, 1976). Biased selection in the specific case of medical care can be initiated either by the insurer (ie GP) or the insuree. Insurer-initiated biased selection may emerge where insurers receive a direct grant from the financing authority for every eligible patient they sign on. If insurers can predict the level of expenditure on each patient more accurately than the financing authority (a crucial assumption, as becomes clear later), they will be able to select those individuals whose levels of expenditure are expected to fall short of the grant and refuse registration to all others.

As a result, an inadequate capitation formula provides insurers with an incentive to concentrate on attracting enrolees whose likely medical care expenditure is below that predicted by the formula, rather than to compete by designing more efficient methods of delivering services. This will create barriers of access to medical care, with some individuals finding it impossible to get insurance coverage, creating both equity and efficiency losses.

Evidence abounds that systems of pre-paid remuneration, such as the Medicare formula used to reimburse HMOs in the USA or the proposed system of payments to competing insurers for the provision of mandatory health care coverage in the Netherlands, leave substantial room for cream-skimming and discrimination against patients (Epstein and Cumella, 1988; van Vliet and van de Ven, 1990). Will the same be true in Britain? The situation is somewhat different in the sense that no fundholding GP should directly lose if his or her practice lands up with a more costly group of patients and this is not reflected in the practice budget. The losers will be the other patients. They will get less than averagely good services. Yet indirectly the GP will lose because potential patients may begin to realise that this is the case. Fewer may register with the practice and the GP's income depends on the capitation fee received for each patient on the list. The indirect loss may be real and the incentive to prevent this happening real too.

Our starting point is that budgets for fundholding practices should be set proportional to the needs of the patients on their list. Even if doctors did not respond to such perverse incentives it would not be fair for patients to suffer poor services just because the formula did not reflect the cost of the patients on the list.

The formula recommended by the Department of Health uses age and sex as the only variables. Is this enough?

In the following section we investigate the extent to which hospital expenditure in a fundholding practice could be attributed to the demographic and behavioural and diagnostic characteristics of its registered population.

## Empirical analysis of patient costs

Since biased selection stems from the inadequate remuneration for patient-specific costs and the superior ability of the insurer (the fundholding GP in this case) to predict these costs, it is necessary to examine the relationship between expenditure in a fundholding practice and the characteristics of its patients.

### Methods

Data on 1,541 patients were collected from the medical records and the financial reports of a large fundholding practice located in an ethnically and socially mixed area in a large English town. The medical records provide general information on patients (eg age, sex, residence), as well as the doctor's notes on their medical history. These notes list episodes of illness, medication regime, details of hospitalisation, and follow-up assessments from GP consultations. From the medical records 16 variables were produced, broadly classified as: 'socio-demographic' factors (age, sex, etc); 'behavioural' or 'risk' factors (smoking, hypertension, etc); and 'chronic health' factors (cancer, heart problems, disability, etc). Variable construction is fully reported in Matsaganis and Glennerster (1993).

Subsequently, the relationship between individual characteristics and patient-specific expenditure was estimated. It was immediately noticed that the distribution of expenditure on hospital procedures covered by fundholding was extremely skewed in our sample.

Table 1 shows that 1% of all patients accounted for more than one-quarter of all expenditure, while about three-quarters of patients did not use any of the hospital services covered by the fund. This implies that the estimation of determinants of expenditure by ordinary least squares (OLS) is inappropriate. In view of that, we decided to use total hospital costs as the dependent variable.

**Table 1:   Cumulative distribution of fundholding expenditure**

| Highest cost patients | Cost (£) | % of total cost |
|---|---|---|
| 1 patient | 4,891 | 5.6 |
| Top 1% (15 patients) | 23,567 | 27.0 |
| Top 5% (77 patients) | 59,785 | 68.4 |
| Top 27% (411 patients) | 87,397 | 100.0 |

In order to diminish the influence of extreme values, a logarithmic transformation of total hospital costs was used. Furthermore, in order to deal with the skewness of the distribution of hospital expenditure, a two-part model was applied. In this, the probability that patients use the relevant hospital services is derived first, following which the expected level of hospital expenditure is estimated, conditional on it being positive (Manning et al, 1987; Duan et al, 1983).

The predictive power of the model is evaluated for specific values of $X$, by comparing actual hospital expenditure, for individuals with certain characteristics, with expected expenditure as estimated by the model. Furthermore, a measure of the overall predictive power can be given by the $R^2$ suggested by Effron (Maddala 1988; Newhouse et al, 1989). The estimation procedures followed here are set out in more detail in the appendix.

## Results

Various different model specifications were estimated, applying the procedure explained above, with combinations of the explanatory variables on the left-hand side of the equations. Table 2 shows the content of the four versions presented here. Note that while models 1 and 2 apply to the full sample of 1,541 patients, because of missing observations models 3 and 4 could only be estimated for the smaller sample of 437 patients. Full results are presented in Tables 3 and 4.

**Table 2:    Specification of estimated models**

| Variables included | Model 1 | Model 2 | Model 3 | Model 4 |
|---|---|---|---|---|
| Demographics | yes | yes | yes | yes |
| Residence | no | no | no | yes |
| Risk | no | no | no | yes |
| Chronic health | no | yes | no | no |
| n | 1,541 | 1,541 | 437 | 437 |

**Table 3:    Predictive power of models 1 and 2**

| | | Average group cost per patient | | |
|---|---|---|---|---|
| | Number of | Expected | | Actual |
| Patient group | patients in group | Model 1 | Model 2 | |
| Clean record | 703 | £45.17 (4.08) | £31.15 (15.67) | £29.49 |
| Diabetes | 37 | £73.98 (3.82) | £163.10 (5.52) | £153.63 |
| Cancer | 28 | £88.94 (3.86) | £168.79 (6.78) | £121.92 |
| Heart/stroke | 205 | £76.31 (3.74) | £104.70 (10.60) | £112.22 |
| Stomach/liver | 94 | £66.86 (3.85) | £81.16 (12.19) | £76.19 |
| Kidney | 48 | £68.38 (3.81) | £111.30 (9.61) | £133.92 |
| Lungs | 173 | £55.40 (3.94) | £73.05 (12.61) | £72.61 |
| Spine | 326 | £71.92 (3.75) | £81.17 (12.28) | £70.18 |
| Minor surgery | 238 | £70.99 (3.84) | £94.41 (11.33) | £112.80 |
| Disability | 19 | £62.80 (3.81) | £99.58 (9.99) | £82.97 |
| Mental disorder | 164 | £59.51 (3.85) | £88.18 (10.86) | £117.75 |
| Moderate deprivation | 97 | £60.34 (3.89) | £66.42 (13.18) | £65.07 |
| Smoking | 159 | £52.55 (3.82) | £56.12 (13.08) | £89.55 |
| Hypertension | 170 | £83.15 (3.70) | £84.48 (12.80) | £106.80 |
| All patients | 1,541 | £55.42 (3.96) | £55.50 (13.89) | £56.71 |
| $R^2$ | | 1.72% | 3.86% | |
| $R^2$ adjusted | | 1.14% | 2.66% | |
| F-statistic | | 2.977 | 3.214 | |
| Prob. of error | | 0.1614% | 0.0004% | |

**Table 4: Predictive power of models 3 and 4**

|  |  | Average group cost per patient | | |
|---|---|---|---|---|
| Patient group | Number of patients in group | Expected Model 1 | Model 2 | Actual |
| Clean record | 234 | £66.20 (14.26) | £67.06 (15.07) | £20.79 |
| Diabetes | 9 | £148.81 (13.79) | £163.42 (15.88) | £270.39 |
| Cancer | 3 | £123.08 (14.93) | £113.44 (16.07) | £219.09 |
| Heart/stroke | 57 | £101.40 (11.95) | £110.98 (13.52) | £142.34 |
| Stomach/liver | 24 | £109.96 (12.80) | £117.62 (14.04) | £112.46 |
| Kidney | 10 | £93.81 (12.07) | £103.74 (13.55) | £284.15 |
| Lungs | 55 | £76.97 (13.27) | £74.22 (13.47) | £126.52 |
| Spine | 50 | £96.42 (12.17) | £101.66 (13.08) | £80.50 |
| Minor surgery | 47 | £96.26 (13.79) | £101.00 (14.83) | £136.38 |
| Disability | 4 | £44.44 (10.75) | £48.91 (12.12) | £18.38 |
| Mental disorder | 46 | £103.18 (13.32) | £100.81 (13.52) | £199.73 |
| Moderate deprivation | 21 | £104.46 (13.61) | £79.94 (10.51) | £92.79 |
| Smoking | 134 | £88.86 (12.56) | £95.96 (13.57) | £96.30 |
| Hypertension | 32 | £125.41 (12.40) | £157.28 (16.73) | £158.67 |
| All patients | 437 | £77.26 (13.72) | £77.29 (14.57) | £64.34 |
| $R^2$ | | 4.03% | 4.67% | |
| $R^2$ adjusted | | 2.00% | 1.97% | |
| F-statistic | | 1.990 | 1.731 | |
| Prob. of error | | 3.9% | 5.8% | |

Table 3 shows predicted average costs and standard errors of the prediction, as derived from models 1 and 2, for fourteen patient groups. The groups selected are: patients belonging in any of the ten 'chronic health' groups, those living in areas of moderate deprivation, smokers, patients with high blood pressure, and patients with a 'clean' medical record.

The performance of model 1 (with only age and sex as explanatory variables) in terms of accuracy of predictions was poor. The model systematically underestimated the expected average costs of smokers, hypertensives, and patients in all chronic health groups except the 'spine' group.

The predictive power of model 2 (with age, sex, and the ten chronic health factors as explanatory variables) was a significant improvement on that of model 1. Not unexpectedly, the two models produced very similar average cost estimates for patients in the risk groups (smoking and high blood pressure), since neither included risk factors as explanatory variables. Nevertheless, expected average costs for patients in the chronic health groups were closer to actual costs in model 2 than in model 1.

Consider the case of the 37 patients suffering from diabetes. The last column of Table 3 indicates that their actual average cost was £153.63. Expected average expenditure for these patients as estimated by model 2 was £163.10 (a 6% overestimate). In contrast, model 1 produced a predicted value of £73.98, underestimating actual costs by 52%. Prediction errors (expected minus actual costs) were £10 and £80 for models 1 and 2 respectively. More formally, the confidence intervals (constructed by multiplying the standard error of the predictions by 1.9615, the t-value for n=1,541 and p=95%) confirm the superiority of model 2 over model 1. Actual average costs for this group (£153.63) lie far outside the confidence interval for model 1 (£66.49 to £81.29), but within that for model 2 (£152.27 to £173.93).

The case of the 'diabetes' patient group was not untypical. Similar results were shown for the 'lungs' group (the prediction error of model 2 was 44p compared with £17 from model 1), the 'minor surgery' group (prediction error £18 compared with £42), or the 'heart/stroke' group (prediction error of £8 compared with £36). On the whole, model 2 effectively eliminated, or considerably narrowed, the difference between expected and actual costs. Examples of the latter are the cases of patients in the 'kidney' group (prediction error £23 compared with £66), and those in the 'mental disability' group (prediction error £30 compared with £58).

Conversely, let us focus on the 703 patients with a 'clean' record, who presumably enjoy good health. While model 2 produced a prediction error of only £1.66, model 1 overestimated their average expected cost by 53%. Confidence intervals (£37.17 to £53.17) failed to include actual average costs (£29.49).

Model 2 was also favoured by Effron's $R^2$, a measure of overall explanatory power. In the context of such a large sample size, the apparently low $R^2$s of both models were in fact highly significant. Still, model 2 achieved much higher levels of statistical significance with a $R^2$ of 3.86% (probability of error 0.0004%) than model 1 with a $R^2$ of 1.72% (probability of error 0.1614%). Adjusted for degrees of freedom, the explanatory power of model 2 remained more than twice as high as that of model 1 (2.66% compared with 1.14%).

Table 4 shows average costs and standard errors of the prediction for the same patient groups, this time estimated by models 3 and 4. Model 4, which includes the risk variables (smoking and hypertension) and residence in addition to age and sex, could only be estimated for a sub-sample of 437 patients because of missing observations. Model 3 includes the same variables as model 1 (age and sex only), estimated for the same sample as model 4 in order to allow a comparison of the two models on an equal footing and enable us to establish whether predictive power improves with the incorporation of risk factors.[1]

The results show that the inclusion of smoking, blood pressure and residence failed to increase the accuracy of predictions and overall explanatory power of model 4 over model 3. In terms of the former criterion, both models perform rather poorly. Large prediction errors can be seen for most patient groups. Actual average costs for most patient groups lie well without the confidence intervals for the predictions of either model. Expected average costs for patients in the 'stomach/liver' group, those living in areas of moderate deprivation and smokers as estimated by both models were not significantly different from actual average costs for the same patient groups. The only result to separate model 4 from model 3 was the former's more accurate prediction of average costs for the 'hypertension' group.

In fact, in terms of overall explanatory power model 3 (age and sex) performed better than model 4. The $R^2$ associated with the former (4.03%) was statistically significant at the 5% level (probability of error 3.9%), while the $R^2$ (4.67%) of the latter, owing to fewer degrees of freedom, failed to reach similar levels of statistical significance (probability of error 5.8%). The inferiority of model 4 is also shown by $R^2$s adjusted for degrees of freedom (1.97%, compared to 2.00% for model 3).

In summary, model 2 (age, sex and chronic health) performed better than model 1 (age and sex alone), which, as model 3 in the smaller sample, performed better than model 4 (age, sex, residence and risk).[2] It is, therefore, unlikely that the predictive power of model 4, had it been possible to estimate it for the larger sample, would have exceeded that of model 2. In view of that, further discussion of the results and their implications will be restricted to the potential benefits of including chronic health factors to the capitation formula in order to narrow the scope for biased selection. The fundamental issues involved are briefly reviewed below.

## The scope for cream-skimming

It is obvious that the scope for cream-skimming allowed by a capitation formula depends on its accuracy. But what does 'accuracy' mean? How is it related to biased selection?

Usually accuracy is assessed in terms of overall closeness of fit. From this point of view, our results are rather unexceptional. Both our main models produced low (though statistically significant) Effron's $R^2$s, with the $R^2$ of model 2 being more than twice as high as that of model 1 (3.86% compared with 1.72%). However, low $R^2$s are far from uncommon in the literature of determinants of medical expenditure. This is because the greatest part of the variation in medical costs is simply unrelated to patient characteristics, and therefore impossible to predict.

The phenomenon of 'regression towards the mean' is a reflection of that. Welch (1985a, 1985b) showed that if a sufficiently large group of patients with medical expenditures of $100 above average is selected, their subsequent costs would be expected to be $20 above average in the first year, $16 in the second year, and $13 in the third year. The extent to which medical expenditures average out over time indicates the random component of the variance. Conversely, the degree to which costs persist at above average levels shows the systematic part of the variance, attributed to patient-specific factors that are constant over time, such as chronic health status.

In view of regression towards the mean, Welch concluded that "one can explain no more than 20% of the variance in such equations" (1985a). In fact, empirical studies in the USA and the Netherlands have estimated this proportion to be around 14% (Newhouse et al, 1989; van Vliet and van de Ven, 1990). The 4% approximated by our model 2 may be an indication of the greater 'randomness' of the narrow range of in-patient procedures covered by fundholding. Further research is needed to clarify this point.

The fact that the distribution of medical expenditure is predominantly random implies that the maximum achievable predictive power of models aimed to explain it will be inevitably low. In view of that, the adequacy of a capitation formula should be judged in comparison to realistic alternatives rather than in absolute terms. Cream-skimming is not, by itself, a result of the low predictive power of the formula, but of the ability of insurers (GP fundholders in our case) better to predict the costs of certain patient groups than the formula. Therefore, the power of a capitation formula to narrow the scope for discrimination against patients depends more on the magnitude and direction of the prediction errors, and less on overall explanatory power as indicated by $R^2$s.

Despite the fact that the fundholding formula is not technically comparable to any of the equations estimated here, we can assume that its performance is similar to that of our model 1, which (like the formula) is based on age and sex alone. On the other hand, the 'intelligence' required in order to engage in biased selection in the context of fundholding can be reasonably assumed to be limited to the information found in medical records.[3] Model 2 replicates the best a GP could do to use the practice's patient record data base to tell him or her what patients to avoid. In view of that, model 2 can be used to estimate the scope for cream-skimming allowed by the Department of Health formula. Therefore, Table 5 may be interpreted as showing the likely implications of a capitation formula adjusted for age and sex only, compared to the predictions of a fundholding practice using information from the medical records on its patients' chronic health status.[4]

Let us again take the example of the 37 patients suffering from diabetes. If a RHA used the age and sex formula to set the budget of the fundholding practice the situation might look like this. The practice would be offered £2,737 towards the anticipated cost of services provided to these patients (the amount allowed for the same number of non-diabetes patients with identical demographic characteristics). The medical records would show that these patients were actually diabetics. The practice would identify these patients as likely to cost considerably more than the formula allowed. A predictive model like our model 2 would raise estimations of expected expenditure to £6,035. Therefore, the financial incentive to exclude diabetes patients from the practice list would be a potential gain of £3,297. The potential gain from excluding other patient groups would also be considerable: £5,820 for the 205 patients in the 'heart/stroke' group, £5,574 for the 238 patients in the 'minor surgery' group, £4,702 for the 164 patients in the 'mental disorder' group, and so forth.

**Table 5:   Incentives for cream-skimming**

| Patient group | Total group costs | | | |
|---|---|---|---|---|
| | Actual | Predicted by | | * Incentive for cream-skimming |
| | | Model 1 | Model 2 | |
| Clean record | £20,731 | £31,755 | £21,898 | £9,857 |
| Diabetes | £5,684 | £2,737 | £6,035 | (£3,297) |
| Cancer | £3,414 | £2,490 | £4,726 | (£2,236) |
| Heart/stroke | £23,005 | £15,644 | £21,464 | (£5,820) |
| Stomach/liver | £7,162 | £6,285 | £7,629 | (£1,344) |
| Kidney | £6,428 | £3,282 | £5,342 | (£2,060) |
| Lungs | £12,562 | £9,584 | £12,638 | (£3,053) |
| Spine | £22,879 | £23,446 | £26,461 | (£3,016) |
| Minor surgery | £26,846 | £16,896 | £22,470 | (£5,574) |
| Disability | £1,576 | £1,193 | £1,892 | (£699) |
| Mental disorder | £19,311 | £9,760 | £14,462 | (£4,702) |
| Moderate deprivation | £6,312 | £5,853 | £6,433 | (£590) |
| Smoking | £14,238 | £8,355 | £8,923 | (£568) |
| Hypertension | £18,156 | £14,136 | £14,362 | (£226) |

Note:     * The incentive for cream-skimming is defined as the
          difference between total costs allowed by the formula
          (approximated by model 1) and total costs as predicted by the
          practice on the basis of patient records (approximated by
          model 2). Positive differences imply an incentive for the
          practice to seek the enrolment of patients in the group under
          consideration, while negative differences (shown in
          parenthese) indicate an incentive to seek their disenrolment.

Naturally, the practice could also gain by discriminating in favour
of healthy individuals, that is, to attract such individuals to its
patient list. A formula similar to model 1 (including age and sex
only) would allocate £31,755 for the anticipated cost of services
provided to the 703 patients with a 'clean' medical record.
Applying a predictive model similar to model 2 would inform the
practice that the cost of these patients is more likely to be around
£21,898. As a result, the practice would stand to make a profit of
£9,857, with the promise of additional profits in the event of more,
similarly healthy individuals registering with it.

Whether potential gains on a £1,500,000 budget would be sufficient to run the risk of professional and customer unpopularity for excluding diabetics, for example, is a moot point but they could be.

In view of the fact that our sample only included about one-eighth of the practice's patient list, the potential financial gains from a discriminating strategy against a single patient group could be up to £50,000. Equally lucrative could be a strategy actively seeking to register healthy individuals.

## Is cream-skimming a real risk in fundholding?

The preceding analysis shows that cream-skimming in the specific context of fundholding is both technically feasible and financially attractive. But will it happen?

Clearly, the ethics of general practice in Britain are a powerful defense against cream-skimming in the short term. However, reliance on medical ethics alone would be ill-advised. Indeed, a set of incentives that reward the devious and penalise the honest might soon promote cynicism and help create a culture of understanding (if not sympathy) for doctors involved in biased selection. On the other hand, the chances of administrative measures against patient discrimination are even slimmer. With time, strategies for biased selection, aimed at encouraging good risks to join the practice and bad risks to leave, will become too subtle for the authorities to detect. The likely failure of medical ethics or administrative regulations to prevent cream-skimming other than in the short term leaves improvements to the capitation formula as the only viable alternative.

### Formula adjustments against cream-skimming

The question arises as to what the appropriate adjustments to the Department of Health formula might be. Both in the USA and the Netherlands, although there is broad agreement that demographic factors are poor predictors of future medical expenses, there is debate on the strengths and shortcomings of prior costs or utilisation on one hand, and health status on the other, as potential candidates for inclusion in a capitation formula.

The use of individual-specific prior costs in budget setting, although likely to remove incentives to cream-skimming, is thought to have negative incentive effects. For example, van de Ven and van Vliet (1990) argued that although prior costs should be used against biased selection in the short term, inclusion of prior costs in the formula would eventually blunt the competitive incentives for efficiency, as it would compensate insurers for factors that are within their control (supply, prices, extent of coverage etc). Moreover, the issues raised by regression towards the mean, as well as more practical considerations, such as the unavailability of data on past expenses incurred by new entrants to the system, are also powerful arguments against reliance on prior costs as a measure against cream-skimming. In any case, information on prior costs of individual patients in the context of fundholding is not yet available for a sufficient number of years. Therefore, the answer must be sought elsewhere.

In our analysis of hospital expenditure in fundholding presented earlier we were able to use chronic health information from the practice's medical records. It is therefore clear that the concern of analysts in other countries that indicators of chronic health status are difficult to collect does not apply to fundholding. It could be made a requirement that practices provide the regulatory authorities (eg FHSAs) with full data on the demographic and chronic health profile of their registered population in a standard format.

However, such a requirement would give rise to doubts about the credibility of data, namely that chronic health indicators could be open to manipulation. That could take forms akin to the phenomenon of 'diagnosis related group (DRG) creep'. The term refers to the re-classification of borderline cases by US service providers in order to maximize reimbursement revenue (Newhouse, 1986; Howland et al, 1987; Epstein and Cumella, 1988; Newhouse et al, 1989; Ash et al, 1989).

In any case, the introduction of chronic health adjusters to the Department of Health formula in Britain would require careful design and reasonable monitoring arrangements. The feasibility of that remains to be seen, but the results of our study indicate that the ability of a formula to eliminate incentives for cream-skimming would be significantly improved, should it be modified to include chronic health status. That our chronic health factors seemed to perform so well is certainly encouraging.

Because of the disadvantages of almost any risk adjuster imaginable, researchers in the USA have drawn attention to the need for further measures to prevent cream-skimming in addition to improvements in the capitation formula. For example, Newhouse

(1986) and Newhouse et al (1989) proposed a blend of capitation and fee for service, in other words a mix of prospective and retrospective reimbursement. Howland et al (1987) argued that re-insurance may be required to address the immediate problems of the Medicare programme. Luft (1986) put forward the idea of separate fee for service payments for specific high cost categories. Wallack et al (1988) discussed the concept of "risk corridors" (whereby profits or losses beyond a specified amount are shared between the HMO and the Medicare programme), and the "outlier approach" (according to which Medicare undertakes to share costs incurred by any individual in excess of a specified amount per year). More recently, Robinson et al (1991) suggested that outlier cases could be reimbursed on a fee-for-service or episode-of-illness basis, rather than through the general risk pool.

In fact, similar risk-sharing arrangements are already in operation in the fundholding scheme (for example, the £5,000 stop-loss ceiling, the effective sharing of surpluses with RHAs, the exclusion of very expensive procedures). The results of our analysis show that such provisions are essential to the smooth running of the scheme.[5] The rules on liability for costs over £5,000 for any one patient in a single year could be modified so that practices contribute, for example, 10% of expenditure over and above that limit, to ensure that cost consciousness does not entirely disappear when doctors deal with very expensive cases.

## Conclusion

The threat of cream-skimming in GP fundholding exemplifies the strategic dilemma left unresolved by the NHS reforms: that is, the choice of purchasing agency between fundholding practices and DHAs. Had the latter been favoured as the sole purchasers, the issue of cream-skimming would never have arisen, but neither would the opportunities for consumer choice and responsiveness have materialised. In introducing a more enthusiastic agent for change in the shape of fundholding, the architects of the reforms created some of the necessary conditions for cream-skimming.

Biased selection has, as the previous analysis suggests, potentially deleterious effects. In a health care system where coverage is not guaranteed, it may lead to the straightforward exclusion of 'non-profitable' patients. In a universal system, those agents unwilling or unable to practice it are left with an expensive mix of patients without the resources to match. To be 'successful', cream-skimming demands effort and resources, expended for no benefit except to those who practice it. In short, cream-skimming results in a 'deadweight' welfare loss, of efficiency as well as of equity.

Cream-skimming is not yet a major issue in GP fundholding. Moreover, this is likely to remain so even after the introduction of an element of formula funding in budget setting. Nevertheless, as this chapter has shown, a formula such as the one used by the Department of Health will inevitably create incentives for cream-skimming. These incentives will be dealt with in the short term in two ways. Ill-structured negotiations and historic cost budgeting will continue to be relied upon, while practices who happen to have a higher than average proportion of expensive patients on their lists without the extra resources required are left to cope as best as they can. Both outcomes are undesirable, the former for perpetuating the inefficiency and inequity of the previous system of budget setting, the latter for preparing the psychological ground for biased selection in the not too distant future.

We have demonstrated that it is possible to benefit from the incentive advantages associated with capitation funding, without at the same time giving hostages to fortune in the form of incentives for discriminatory behaviour against certain patient groups. Our analysis showed that the potential benefits in terms of reducing the opportunities for cream-skimming can be quite considerable. In view of that, we recommend the use of chronic health factors as adjusters to the capitation formula.

## Appendix

### The estimated equations

The probability $P_i$ of positive medical costs for a patient with a vector of characteristics $X_i$ is:

$$P_i (Y_i > 0 \mid X_i)$$

The individual probabilities of positive medical costs can be calculated from a logit equation for the *full sample of patients* (Maddala, 1983):

$$I = \alpha + \beta X + \varepsilon$$

The errors $\varepsilon$ are distributed as $N(0,1)$.

Since $$I_i = \log_e (P_i / (1 - P_i))$$

it follows that $$P_i = e^{li} / (1 + e^{li})$$

Once the individual probabilities have been computed, a linear model on the logarithmic scale can estimated by OLS for *patients with positive expenditure only*:

$$\log (Y \mid Y > 0) = \gamma + \delta X + \eta$$

The errors $\eta$ are distributed as $N(0,\sigma^2)$.

Expected expenditure $E (Y \mid X)$ for the $i$ individual is calculated as:

$$E (Y_i \mid X_i) = P_i . Z_i . \phi$$

$Z_i$ is the logarithmic retransformation of the estimates of log $(Y_i \mid Y_i > 0)$, and $\phi$ denotes the retransformation factor needed to correct for the residuals $\eta$ in the OLS equation (see below).

The confidence intervals for average *expected* expenditure are given by:

$$E (Y_i) \pm t . SE [E (Y_i)]$$

where $t$ is the value of the $t$-statistic at the relevant level of statistical significance.

Effron's $R^2$, a measure of overall explanatory power, is:

$$Effron's\ R^2 = 1 - [\Sigma(Y_i - EY_i)^2 / \Sigma(Y_i - \Sigma Y_i / n)^2]$$

Statistical significance can be assessed through the $F$-statistic as usual.

## The retransformation factor

If the errors $\eta$ are normally distributed, $\phi$ can be estimated by the normal correction term, which is equal to the base 10 exponential of ($\sigma_\eta^2 / 2$). However, if the normality assumption is not satisfied, this retransformation is incorrect. The retransformation factor $\phi$ can be approximated by the *smearing estimate*, as developed by Duan (1983) and Duan et al (1983, p 120).

The smearing estimate is a non-parametric estimate of the retransformation factor $\phi$, applicable when the distribution of the errors does not depend on the individual characteristics (the values of $X$). The smearing estimate of the retransformation factor $\phi$ is a constant, equal to the sample average of the exponentiated OLS residuals:

$$\phi = (1 / n) \cdot \Sigma(10^{ni})$$

It was shown by Duan (1983) that the smearing estimate is statistically consistent for the retransformation problem if the distribution of the errors is independent of the vector of characteristics $X_i$. The smearing estimate has higher efficiency than the normal retransformation factor even when the normality assumption holds.

## The standard error of the prediction

The standard error of the prediction is a function of the standard errors of all the parameter estimates involved. In a two-part model, where the prediction is derived from combining the results of two estimates and the retransformation factor, the standard error of the prediction needs to combine the standard errors of the parameter estimates in each of the two equations of the model.

More specifically, the standard error of the prediction in this context can be asymptotically estimated by the *delta method* (Duan et al, 1982, p 48). According to the delta method, the variance of the prediction is approximately equal to the sum of the products of the partial derivative of the function with respect to each parameter estimate multiplied by its covariance. In other words:

$$\text{Var} \left[ E \left( Y_i \right) \right] = \text{Var} \, f(\beta_1, \beta_2, ...)$$

$$\div \left[ (\theta f / \theta \beta_1) \cdot \text{cov} \left( \beta_1 \right) (\theta f / \theta \beta_1) \right] + \left[ (\theta f / \theta \beta_2) \cdot \text{cov} \left( \beta_2 \right) (\theta f / \theta \beta_2) \right] + ...$$

The separability of the likelihood function implies that the estimated coefficients in the different equations are asymptotically uncorrelated.

The standard error of the prediction, is the square root of the above expression. The confidence intervals are given by:

$$E(Y_i) \pm t \cdot SE \left[ E(Y_i) \right]$$

where $t$ is the appropriate $t$-value.

**Notes**

1. Significantly, some patient groups in this sample number only a very small number of patients (ten or less on four occasions). The lack of an adequate number of positive values in the relevant explanatory variables lends itself to the risk of extremely high variance for these variables. This problem, apart from greatly affecting the stability of predictions, made impossible the estimation of any model which included the chronic health variables on the sample of 437 patients (the maximum likelihood function for the logit equations failed to converge).

2. Even if the residence and risk factors performed better than they did, it would be inappropriate to compare directly the performance of models 3 and 4 to that of models 1 and 2, as the samples contain different populations. For example, the mean age of the 437 patients was 26.3 years, compared to 40.6 years for the 1,541 patients, while average costs for the same patient groups differed across samples.

3. This is particularly true in the short term. In the long term, practices will be able to collect data on previous costs as well as chronic health of individual patients if they so wish.

4. The way our models have been specified does not allow for an examination of the implications of co-morbidity on hospital costs. The costs incurred by patients suffering from conditions in more than one diagnostic group are assumed here to be the sum of the component extra costs for each such group. However, it is likely that a non-additive pattern is in operation. Clearly, the issue deserves more attention in future research into individual-specific determinants of expenditure.

5. It is characteristic that all models underestimated the average costs of female patients in the age group 35-44 (for full results, see Matsaganis and Glennerster, 1993). In fact, the unusually high costs of that group (£118 per patient) were caused by one patient who incurred costs of £4,890. Without her, the average cost for the group would be less than £66. This shows the inability of any model to predict outliers, and the need for arrangements separate from the capitation formula to deal with the problem.

## References

Akerlof, G.A. (1970) 'The market for 'lemons': qualitative uncertainty and the market mechanism', *Quarterly Journal of Economics*, vol 84, no 3, pp 488-500.

Ash, A., Porell, F., Gruenberg, L., Sawitz, E. and Beiser, A. (1989) 'Adjusting Medicare capitation payments using prior hospitalization data', *Health Care Financing Review*, vol 10, no 4, pp 17-29.

Bartlett, W. (1991) 'Quasi-markets and contracts: a markets and hierarchies perspective on NHS reforms', *Public Money and Management*, vol 11, no 3, pp 55-61.

Crump, B.J., Cubbon, J.E., Drummond, M.F., Hawkes, R.A. and Marchment, M.D. (1991) 'Fundholding in general practice and financial risk', *British Medical Journal*, vol 302, pp 1582-84.

Department of Health (1989) *Working for Patients - White Paper on the NHS*, Cm 555, London: HMSO.

Department of Health (1992) *Guidance on setting GP fundholder budgets in 1993-94*, EL(92)83, London: HMSO.

Duan, N. (1983) 'Smearing estimate: a non-parametric retransformation method', *Journal of the American Statistical Association*, vol 78, no 3, pp 605-10.

Duan, N., Manning, W.G., Morris, C.N. and Newhouse, J.P. (1982) *A comparison of alternative models of the demand for medical care*, R-2754-HHS, Santa Monica, California: The Rand Corporation.

Duan, N., Manning, W.G., Morris, C.N. and Newhouse, J.P. (1983) 'A comparison of alternative models of the demand for medical care', *Journal of Business and Economic Statistics*, vol 1, no 2, pp 115-26.

Enthoven, A. (1985) *Reflections on the management of the NHS*, London: Nuffield Trust.

Epstein, A.M. and Cumella, E.J. (1988) 'Capitation payment: using predictors of medical utilization to adjust rates', *Health Care Financing Review*, vol 10, no 1, pp 51-69.

Glennerster, H., Matsaganis, M. and Owens, P. (1992) *A foothold for fundholding*, Research Report 12, London: King's Fund Institute.

Glennerster, H. and Matsaganis, M. (1993) 'The UK health reforms: the fundholding experiment', *Health Policy*, vol 23, no 3, pp 179-92.

Ham, C. (1993) 'How go the NHS reforms?' *British Medical Journal*, vol 306, pp 77-78.

Howland, J., Stokes, J., Crane, S.C. and Belanger, A.J. (1987) 'Adjusting capitation using chronic disease factors: a preliminary study', *Health Care Financing Review*, vol 9, no 2, pp 15-23.

Le Grand, J. (1991) 'Quasi-markets and social policy', *Economic Journal*, vol 101, pp 1256-67.

Lubitz, J., Beebe, J. and Riley, G. (1985) 'Improving the Medicare HMO payment formula to deal with biased selection', in R. Scheffler and L. Rossiter (eds) *Advances in health economics and health services research*, vol 6, pp 101-22, Greenwich, Connecticut: JAI Press.

Luft, H.S. (1986) 'Compensating for biased selection in health insurance', *Milbank Quarterly*, vol 64, no 4, pp 566-91.

Luft, H.S. and Miller, R.H. (1988) 'Patient selection in a competitive health care system', *Health Affairs*, vol 7, no 3, pp 97-119.

Maddala, G.S. (1983) *Limited-dependent and qualitative variables in econometrics*, Cambridge: Cambridge University Press.

Maddala, G.S. (1988) *Introduction to econometrics*, New York: Macmillan.

Manning, W.G., Newhouse, J.P., Duan, N., Keeler, E.B., Leibowitz, A. and Marquis, M.S. (1987) 'Health insurance and the demand for medical care: evidence from a randomized experiment', *American Economic Review*, vol 77, no 3, pp 251-77.

Matsaganis, M. and Glennerster, H. (1993) 'Patient characteristics as determinants of hospital expenditure in general practice fundholding', Paper presented at the Commissioning for Health Conference, Health Economists Study Group and Faculty of Public Health Medicine, York.

Maynard, A. (1986) 'Performance incentives', in G. Teeling Smith (ed) *Health, education and general practice*, London: Office of Health Economics.

Maynard, A. (1993) 'Competition in the UK National Health Service: mission impossible?', *Health Policy*, vol 23, no 3, pp 193-204.

Newhouse, J.P. (1982) 'Is competition the answer?', *Journal of Health Economics*, vol 1, no 1, pp 109-16.

Newhouse, J.P. (1984) 'Cream-skimming, asymmetric information, and a competitive insurance market', *Journal of Health Economics*, vol 3, no 1, pp 97-100.

Newhouse, J.P. (1986) 'Rate adjusters for Medicare under capitation', *Health Care Financing Review Annual Supplement*, pp 45-55.

Newhouse, J.P., Manning, W.G., Keeler, E.B. and Sloss, E.M. (1989) 'Adjusting capitation rates using objective health measures and prior utilization', *Health Care Financing Review*, vol 10, no 3, pp 41-54.

Robinson, J.C., Luft, H.S., Gardner, L.B. and Morrison, E.M. (1991) 'A method for risk-adjusting employer contributions to competing health insurance plans', *Inquiry*, vol 28, pp 107-16.

Rothschild, M. and Stiglitz, J. (1976) 'Equilibrium in competitive insurance markets: an essay on the economics of imperfect information', *Quarterly Journal of Economics*, vol 90, no 4, pp 629-49.

Scheffler, R. (1989) 'Adverse selection: the Achilles heel of the NHS reforms', *Lancet*, 29 April, pp 950-52.

van de Ven, W.P.M.M. (1991) 'Perestroika in the Dutch health care system: a demonstration project for other European countries', *European Economic Review*, vol 35, no 2/3, pp 430-40.

van de Ven, W.P.M.M. and van Vliet, R.C.J.A. (1990) 'Towards a budget formula for competing health insurers', Paper presented at the Second World Congress on Health Economics, Zurich.

van Vliet, R.C.J.A. and van de Ven, W.P.M.M. (1990) 'How can we prevent cream-skimming in a competitive health insurance market?', Paper presented at the Second World Congress on Health Economics, Zurich.

Wallack, S.S., Tompkins, C.P. and Gruenberg, L. (1988) 'A plan for rewarding efficient HMOs', *Health Affairs*, vol 7, no 3, pp 80-96.

Weiner, J. and Ferriss, P. (1990) *GP budget holding in the UK: lessons from America*, Research Report 7, London: King's Fund Institute.

Welch, W.P. (1985a) 'Medicare capitation payments to HMOs in light of regression toward the mean in health care costs', in R. Scheffler and L. Rossiter (eds) *Advances in health economics and health services research*, Greenwich, Connecticut: JAI Press, pp 75-96.

Welch, W.P. (1985b) 'Regression toward the mean in medical care costs: implications for biased selection in health maintenance organizations', *Medical Care*, vol 23, no 11, pp 1234-41.

*conclusion*

# WHERE NEXT?

## Will Bartlett, Julian Le Grand and Carol Propper

### Introduction

The chapters in this volume have brought to the surface a number of hitherto unexplored issues and have highlighted some of the main areas in which further research is needed. In this concluding chapter we set out the most important areas for further research as we see them. The first area concerns the development of the theory of quasi-markets and the consideration of alternative theoretical approaches. The second concerns the need for more empirical studies. A number of initial studies have begun, some of which are reported on in this book. But there is a need for further policy studies centring upon the appropriate institutional design for the improvement of quasi-market performance. In what follows we discuss these three areas in more detail.

### Developing the theory

Thus far the study of the operation of quasi-markets in the UK has relied largely upon theorising the potential effects of the institutional changes which have been introduced since the late 1980s. Evaluation of the reforms has been conducted mainly through an indirect approach, establishing the conditions that would be required for the new set of institutional arrangements to meet certain criteria, and then examining the evolution of the quasi-markets with respect to their ability to meet these conditions. For example, in an earlier work Le Grand and Bartlett (1993) identified five conditions which would be required for quasi-markets to achieve the objectives of increased efficiency, responsiveness and choice without having adverse effects on equity, as mentioned by several of the contributors in this volume. These conditions related to market structure, information, motivation, and cream-skimming. In a subsequent study (Robinson and Le Grand, 1994, Chapter 10) the objectives were expanded to include a direct consideration of quality. The use of this indirect approach was necessitated by the early stage of implementation of the reforms and the consequent lack of hard data with which to conduct more direct tests of various hypotheses concerning the performance of the new quasi-market institutions with respect to the objectives. However, as several of the chapters in this book demonstrate, the early findings from a number of more direct empirical studies are beginning to emerge.

The theoretical structure outlined in Le Grand and Bartlett (1993) focuses on the conditions which affect the performance of quasi-markets. The chapters in the present volume suggest a number of issues that move the debate forward and identify potential new areas for new theoretical research on quasi-markets. Broadly, these issues concern:

● the extent to which standard economic theory can be, and is, used to model behaviour in quasi-markets;

● the ability of economic theory to deal with the complexity of the institutional changes which have been introduced into the provision of welfare services through the quasi-market reforms.

## Economic theory and behaviour in quasi-markets

This group of issues includes the way in which not-for-profit enterprises are expected to behave, and what their economic motivation is; how central regulation affects the behaviour of both providers and purchasers; and how the devolution of managerial autonomy affects the internal efficiency of individual provider units.

Many of the provider organisations in the new quasi-markets are not-for-profit organisations. That is, they are constrained by their form of incorporation, their statutes or regulation in the extent to which they are able to distribute their profits or surpluses. Examples include NHS trusts, residential care homes registered as charities, grant-maintained schools and housing associations. Alongside these are other providers, including private for-profit organisations and provider units still owned and managed by the purchaser of the service. Examples of the first include private nursing and residential homes registered under company law; examples of the second include local authority residential homes, the few remaining directly managed units in the health service, locally managed primary and secondary schools and local authority housing departments.

This variety of provider organisations raises a number of issues. First there are questions concerning its desirability and its stability. Taylor and Hoggett in Chapter 8 map the range of providers in the community care field and argue that this diversity is a positive feature of the system. However, can not-for-profit (including public sector) and for-profit organisations compete, without being driven to adopt similar patterns of behaviour? That is, will not the competitive requirements of the market eventually eliminate the diversity? This appears to have been one of the results of 'contracting out' of local government services in the USA (Propper, 1993a).

Associated with the recognition of diversity is the issue of the motivation of the providers, particularly the not-for-profit organisations. As yet we do not have a good theory of how these organisations behave in a quasi-market setting. Johnes and Cave use a model of surplus-maximising universities to good effect in Chapter 5, but it is an open question whether surplus maximisation accurately reflects the motivation of not-for-profit providers. The traditional theory of not-for-profit organisations (Hansmann, 1987) suggests that they may reflect some preferences to promote (directly) user benefit, subject to the constraint that they should not make a loss. In this case, some measure of user benefit ought to be reflected in the objective function. This may even be appropriate in the case of some for-profit providers, and Wilson and Bartlett (1994) have suggested that a measure of patient benefit should enter directly into a GP objective function. However, where there are both for-profit and not-for-profit providers available, Hansmann's theory of contract failure suggests that purchasers may prefer to contract with not-for-profit providers who they regard as being less likely to behave in an opportunistic manner than similar for-profit providers (and hence less likely to engage in cream-skimming, or taking advantage of information asymmetries to boost profits). Taylor and Hoggett (Chapter 8) carry this forward by suggesting that the introduction of market incentives in such a context may be counter-productive if it were to undermine the willingness of not-for-profit providers to supply voluntary effort on behalf of users (see also Frey, 1993, for a related argument concerning the effect of performance related pay on work incentives).

Clearly, the issue of motivation structure of both not-for-profit and welfare-minded for-profit providers will need to be taken into account in developing the theory and predicting the performance of quasi-market institutional arrangements. And there are potentially interesting issues in modelling the strategic reactions of not-for-profit providers to the performance of for-profit providers in a quasi-market setting, and vice versa.

Further research is also needed into the need for, extent and form of regulation in quasi-markets. Regulation of those services now traded in quasi-markets has historically been high, so high in fact that the regulator (central government) directly determined the nature of the goods produced and their allocation. In addition, regulation by professionals, mainly of quality, was also widespread. The establishment of quasi-markets was part of an economy-wide move towards deregulation, but the issue of what regulation should remain was not directly tackled in the separation of provider and purchasers. While the reforms can broadly be seen as an attempt to loosen controls on entry, other issues of structure such as merger and exit have not been addressed. Nor has the role for regulation of conduct.

In the little research carried out directly in this area to date, Propper (1993b) argued that the extent of conduct regulation is already high and that further regulation of price and quality may have an adverse effect on incentives. In a more detailed examination of the health sector Propper (1994) argued that the regulatory tools being used in the NHS quasi-market were unlikely to encourage efficiency or consumer responsiveness. Challis et al (Chapter 1) examine quality regulation and conclude that in quasi-markets there is more need for regulation where competition is high. This finding is somewhat at odds with the generally accepted role for greater regulation where providers have market power (see for example Tirole, 1990). It may reflect the importance of the role of the agent in quasi-markets. A better theoretical understanding of the interaction between regulation and a quasi-market is needed as the extent and form of regulation is likely to be a key issue in the performance of quasi-markets. The role of regulation in markets where some providers remain government owned and others are financed by private capital, where funding for the purchase of services is to a large extent provided by the state and where equity goals exist alongside goals of efficiency, consumer choice and responsiveness needs to be examined. Specific issues include the extent to which regulation of structure (entry, exit, merger) is sufficient to prevent the acquisition, maintenance and exploitation of monopoly power; the interaction between professional self-regulation and government regulation; the interaction between incentives provided by contracting for services and regulatory control on rates of return, modes of production and price; the ability of the regulator to influence behaviour in increasingly decentralised markets where providers are both public and private and have profit and not-for-profit motives and the interaction between regulation and social norms.

A third area of theoretical interest within this group concerns the way in which devolution of managerial autonomy affects the internal efficiency of individual provider units. This issue was brought up by Levacic (Chapter 2) who points out that, whilst devolution of managerial autonomy is generally welcomed by headteachers in LMS schools, there is no clear evidence that this devolution actually changes educational outcomes. Levacic identifies a potential conflict between a headteacher's effectiveness in delivering educational services and his or her effectiveness in budget management. Time spent on one activity may detract from attention to the other, and so devolution may actually be counter-productive in terms of service outputs to the same extent as it is effective in budgetary terms.

### Economic theory and institutional change

This group of issues reflects the search for a possibly more appropriate theoretical framework, and draws on a wide set of alternative approaches from economics and the sociological and organisational studies literatures.

Three separate approaches, each addressing rather different issues, seem to offer promise here. The first is the idea of 'social embeddedness' developed by Granovetter (1985). Ferlie (Chapter 9) and Ball et al (Chapter 4) both stress the importance of the legacy of the past in the differentiated development of quasi-markets across different markets, and within markets across localities. The state has not been able to create the new institutions on a clean slate but has had to deal with the structures and behavioural codes bequeathed by the previous administrative system of welfare service provision. This affects the ability of the new systems to achieve policy objectives. For example, user choice is heavily structured by social class and by the cultural expectations generated by the previous system. Similarly, some provider organisations may have a greater ethos of public service than others, and this may affect their reaction to the new quasi-market incentives. Because of these differentiated responses, conventional theory may find it hard to make sensible predictions about the impact of defined institutional changes. The problem is exacerbated by the fact that expectations are dynamic and change over time in response to the unfolding of the new institutional set up which is undergoing constant change. To give only one example, as a greater proportion of NHS purchasing is carried out by GP fundholders, the quasi-market for primary care becomes more competitive for some users who are registered with fundholding GPs, but for other users the quasi-market becomes less competitive as the pool of funds held by DHA purchasing authorities diminishes. What effect this is likely to have on the efficiency and equity of the system,and on the satisfaction of consular choice is an unexplored area.

Related to this approach is the important issue of the role of social networks in the performance of the quasi-market identified by Taylor and Hoggett (Chapter 8) as an alternative (or additional) paradigm to the idea of markets and hierarchies (Williamson, 1975) as the basic organising principles through which to understand the significance of the quasi-market reforms. Hypotheses associated with both social networks and social embeddedness theories are probably best tested by means of case study approaches.

Another potential fruitful area for the development of theory in the general area of service delivery is introduced by Means et al in Chapter 7. Instead of emphasising competition and the associated importance of users shopping around between providers in an apparent exercise of choice (the 'exit' mechanism of quasi-markets), they place emphasis on the importance of user participation, or more general 'voice' mechanisms, as a means of improving the type or quality of service provision delivered by a provider without the necessity of searching for a new provider (Hirschman, 1970). Voice can either be expressed individually, through complaints procedures for example, or collectively, through collective entities such as pressure groups, consultative councils or executive authorities (elected or non-elected).

Although primarily concerned with exit strategies of the quasi-market type, the current British Government has not totally neglected voice strategies for empowering users of welfare services. The Government's Citizen's Charter initiative is a way of strengthening voice at an individual level; there are now some 20 published charters for various parts of the public sector, including several in welfare areas. There has also been a strengthening of parental involvement in, and the powers of, school governing bodies in the education system (replacing the 'right to gripe' with the 'right to control').

However, the effectiveness of voice mechanisms has been reduced in other ways, including the removal of elected representatives from health authorities, and the reduction in local authority powers over education and housing. Increasingly, power over the planning, purchase and provision of welfare services is in the hands of non-elected boards. Moreover, even where voice mechanisms have been strengthened, they may be overridden by the operations of the relevant quasi-market; how long could school governors, however powerful, keep open a school that was losing pupils due to the open enrolment scheme and hence funding due to the operation of formula funding?

Not surprisingly there is interest in voice mechanisms in other parts of the political spectrum. The centre/left think tank, the Institute for Public Policy Research, has produced a volume advocating a wider use of citizens' rights as a means of giving power to users (Coote, 1992). More generally, as the quasi-markets develop, there is a growing interest in voice mechanisms as a way of correcting some of the problems that are beginning to emerge, both as complementary to the quasi-market, for instance in improving the ability of large-scale purchasers to reflect the needs and wants of the population they serve, and as alternatives to it.

With respect to the role of voice as an alternative, voice mechanisms are crucial for those who cannot 'exit' or who face very high costs of doing so (examples include older people in residential homes, or children in rural schools). Also, many forms of welfare service are 'one-off', hence reducing the ability to shift business elsewhere that is an essential part of the incentive mechanism of quasi-markets. Even in areas where exit is not so great a problem, voice mechanisms have advantages over exit ones. They allow for the interests of non-users of services to be taken into account; and, as Hirschman (1974) argues, the very act of engaging in user participation can yield benefits in and of itself. However, they also have their disadvantages; principally, that their effectiveness depends on the exercise of certain resources by those who activate them, such as confidence and time, the possession of which may not be correlated with the intensity or even the direction of the needs and wants of users. Whether and where voice or exit mechanisms are superior as methods of user empowerment remains an open theoretical and empirical question.

However, the theory of voice is even less developed than that of quasi-markets; and until its development is under way, assessing the relative merits of the different mechanisms and their appropriateness in different situations is very difficult. Here is an area ripe for theoretical development.

## Empirical research issues

As already noted, the quasi-market reforms have now been running for over three years (implementation beginning in the field of health and education around 1990, although only really in 1993 in the field of community care). The results of some early studies are beginning to emerge, and some are reported in this volume. In this section we highlight some of the key issues which we feel empirical studies should address. These issues are associated with the theoretical developments outlined in the previous section.

First, there is the issue of direct analysis of the emerging structure of the quasi-market and its performance in terms of quality, efficiency, choice, responsiveness, and equity. Some of the chapters in this volume have begun this kind of analysis, notably in the chapters on education. But a host of issues need to be addressed in other areas, many of which are very basic. For example, there is a need for data on the market structure and the degree of competition in different markets. Taylor and Hoggett (Chapter 8) report on some work to map the variety of types of providers operating in community care. As yet such basic information is scarce or simply not available. Clearly, until more is known on this important issue it will not be possible to draw firm conclusions concerning the validity of predictions from theoretical research.

Second, there is a need for more information on the motivations and objectives of the provider organisations. This can only really be satisfactorily investigated on the basis of sample surveys and possibly case studies. There is a need for analysts to go directly to practitioners to discover the extent to which they are adapting to the new quasi-market environment of financial incentives. Are they at all motivated by such mechanisms? Or do they operate on a more altruistic basis, putting service for the user to the fore? The importance of this type of research is not just permitting more accurate development of abstract models, but also has direct policy relevance. If provider motivations are not primarily based on monetary gain, then financial incentives may at best be weak and or at worst counter-productive if they undermine the willingness to offer services based upon altruistic motives.

Third, there is a need for a study of the costs of introducing quasi-market arrangements. Are the transactions costs of operating a quasi-market high relative to the possible gains? There are currently newspaper reports concerning the increase in the number of administrative and managerial personnel in the NHS, for example - how far are these the results of reclassification, and how far do they represent genuine increases? Has the increase in administrative costs outweighed any cost reduction due to competitive pressures of the market, and has the overall cost of providing services risen as a result?

If these costs have risen, what about the corresponding benefits to users? Little is known about whether these benefits have increased, in large part because of the difficulty of obtaining satisfactory outcome measures. There has been an apparent increase in activity in hospitals, for example. But is this just a statistical illusion, as recording systems change and possibly improve, or does it represent a real increase in activity? And is an increase in activity associated with an increase in patient benefit, or does an increasing rate of throughput lead to an increasing rate of re-admission reflecting an actual decrease in patient benefit? We will only really be able to assess the answers to these sorts of questions on the basis of large scale user surveys. Some progress in this direction is being made, as is evident from the results reported by Glatter and Woods (Chapter 3) on the PASCI study of user choice in education. However, there is a clear need for more work in this direction.

Associated with this is the issue of equity. The key issue is of course whether inequity has increased as a result of the introduction of quasi-markets. There is some evidence that the introduction of GP fundholding has led to a two-tier service, with the patients of fundholders receiving more and better hospital treatment than the patients of non-fundholders (Whitehead, 1993).   A study of outpatient referrals came to the opposite conclusion (Coulter and Bradlow, 1993).   On the other hand, there is no evidence so far of cream-skimming by fundholders, probably because, as pointed out by Matsaganis and Glennerster (Chapter 11), there is a £5,000 limit on the amount a fundholder has to pay.   But will this feature be continued, and if removed, what will be the effect?   In education, have inner city schools lost out as a result of changes in the funding system compared to schools in more favoured locations?   These and other equity issues will need to be closely examined before any final judgement can be made concerning the success or otherwise of the quasi-market reforms.

Finally, we would expect the nature of the quasi-market to change over time, in response to the incentives established by contracting for services, the allocations to purchasers and the regulatory framework.   There is a need for descriptive studies on a scale large enough to isolate the impact of each of these (and other) forces upon the market structure and the services delivered by the market.   There is also a need for greater understanding of the dynamic properties of the incentive mechanisms that are in operation in these markets.

## Policy analysis

Three issues that appear to us to be particularly important in this area concern the encouragement of entry and exit of providers, the determination of the funding for purchasers and the evolving regulatory regimes.

Knapp et al in Chapter 6 draw attention to the barriers to entry that new providers face in the quasi-market for community care. These include lack of size, the absolute cost advantages of existing providers due to the existence of 'sunk costs' and other factors, resource constraints of factor supplies (both labour and capital) and the contractual arrangements that local authorities may impose on unwilling voluntary agencies.   All of these problems face new entrants in the other quasi-markets, and may need to be addressed by appropriate policy measures.   But the form these should take has yet to be spelt out.

In addition to the problem of entry, there is the problem of exit. What policies are appropriate for dealing with provider units that are losing business? At present, a variety of ad hoc strategies are being pursued, including mergers with more successful units or straightforward 'bail out' subsidies. However, remedies such as these can undermine the incentive structure of the market and cannot be resorted to indefinitely. The development and evaluation of more systematic policy alternatives, such as franchising, are urgently needed.

If one key element in the new pattern of quasi-markets is competition between relatively independent service providers, the other is the means by which these agencies are financed. The introduction of quasi-markets means funding mechanisms are the principal means by which governments can secure national policy objectives, including efficiency, performance and equity goals. Governments will become increasingly dependent on the incentive structures built into these funding mechanisms. But as yet they are poorly understood.

In discussions with different government departments devising these funding formulae in the new world of purchaser and provider, we have been struck by the extent to which several are re-inventing the wheel. Many of the incentive issues involved in devising formulae for funding opted out schools, for example, are identical to those involved in funding GP fundholders; yet there appears to be little communication between the relevant departments, and little awareness of the similarity of the principles involved. More generally, we know from past work on local government finance that formula funding can have unexpected and perverse consequences both on efficiency and equity, (Bramley, 1990; Hills, 1991); but again there seems to be little knowledge of this literature or its conclusions in key areas of policy making.

There are three basic methods of allocation. One sets out to achieve territorial equity through area-based needs formulae. Another more radical approach is to finance competitive purchasers and providers on a weighted capitation basis. This model produces a voucher-like effect; when a user signs on, this triggers a payment to the institution (Le Grand, 1991). A third approach essentially eschews codified principles and allocates resources through a judgemental process.

Behind all three of these approaches lie implicit assumptions about the responsiveness of receivers to the incentives embedded in the scheme. The intended results may not happen either because the relevant formulae were poorly designed or because local agents' motivations were poorly or wrongly understood. Allocation rules may vary over time and lead to dynamic inconsistency. Formulae often ignore the behaviour of other agents in the market and other complementary services and funding mechanisms. The extent of competition in the market and the level of risk agents will have to bear will affect their response. All these issues need both further study and greater consideration in policy design.

A third key element for policy to address is the form and extent of regulation. Despite the rhetoric of deregulation which accompanied the introduction of quasi-markets, in many of these markets the extent of regulation remains high and in some cases is increasing. There is a lack of coordination between the regulatory actions of central government, local government and professional bodies. New performance regulations such as those embodied in the various Citizens' Charters are introduced with little apparent consideration of how these fit with (a) existing regulations and (b) the contracting requirements of purchasers. There is heavy emphasis on conduct regulation with lack of attention to the importance of regulation of structure. The form of regulation may be inappropriate, with excessive emphasis on static efficiency and too little focus on incentives for efficiency over time. For example, the regulation that NHS health care providers must set price equal to short run average cost gives little incentive to make efficiency gains, whilst also being relatively easy to evade. It is also applicable to only part of the market, as private suppliers are not subject to any price regulation. A lack of clear exit mechanism for public providers dampens incentives for efficiency. Given the importance of the regulatory regime in quasi-markets, there is a need for policy to develop in a more coherent fashion, and to be informed by theory and the lessons from other markets, inside and outside the UK.

## Conclusion

The studies presented in this volume lay an initial groundwork for some of the emerging findings in this new and exciting field for social policy research; one which will no doubt dominate the policy agenda for the next decade as the quasi-market reforms work themselves through and assessments of their effectiveness become more well grounded in research. However, it is essential that this work is done, and that it is done systematically and comprehensively. Part of the significance of this book lies in the areas that it does not cover; it is hoped that others will be encouraged to try to begin the process of filling the gaps.

## References

Bramley, G. (1990) *Equalisation grants and local expenditure needs*, Aldershot: Avebury.

Coote, A. (ed) (1992) *The welfare of citizens: developing new social rights*, London: IPPR/Rivers Oram Press.

Coulter, A. and Bradlow J. (1993) 'Effect of NHS reforms on general practitioners' referral rates', *British Medical Journal*, vol 306, 13 February, pp 433-37.

Frey, B.S. (1993) 'Shirking or work morale? The impact of regulating', *European Economic Review*, vol 37, no 6, pp 1523-32.

Granovetter, M. (1985) 'Economic action and social structure: the problem of embeddedness', *American Journal of Sociology*, vol 91, no 3, pp 481-510.

Hansmann (1987) 'Economic theories of non-profit organisations', in W. Powell (ed) *The non-profit sector*, New Haven and London: Yale University Press.

Hills, J. (1991) *Unravelling housing finance: subsidies, benefits and taxation*, Oxford: Clarendon Press.

Hirschmann, A. (1970) *Exit, voice and loyalty*, Cambridge, Mass: Cambridge University Press.

Le Grand, J. (1991) 'Quasi-markets and social policy', *Economic Journal*, vol 101, pp 1256-67.

Le Grand, J. and W. Bartlett (eds) (1993) *Quasi-markets and social policy*, London: Macmillan.

Propper, C. (1993a) 'Quasi-markets, contracts and quality: lessons from the American health and social service markets', in J. Le Grand and W. Bartlett (eds) *Quasi-markets and social policy*, London: Macmillan.

Propper, C. (1993b) 'Is there a need for further regulation of quasi-markets?', in J. Le Grand and W. Bartlett (eds) *Quasi-markets and social policy*, London: Macmillan.

Propper, C. (1994) 'Incentives in the NHS internal market, Discussion Paper, Department of Economics, University of Bristol.

Robinson, R. and Le Grand, J. (eds) (1994) *Evaluating the NHS reforms*, London: King's Fund Institute.

Tirole, J. (1990) *The theory of industrial organisation*, Cambridge, Mass: MIT Press.

Whitehead, M. (1993) 'Is it fair? Evaluating the equity implications of the NHS reforms', in R. Robinson and J. Le Grand (1994) *Evaluating the NHS reforms*, London: King's Fund Institute.

Williamson, O.E. (1975) *Markets and hierarchies: analysis and anti-trust implications*, New York: The Free Press.

Wilson, D. and Bartlett, W. (1994) 'Partnerships and incentives in health care: the case of general practice in the UK', Paper presented to the Health Economists Study Group, London, January.

# INDEX